Imagining the Ideal Pension System

Imagining the Ideal Pension System

International Perspectives

Dana M. Muir
John A. Turner
Editors

2011

W.E. Upjohn Institute for Employment Research
Kalamazoo, Michigan

Library of Congress Cataloging-in-Publication Data

Imagining the ideal pension system : international perspectives / Dana M. Muir, John A. Turner, editors.
p. cm.
"This book is based on the 2010 conference of the European Network for Research on Supplementary Pensions (ENRSP), held at the Economic Policy Institute in Washington, D.C., on September 10, 2010"—Foreword.
Includes bibliographical references and index.
ISBN-13: 978-0-88099-381-4 (pbk. : alk. paper)
ISBN-10: 0-88099-381-2 (pbk. : alk. paper)
ISBN-13: 978-0-88099-382-1 (hbk. : alk. paper)
ISBN-10: 0-88099-382-0 (hbk. : alk. paper)
1. Pensions. I. Muir, Dana M., 1958- II. Turner, John A. (John Andrew), 1949 July 9- III. European Network for Research on Supplementary Pensions.
HD7091.I464 2011
331.25'2—dc23
2011038440

W.E. Upjohn Institute for Employment Research
300 S. Westnedge Avenue
Kalamazoo, Michigan 49007-4686

Cover design by Alcorn Publication Design.
Index prepared by Diane Worden.
Printed in the United States of America.
Printed on recycled paper.

Contents

Foreword

This book is based on the 2010 conference of the European Network for Research on Supplementary Pensions (ENRSP), held at the Economic Policy Institute in Washington, D.C., on September 10, 2010. The ENRSP is a research network for independent researchers in the field of private pensions. This conference was the first conference of the network held outside Europe. Financial support for the conference was provided by the Stephen M. Ross School of Business at the University of Michigan and IBIS Advisors Co., as well as from funds from the network.

In part because of population aging, many countries are considering reforms of their pension systems. For that reason, the conference addressed the issue of what pension experts in different countries thought would be the ideal pension system for their countries. As discussed in the overview chapter and in the individual country chapters, it is clear that the authors differ as to the role of the government and capital markets in providing retirement income, as well as on issues relating to what age retirement benefits should be available.

1
Constructing the Ideal Pension System

The Visions of Ten Country Experts

Dana M. Muir
Stephen M. Ross School of Business,
University of Michigan

John A. Turner
Pension Policy Center

At a time when many countries have aging populations and economies continue to struggle in the aftermath of the global financial crisis, the improvement of pension systems is especially important. Pensions often are critical in preventing retirees from living in poverty. Pensions enable older workers to retire. In order for retirees and workers to rely on pensions, the funding and administration of those pensions must be affordable and sustainable for workers, business, and society.

The theme of the 2010 conference of the European Network for Research on Supplementary Pensions (ENRSP or the Network) was an exploration of how and why the image of the ideal pension system differs across countries. The organizers recognized that views on the ideal pension system for a country may evolve in reaction to changes in the economic and demographic environment. The conference recognized the importance of the various long-run goals that different actors have for the pension system. The conference focused on country-by-country studies. It was expected that the conference authors would have very different approaches to thinking about the characteristics of the ideal pension system, and the authors did not disappoint.

This introductory chapter begins with a brief overview of the country studies. By necessity this overview omits much of the nuance of the chapters—the goal is to provide a short explanation of each country's pension system and summarize the reforms proposed by the author of the country study.

The summaries are intended to establish some background for the second section of this chapter in which we address some broad themes drawn from the country studies. We consider the authors' views on the importance of culture in explaining differences in approaches to pension issues. We also reflect on four primary goals for any pension system:

1) coverage of the population so that pensions are broadly available,
2) risk sharing so that the many risks inherent in any pension system are appropriately shared,
3) adequate benefits to meet the country's goal of sufficient retirement standards, and
4) approaches to respond to increases in longevity.

Given our backgrounds, we view the complex pension systems described in this chapter through a U.S. lens.

To decrease the confusion that results from using different terms for essentially similar pension concepts, we adopt U.S. terminology in this chapter and throughout the rest of the book, even when different terminology would typically be used elsewhere in the world. So, for example, pension schemes (British terminology) are referred to here as pension plans or pension systems. And the government-administered portion of a country's pension system is typically referred to as social security.

NORTH AMERICA

United States, John A. Turner and Dana M. Muir

The U.S. pension system is the only North American system covered in this book because, given the focus of the Network, the emphasis is on European pension systems. The U.S. and Japanese systems are included in the volume as points of comparison and discussion.

The U.S. pension system requires nearly all workers to participate in the social security system, which provides a defined benefit pension to workers who meet minimum criteria. In addition, the U.S. provides tax incentives for employer-sponsored pension plans, which may be defined benefit or defined contribution plans, and for individual retirement savings in accounts such as Individual Retirement Accounts (IRAs). The social security plan is the only mandatory plan. Sponsorship of defined benefit or defined contribution plans by employers is voluntary, as are individual savings accounts. Employer-sponsored plans have been heavily regulated since 1974. In spite of various incentives intended to increase coverage of employer-sponsored plans, however, coverage rates have never exceeded much more than 50 percent.

Numerous interest groups recognize that planned and potential reductions in the social security system, limited coverage of employer-sponsored plans, poor uptake of individual plans, and the transition from defined benefit to defined contribution plans means that the U.S. pension system needs reform. Turner and Muir briefly discuss some of those proposals, which advocate very different approaches. Turner and Muir conclude that the importance of individual freedom in U.S. culture means that the voluntary nature of the employer-sponsored pension system should be retained. Still, Turner and Muir believe that the current system can be modified to enhance coverage, better allocate risks, and increase adequacy of benefits. As an example, they advocate measures, including changes in tax and funding rules, that would help equalize the attractiveness to employers of defined benefit and defined contribution plans. One example is a recommendation to permit employee tax-deductible contributions to defined benefit plans. They also suggest that the demographic issue of an aging population that is so costly to employer-sponsored defined benefit plans could be addressed in part by reallocating some of the demographic risks. The plans could retain the idiosyncratic risk of longer than average life expectancies for individual workers, while the cohort risk could be shifted to plan participants as a group.

EUROPE

Although the eight European countries studied in this volume (except Switzerland) all are members of the European Union (EU), the pension systems vary considerably in terms of structure, coverage, risk sharing, adequacy, and approach to increasing longevity.

United Kingdom, Bryn Davies

The United Kingdom (UK) has a two-part mandatory pension system administered by the government (social security) that in combination applies to all employees, is earnings related, and provides a defined benefit pension. A move is under way to transform the earnings-related benefit to a flat-rate benefit (not related to earnings but increasing with years of contributions) and to increase the retirement age. The United Kingdom also has a system of voluntary employer-sponsored pension plans, which may be either defined benefit or defined contribution plans. Beginning in 2001, most employers that do not offer a pension plan meeting minimum standards must designate what is known as a "stakeholder" plan to receive employee contributions from those employees who wish to contribute, although neither employers nor employees are required to contribute to these plans. The UK pension system, other than the social security pension, essentially remains a voluntary system of defined benefit or defined contribution plans where risks are borne almost completely by the employer or the employee depending on the type of plan.

Davies advocates a four-part system. The first two parts would be mandatory systems administered by the government (social security). Together they would provide a flat-rate benefit at 60 percent of median household income for a single person and an additional amount depending on the individual's lifetime earnings. In addition, Davies proposes an incentivized pension at the occupational or other collective level. The combination of this collectively based earnings-related pension and the social security benefits would provide individuals with a pension that would meet the target replacement ratio. Finally, Davies's proposal calls for a fourth component for individuals who desire a more generous pension. The government would facilitate that component through regulation but would not necessarily encourage savings into that component.

Ireland, Gerard Hughes and Jim Stewart

Ireland's pension system has a mandatory government-administered pension (social security) that is paid as a flat-rate defined benefit. It has an additional two-part system for private sector employees. Employers may provide either defined benefit or defined contribution plans for their employees. The trend has been for employers to shift their sponsorship from defined benefit to defined contribution plans. Individuals not covered by an employer-sponsored pension plan may establish an individual pension plan. Over the past 10 years, the pensioner poverty rate has been volatile. In recent years, the social security benefit has increased more quickly than workers' earnings, and the at-risk-of-poverty rates for pensioners decreased to slightly more than 11 percent in 2008.

Hughes and Stewart propose a universal social security system that would further decrease or eliminate the risk of poverty for pensioners in Ireland. They show that the current social security system provides most of the income for most pensioners, and only those in the top quintile of the income distribution derive a significant portion of their total pension income from an employer-sponsored or individual pension plan. Hughes and Stewart advocate decreasing the tax relief for employer-sponsored and individual pension plans and suggest reallocating those resources into the social security system to improve that system's ability to support pensioners in an equitable and sustainable manner.

Denmark, Finn Østrup

The government of Denmark administers a universal social security pension system that provides defined benefits. Also, the Danish pension system includes employment-based defined contribution plans that cover nearly all employees. These plans arise from centralized wage agreements or company policies and have guaranteed minimum rates of interest. In addition, workers are encouraged to participate in personal pension plans by tax incentives.

In addressing risks to pensioners, Østrup observes and criticizes the political uncertainty in the Danish pension system. He explains multiple instances where the government of Denmark has changed the taxation of plan benefits and sought to use pension plan assets to fund business enterprises, including troubled financial institutions in 2008. Østrup points out that, compared to other industrial countries, Denmark has a very low household savings rate. Østrup also concludes that the complexity of the Danish pension system results in a lack of transparency. After detailed analysis comparing funded and unfunded pension systems as well as defined benefit and defined contribution benefit structures, Østrup concludes that there is no single optimal pension system. In his view, optimality in a pension system depends on the broad spectrum of goals of the pension system, including not just income replacement after retirement but also effects on labor supply and financial markets.

Germany, Markus Roth

Germany has the oldest social security system in the world. It provides an income-related defined benefit. It also has a voluntary system of pensions that is made up of employer-sponsored plans and individual pensions, but that system is moving from an employer-sponsored system to one that has elements of employee financing. The voluntary system covers approximately 60 percent of the German workforce but often provides only a small benefit. New forms of plans have been introduced in Germany, such as a defined benefit with a guaranteed return.

Roth observes that the German law on both individual and occupational pensions needs to be systematized. His view is that defined benefit plans are not categorically more appropriate than defined contribution or hybrid plans for individual and occupational pensions. Roth advocates use of a pension protection triangle and a loyally administered separate fund to model protective principles. Roth's pension protection triangle is formed by consideration of exit (termination of a pension contract), voice (consultation), and guarantees. He makes a number of specific suggestions to improve Germany's occupational pensions, including recommending the use of automatic enrollment in defined contribution occupational pension plans.

Belgium, Kim De Witte

Belgium's pension system has a mandatory government-administered component (social security) that covers all workers, is income-based, and is paid as a defined benefit. In addition, employers may, but are not required to, sponsor defined benefit or defined contribution plans for their workers. Approximately 60 percent of workers are covered by a work-related pension plan. Many of these plans are industry-wide plans that arise from collective bargaining rather than plans that are sponsored by individual employers. One somewhat unusual provision of Belgium's pension regulation is a requirement that defined contribution pensions include a minimum guarantee rate, currently 3.25 percent for employer contributions and 3.75 percent for employee contributions. Finally, in addition to the social security and work-based pension plans, Belgium permits voluntary individual pension savings arrangements on a defined contribution basis.

After discussing the shortcomings of the current pension system in Belgium, De Witte explains the reform proposals advocated by the main social and political groups. De Witte then develops a comprehensive set of criteria to evaluate the reform proposals and evaluates various approaches to pension accrual against the broad categories of

- degree of redistributive solidarity,
- scope of risk sharing, and
- protection of pension rights.

Each of these broad categories is defined by subcategories. So, for example, longevity is an explicit factor in the scope of risk sharing category and an implicit factor in the protection of pension rights category through subcategories that differentiate between lump sum and annuitized benefit entitlements. De Witte advocates an ideal system for Belgium that would include a social security benefit of 60 percent of final salary and an additional amount of up to 15 percent (for a maximum total of 75 percent of final salary) from tax-incentivized individual or work-related pensions.

France, Lucy apRoberts and Pierre Concialdi

The French pension system is a government-administered mandatory system that covers all private sector workers by providing a means-tested minimum pension and work-related pensions as defined benefits (social security). Fewer than 8 percent of retirees receive the minimum means-tested benefit. Mandatory work-related supplementary plans provide about one-third of the pension benefits received by the average retiree. The supplementary work-related plans are organized along occupational lines, but the plans have been increasingly consolidated. The replacement rate achieved by the French system is among the highest in Europe.

apRoberts and Concialdi preface their discussion of prospective changes in the French social security system with a concise history of the development of the current system. They then take issue with the French government's projections for the future of the country's pension system and state that the government believes that it is not possible to increase pension contributions. apRoberts and Concialdi believe that the cumulative nature of the many changes that have taken place in the French pension system will, if left unchanged, result in drastically reduced pensions in the future. They argue that the French social security system can and should be reinforced to receive increased revenues and pay appropriately generous benefits. They also point out the linkage between full and well-paid employment and levels of retirement income security. In any pension system with a work- and income-based pension component, unemployed and underemployed individuals will not earn the pension benefits they would in a system of full employment with well-paid jobs.

Switzerland, Matthieu Leimgruber

Switzerland has two mandatory components to its pension system and a voluntary third component. The Swiss government administers a mandatory social security plan that covers all workers and pays earnings-related defined benefits. In addition, the mandatory work-related benefit plans cover approximately 90 percent of the workforce and constitute an increasingly large proportion of the expenditure in Switzerland on pensions. Coverage by this component of the Swiss system is less than universal because there is a wage floor, which results in the exclusion of low-wage and temporary workers. The work-related plans are required to provide a minimum guaranteed return on invested assets. The third component of the Swiss pension system is made up of voluntary individual pensions.

Leimgruber engages in a historical analysis of the Swiss pension system, concentrating on the work-related pensions that have attracted significant controversy in recent years. He argues that specific pension reforms that may appear merely technical matters must be understood in the larger context of the multiple components of the Swiss pension system and the dynamics that affect that system. In early 2010, Swiss voters rejected a proposal that would have reduced those benefits. Leimgruber observes that the development of the mandatory work-related pension system was designed in part to improve the levels of pension benefits and in part to discourage the enhancement of the social security system. He explains the important role he believes that business forces, including the providers of pension investments and services, such as life insurers that provide group pension contracts, have played in the structure of the Swiss pension system. Leimgruber expects that the work-related component of pensions will become increasingly important in debates over the provision of pensions.

Poland, Marek Szczepański

The pension system in Poland underwent significant reform in 1999, resulting in two side-by-side systems. Szczepański addresses only the structure of the pension system as it applies to individuals who were below age 30 at the time of the reform. The government of Poland administers a mandatory notional defined contribution system (social security). A second component provides funded defined contribution benefits and a third component that is voluntary also is defined contribution. The pension system is made up of both work-based pension plans and individual pension plans. The voluntary third component covers only about eight percent of the workforce. Szczepański concentrates his analysis on the problems associated with the voluntary defined contribution component of the Polish pension system. He establishes an analytic framework that divides the barriers for development of the occupational portion of the voluntary component into exogenous and endogenous factors. He further divides exogenous factors into variables of institutional or noninstitutional character. Szczepański divides the endogenous factors into employer- and employee-related variables. He concludes with specific recommendations for improving pension coverage, improving adequacy of pension benefits, and mitigating both financial market and longevity risks. For example, he suggests that workers could be automatically enrolled, with an opportunity to opt out, into voluntary work-based plans to increase coverage. To increase the adequacy of pension benefits, he suggests equalizing the statutory retirement age of women with the retirement age for men, which currently is 65. Finally, he observes the importance of limiting fees and charges in a defined contribution system.

ASIA

Japan, Noriyasu Watanabe

Understanding the Japanese pension system provides context for the views of the European contributors to this volume. Japan administers a compulsory earnings-related pension plan paid as a defined benefit that supplements the basic pension, also provided through the government (together forming social security). Two different types of work-related pension plans may be established by employers. Both types are defined benefit and played an important role until 2001, when pension reform first permitted defined contribution plans, amended work-related pension systems, and introduced a new corporate defined benefit plan. The new defined contribution plans may be either work related or set up by an individual.

Watanabe's analysis shows a number of weaknesses in the 2001 reform. For example, he notes two problems with defined contribution plans. First, Japan does not have the strict fiduciary responsibility regulations that are important in maintaining the integrity of any defined contribution system. Second, the lack of transparency and fairness in the Japanese financial markets is dangerous for defined contribution plans. Watanabe particularly criticizes the past approach to corporate pension policy for its concentration on addressing minor technical issues instead of the broader structural issues. His recommendations include a call for greater understanding of the importance of strong employee welfare systems in contributing to profitable corporations and the role for pension plans in those systems. Among other recommendations, he also calls for a full review and reconstruction of all social security systems in Japan.

BROAD THEMES DRAWN FROM THE COUNTRY STUDIES

Although the country studies are intended to stand alone, in this section, we draw some broad themes from the country studies. One of the many advantages of the Network is the ability to exchange ideas on common approaches, issues, and solutions. Similarly, the Network provides a forum for respectful professional debate and disagreement.

Importance of Culture in Explaining Differences in Approaches

Underlying pension systems is a complex web of cultural considerations. Those considerations may affect the technical choices of a pension system, and they may also affect the broader policy goals that are inherent in the structure of pension systems. A careful reader will see, sometimes explicitly, but more often implicitly, the effect of culture on the various country systems studied here.

For example, Turner and Muir believe that the high priority placed on individualism in U.S. culture should constrain the mandates imposed on U.S. employment-based and individual retirement plans. In contrast, in Watanabe's study of Japan, he observes the importance of the large number of companies that have been in business for hundreds of years. This pattern of business longevity is often attributed to harmony between a company and its employees (as well as between the company and its customers and society) and a history of lump-sum severance payments that dates from the seventeenth century. The importance placed on the relationship between a company and its current and past employees can be seen in Watanabe's recommendation that stable employee welfare systems, particularly pension plans, contribute to corporate profitability.

These cultural norms of individualism in the United States and of corporate responsibility in Japan stand in stark contrast with the current and ideal systems discussed in some of the European country studies in which government programs are recognized as being the primary route to reliable and reasonably generous pensions. In France, the government plays the primary role in the provision of pension benefits. The mandatory defined benefit pensions provided through the programs of the French government, combined with marginal employer-provided and individual pensions and property income, provide a standard of living for pensioners equivalent to that of other French households. apRoberts and Concialdi argue that the French system of governmental pension provision should be retained and cutbacks that have occurred over time should be rescinded.

Similarly, Hughes and Stewart show that the government-provided social security pension in Ireland provides the largest share of income for households headed by a person aged 65 and over. Not only are government-provided pensions viewed as an acceptable source of pension income in Ireland, Hughes and Stewart argue that resources from the current tax support of nongovernmentally provided pensions should be shifted to government pensions because it would result in a fairer and sustainable pension system.

Even in the United Kingdom, which perhaps has the closest historical and cultural position to the United States among the countries considered in this book, the Pension Commission suggested in 2005 that the government should provide a flat-rate pension at a level that would prevent pensioner poverty. The Pension Commission then suggested an opt-out earnings-related pension for the next supplemental tier of the pension system. The findings to date of behavioral economics teach us that in operation an opt-out system comes very close to being a mandatory system. Davies goes even further and argues that second tier earnings-related pensions should be mandatory.

In contrast with these other European countries, Szczepański argues that Poles do not want to rely on the government of Poland exclusively for pension provision in part because of historical experience. In 1999, Poland put into effect a complicated new pension system, leaving in place the old system for individuals who were aged 50 or older on the date of implementation. The new individual and work-related pensions authorized and encouraged by that reform have not resulted in significant rates of coverage by those plans. The Polish people, thus, appear to have become skeptical of relying too heavily on government involvement in the pension system.

In addition to the European cultural acceptance of a larger role of government in pension provision than in the United States, solidarity is also an important norm in many European countries. This norm can be seen in the Belgian system. Solidarity across workers is reflected in the industry-wide pension plans that cover approximately 60 percent of the workforce in Belgium. De Witte identifies three types of redistributive solidarity and categorizes alternative types of pension accrual, in part, according to the type of redistributive solidarity provided. Ultimately, redistributive solidarity is one of the evaluative criteria De Witte suggests be used in identifying an ideal pension system for Belgium. Davies states that some redistribution is appropriate for pension systems and that it plays an especially important role in pensions for women because of their lower average wages.

Insights on Specific Topics

Improving coverage

Although widespread pension coverage through nongovernmental pension programs is not unheard of, most of the countries studied in this book have voluntary employment-based pension systems that achieve only moderate levels of workforce coverage. Switzerland, however, mandates work-based pension systems and has achieved coverage of about 90 percent of its workforce. The exceptions are low-wage and part-time workers because the Swiss mandate has a wage floor. Belgium also appears to have one of the strongest systems of workplace pension provision. De Witte attributes its high coverage rate at least in part to the fact that many of the plans are industry-wide collectively bargained plans.

In contrast to Switzerland and Belgium, less than half of Irish retirees over age 65 reported receiving a work-related pension. Poland is an even more extreme example of the low end of the coverage spectrum—only 2 percent of workers are covered by work-related pension plans. The country experts appear to be in general agreement that there are three ways to increase coverage rates in work-related pensions. Pension systems could do three things:

1) make work-related pension provision mandatory,
2) make participation in work-related pensions the default with an opt-out opportunity, or
3) increase the incentives for sponsorship and participation in work-related pensions.

A number of countries, including Ireland and the United States, have tried the third approach (i.e., tax incentives) for a number of years. The problems observed with this approach include that tax incentives are of less value to lower paid workers than to higher paid workers and that lower paid workers have less disposable income to contribute to retirement plans.

Not surprisingly, then, given the cultural norms against mandates in some countries, multiple country experts suggest that the second approach, that of coverage defaults with opt-out opportunities, could be an appropriate way to increase pension coverage. Interestingly, this approach is suggested in countries that have quite different pension systems and cultural histories. For example, Szczepański believes that defaults may be useful in Poland, and Turner and Muir make a similar suggestion for the United States. Turner and Muir also acknowledge, though, that there is a danger in defaults in the United States because the system permits distributions from plans for hardships or when workers change employers. If individuals are not committed to pension savings, they may decide to take early distributions, even though they are penalized by the U.S. tax system.

Sharing risks

The global financial crisis reinforced the importance of risk in pension systems. All of the country experts raised concerns about a broad spectrum of risks. The global financial crisis highlighted the risk that an employer might voluntarily, or upon its bankruptcy, terminate a defined benefit plan, resulting in reduced benefits for current or future retirees. In defined contribution plans, the decline of financial markets has resulted in lower account asset levels and dropping interest rates.

Financial market risks and reform proposals related to the benefits provided by defined benefit and defined contribution plans are somewhat difficult to categorize because, in part, they are specific to the details of a country's pension system. Nuances that are important in a given country are lost as this summary becomes quite general. As an example, the United States, the United Kingdom, Germany, and Japan are the only countries with a formal insurance program for defined benefit plans, and those programs decrease the employee risk of employer bankruptcy in those countries. But other countries widely use insurance contracts that are quite stable to prefund work-based defined benefit plans, and these contracts also reduce plan risks. Roth discusses the use of book reserves recorded on a company's balance sheet in lieu of a separate fund for occupational pensions in Germany. This is changing as German companies, especially large ones, revise their approach to meet international accounting standards.

Financial market risks are not the only pension plan risks observed. Both Szczepański and Watanabe suggest that financial market regulations in their respective countries, Poland and Japan, are insufficient to appropriately protect individuals who depend on defined contribution plans for their pensions. Szczepański and Østrup note that a history of governmental amendment or proposed amendment of pension regulations in Poland and Denmark, respectively, imposes risks on the pension systems. Szczepański explicitly recognizes the skepticism of Poles toward government policymakers and states it is a source of Poles' preference not to be entirely dependent on a government-provided pension system. apRoberts and Concialdi discuss the series of technical changes made by the French government to its pension system that are projected to significantly reduce future pensions. They counter this risk by arguing that the governmental system is the safest and most appropriate choice for France, but that it needs to be restored to prior levels. Relating to the political risks affecting benefit levels, Leimgruber recounts the recent rejection by Swiss voters of provisions that would have decreased pension benefits.

Providing adequate benefits

Most if not all of the country studies discuss the question of how much pension is required to provide adequate benefits. In accordance with traditional concepts in pension policy, most country experts write in terms of replacement income. That, of course, simply rephrases the real question as: what level of replacement income is necessary to provide adequate benefits? The authors consider the answer to that question as a percentage, often relying on policy documents or studies in their home countries to set an approximate appropriate standard. Davies's discussion for the United Kingdom is reasonably indicative. He looks to World Bank policy and a 2004 UK Pensions Commission report to conclude that replacement rates should be between 65 and 75 percent for those earning median incomes. In the proposed system, replacement percentages would be set to provide higher percentages for low-income earners, and there would be a flat-rate floor to prevent pensioner poverty. Østrup, in comparison, approaches the question from the perspective of the goals of the pension system and Danish culture. He points out that consumption goals in retirement may be highly individualized, may depend on a standard of living relative to a reference group such as those who practice the same profession as the retiree, or may depend on the standard of living the retiree enjoyed while employed.

Even to the extent that country experts agree as a general matter with this approach, they do not necessarily agree on how to calculate the replacement percentages and what should happen after the pension begins. Should replacement percentages be determined on the last wage earned, or should there be some averaging of earnings over a preretirement period? And, if the pension is indexed once payments begin, how should that indexation occur? apRoberts and Concialdi argue that France's change from indexing to current wages to indexing to current prices will result in lower pension payments and will deprive French retirees of their fair share of gains in labor productivity.

Responding to increased longevity

Increased longevity may affect pension plans on the previously discussed aspects of dimensions of risk and provision of adequate benefits. From a risk standpoint, in a defined benefit plan where the pensioners outlive the expectations under which the plan was funded, costs will be higher and additional funds will need to be contributed to the plan. In an unfunded defined benefit plan, costs similarly increase, perhaps beyond the ability or willingness of the funding entity to maintain the plan and benefits. In a government-funded plan, this may raise the specter of political risk. And, if indexation is insufficient, pensioners receiving defined benefits will see their pension income whittled away by inflation.

In a defined contribution plan, the risk is that an especially long-lived pensioner might outlive the account assets even if the pensioner is reasonably conservative in making account withdrawals. That, of course, overlaps with adequacy risk. Similarly, since many defined contribution plans permit benefits to be paid as a lump sum, pensioners may have the choice to be the opposite of conservative, resulting in a decreased or completely exhausted pension in later years.

Turner and Muir offer a proposal to help counter the longevity risk of increased defined benefit plan costs. They suggest that U.S. law be amended to permit defined benefit plans to shift the cohort risk to plan participants, who are better able than employers to bear that risk. They observe that the idiosyncratic risk of longer-than-average life expectancies should remain on the plan, which is better able than individuals to bear that particular risk.

CONCLUSION

In this chapter we briefly summarized the pension systems of the countries studied as well as examined some of the most significant themes that we observed in the studies. We provide these summaries not as a digest of all of the important ideas that can be drawn from the individual chapters, because the country experts provide a wealth of insights and thoughts about the ideal pension system for each of their countries. Instead, we hope the themes provide a basis for our readers to delve deeper into this book and a platform to compare the proposals and perspectives of this group of pension experts.

2
Imagining the Ideal U.S. Pension System

John A. Turner
Pension Policy Center

Dana M. Muir
Stephen M. Ross School of Business, University of Michigan

Pension systems evolve over time as the economic and demographic environment in which they operate changes and as human institutions and ideas develop. Their structure is influenced by competing political forces, with differing ideological goals and economic interests. The ideal pension system from the perspective of workers may differ from that of employers, and indeed, not all workers nor all employers hold the same views. Systems in different countries may differ because of different national values, philosophies, and economic histories.

This chapter focuses on the long-run goals that different actors have for the U.S. pension system and the differing views on the ideal U.S. pension system. It examines the underlying values and philosophies of different actors affecting the U.S. pension system, with a focus on pensions in the private sector that supplement the national social security system, which are referred to as the private pension system. This private system includes both employer-provided pensions and individually provided pensions. The chapter critiques the current system and suggests policy options for improvements that would move the current system toward an ideal system.

The primary goals of the U.S. pension system from the perspective of workers arguably are to provide secure and adequate retirement income and to cover most workers. In all three respects, the U.S. system needs better solutions. With the decline in defined benefit plans and the increasing reliance on defined contribution plans, some analysts believe that future retirees will have less secure and less adequate retirement income than current retirees.

This chapter is structured as follows. First, it discusses the necessity of balancing the interests of workers and employers in a voluntary pension system. Second, it examines several recent pension policy initiatives. Third, it discusses policy issues relating to the goals of increased coverage, sharing of risks, and adequacy in the U.S. pension system. Fourth, it examines the extent to which other goals play a role in policy debates. Fifth, it presents specific proposals for reforming defined benefit plans and 401(k) plans, the major type of defined contribution plan. Sixth, it presents conclusions.

U.S. PENSION POLICY IN A VOLUNTARY PENSION SYSTEM

American exceptionalism is the concept that the American culture places a much higher weight on individualism—individual freedom and individual responsibility—than do the cultures in most other high-income countries. In those countries, social solidarity, shared responsibility of workers and employers, and the responsibility of the state are given more prominence (Muir 2006). This difference causes the American pension system to differ in some ways from those in other countries, with a greater emphasis on individual choice and individual responsibility.

The United States has a voluntary pension system, which limits the ability of policymakers to make changes that would be in the interest of workers but would increase the costs or risks borne by employers. Employers are not required to provide a pension plan. Any change within this voluntary framework that reduces risk for workers while increasing risk for employers, or that makes benefits more generous for workers while raising costs for employers, may ultimately not serve the interest of workers because it may lead employers to not offer pensions. Employers, however, have other ways of adjusting to increased risks or increased costs in pension plans, but these adjustments also may be adverse to the interests of workers. For example, employers may hire fewer workers, pay less generous wages, or provide less generous benefits in other forms.

Public policy in a voluntary system thus can have the adverse effect of causing employers not to provide pensions. However, these considerations do not imply that no changes should be made that raise costs to employers or that increase the risks they bear. Often, such changes can be made within a balanced package that takes into account the interest of employers by reducing their risks and costs in other ways. Thus, when considering policy options, an option should not be considered in isolation and rejected because of its particular allocation of costs and risks. Such an option could be part of a balanced package of changes that takes into account the interests of both employers and employees.

INITIATIVES FOR THE IDEAL PENSION SYSTEM

In recent years, a broad consensus has emerged that changes are needed in the U.S. pension system, though a consensus as to what those changes should be has not developed. Several organizations have been active in encouraging discussion of the ideal pension system. The Society of Actuaries' Retirement 20/20 initiative (Retirement 20/20 2011) has established principles for the ideal pension system. The Pension Rights Center, which is a pension participants' rights organization, along with a number of other organizations, has established the Retirement USA initiative, which has also established principles for an ideal pension system (Retirement USA 2011). Both groups have held conferences and have issued calls for proposals for new types of pension plans. The ERISA Industry Committee (ERIC), an employers' group, has also issued a proposal for reform—a report titled *A New Benefit Platform for Life Security* (ERIC 2009). The Retirement Security Project, associated with the liberal think tank the Brookings Institution, has focused on reforming 401(k) plans using insights from behavioral economics about the importance of the choice of defaults by plan sponsors (e.g., Iwry and Turner 2009).

Retirement 20/20

Retirement 20/20 has focused on the development of new types of pension plans. To evaluate proposals for new types of plans, it has an elaborate rating system with four key criteria:

1) The plan is self-adjusting to maintain adequate funding and automatically adjusts to changing economic and demographic conditions.
2) The plan aligns roles of different stakeholders with their skills.
3) The plan recognizes new norms for work and retirement, so that it could support flexible work arrangements, such as phased retirement or return to work after a trial retirement.
4) The plan is appropriately aligned with markets and uses market mechanisms effectively to hedge risks.

The Retirement 20/20 initiative recognizes four stakeholders: participants, employers, markets, and society.

Retirement USA

The Retirement USA initiative has three key principles—the retirement system should provide universal coverage, pension benefits should be secure, and pension benefits should be adequate. It has nine other core principles.

1) **Shared responsibility.** Retirement should be the shared responsibility of employers, employees, and the government.
2) **Required contributions.** Employers and employees should be required to contribute a specified percentage of pay, and the government should subsidize the contributions of lower income workers.
3) **Pooled assets.** Contributions to the system should be pooled and professionally managed to minimize costs and financial risks.

4) **Payouts only at retirement.** No withdrawals or loans should be permitted before retirement, except for permanent disability.
5) **Lifetime payouts.** Benefits should be paid out over the lifetime of retirees and surviving spouses, domestic partners, and former spouses.
6) **Portable benefits.** Benefits should be portable when workers change jobs.
7) **Voluntary savings.** Additional voluntary contributions should be permitted, with reasonable limits for tax-favored contributions.
8) **Efficient and transparent administration.** The system should be administered by a governmental agency or by private, nonprofit institutions that are efficient, transparent, and governed by boards of trustees that include employer, employee, and retiree representatives.
9) **Effective oversight.** Oversight of the new system should be by a single government regulator dedicated solely to promoting retirement security.

ERISA Industry Committee (ERIC)

In its proposal, ERIC argues that the issues of health security and income security in retirement are so deeply intertwined that any broad revisions should address both components of retirement security. ERIC uses 11 basic principles to evaluate potential benefit plan systems. Employers could continue to offer their current plans rather than developing plans to fit within what ERIC terms a "new benefits platform." The platform for retirement benefits has three parts: a guaranteed benefit plan (modeled on defined benefit plans and including the possibility of hybrid plans), a retirement savings plan (modeled on 401(k) plans), and a short-term security account (which could be used for life event expenses or saved for retirement).

ERIC's proposal envisions benefit administrators who would compete at an individual participant level to provide plan services. This structure is intended to create economies of scale by developing larger pools of plans than individual employers, particularly small employers, could develop on their own. The benefit administrators, not employers, would assume the primary fiduciary and contractual obligations to employees. This feature would reduce legal and administrative burdens on employers. Tax treatment of benefits would be uniform for all workers. Employers would be permitted to retain their current benefit plans rather than being required to switch to the new benefits platform.

COVERAGE, RISK SHARING, AND ADEQUACY

This section examines policy issues in the U.S. pension system concerning extending coverage, risk sharing between employees and employers, and the adequacy of benefits.

Increased Coverage and Participation

A worker is covered by a pension plan if the worker has the option of participating in the plan. A worker is a plan participant if the worker actually is accruing future pension benefits. The distinction between coverage and participation arises in 401(k) plans, where not all workers who are covered participate because they do not contribute, which some plans require for participation.

Few countries with voluntary pension systems similar to the U.S. system have achieved participation rates greater than 50 percent of the workforce. Countries that have higher participation rates generally have mandates (Australia, Switzerland) or widespread collective bargaining (Sweden), neither of which applies in the United States (Turner 2010). Only about half of the U.S. private sector workforce participates at any point in time in an employer-provided pension.

Workers not covered tend to be low-wage, part-time, young, nonunionized, and work for small employers and in the service industry. Women and minorities tend to have lower coverage rates than men and whites.

Many U.S. policymakers and policy experts have long wished to improve the coverage provided by the private sector employer-sponsored pension plans. The federal government has enacted numerous reforms having that goal over the past 30 years. A variety of policy issues apply to reforms targeted at increasing coverage.

The following sections consider policy options for increasing pension coverage and participation.

Mandates

The policy value placed on individualism and individual responsibility is held by many people and limits the options for raising coverage. Underlying many of the policy debates in the United States is the issue of mandates versus free choice. Some people oppose mandates on employers and favor a labor market with less intervention by the government. Those opposing mandates argue they are an unwanted government intrusion in the labor market, interfering with the ability of workers and employers to freely negotiate employment contracts.

Some policy experts argue that universal coverage is neither necessary nor desirable because Social Security provides a high replacement rate for low-wage workers. They argue that the low level of benefits paid to these workers by Social Security is due to the low wages on which the Social Security benefit is based. Thus, according to this view, the proper focus for reform should be on improving wages.

Others, such as the Retirement USA initiative, argue that the goal of the private pension system should be universal coverage, based on the rationale that everyone needs a supplement to Social Security. The generosity of Social Security is being reduced, with benefit cuts due to the legislated increase in the Normal Retirement Age (rising to 67 in 2022) for Social Security, and with Medicare tax increases that are paid out of Social Security benefits. The reductions in Social Security benefits increase the importance of supplemental pension benefits.

Those favoring mandates argue that mandates are the only way to achieve a substantial improvement in pension coverage. Some argue that the mandate should include mandatory annuitization of account balances and no preretirement withdrawals.

Mandates can have different options, including whether employers should be mandated to provide a pension, whether they should be mandated to contribute to a pension or just offer one for employee contributions, and whether mandates should exclude small employers including household employers of domestic help, such as nannies and housekeepers. Often, proposed mandates exclude small employers because the administrative burden on them is greater than on larger employers with human resources departments and benefits specialists. Some people who work at small employers may be covered by pension plans if they are employees of a larger company that provides a service instead of being employed directly by the small employer.

Given that the entire U.S. workforce has access to a tax-favored pension plan—those not covered by an employer plan can contribute on a tax-deferred basis to an Individual Retirement Account (IRA)—the question arises as to what the justification is for more aggressive government policies on coverage by plans sponsored by private sector employers. The counterargument is that few people who lack a pension plan actually set up IRAs.

Paternalism ultimately is a justification for much of retirement income policy. Many people do a poor job of saving for retirement on their own. Even if they have the opportunity to participate in a tax-favored pension plan, such as an IRA, they do not voluntarily do so. That argument takes on greater weight as a reason for aggressive government policies intended to increase pension coverage with the cutbacks in Social Security.

One soft mandate in the United States is found in what are referred to as nondiscrimination rules. These rules require firms that provide a pension to treat lower paid and higher paid workers similarly in terms of percentages of both groups covered and the generosity of the benefits provided relative to wages.

Incentives

Raising pension coverage has proven to be more difficult than once thought by policy experts. Tax incentives to encourage participation in a pension have long been an aspect of the pension system. With the passage of the Employee Retirement Income Security Act of 1974 (ERISA), all workers have had access to a tax-favored pension in that any worker not otherwise participating in a pension plan can make a tax-deductible contribution to an IRA. In the late 1990s, the Roth IRA was established. This type of IRA expanded the options available to some workers, who pay taxes on their contributions but receive their benefits tax free. In a traditional IRA, the pattern is reversed, with qualifying workers not paying taxes on contributions, but receiving taxable benefits. Yet, even with this expansion in options, relatively few workers have set up accounts in either type of IRA for the purpose of contributing to them. Account balances in IRAs have grown considerably, but that is largely a result of contributions from rollovers from 401(k) plans made by workers changing jobs.

Many employers have added a further incentive for workers to participate in the defined contribution plans they provide by matching contributions in 401(k) plans. Some employers do this because of nondiscrimination rules, which require that a minimum percentage of low-wage workers participate or that the employer provide either a contribution to all employees or a minimum matching contribution. Still, roughly a quarter of workers who have the opportunity to participate in those plans forgo both the tax incentive and the matching contribution (Turner and Verma 2007).

New types of plans

A major example of reforms to improve coverage has been the enablement of new types of pension plans. Some reforms have provided new types of pensions for small employers, such as the Simplified Employee Pension and the Savings Incentive Match Plan, recognizing that the pension coverage rate for small employers is low and that the administrative and compliance costs per employee of providing pensions are higher than they are for large employers. These reforms have sought to reduce the regulatory burden placed on small employers relative to large employers. Based on limited data available, it appears that the rate of participation in Simplified Employee Pension plans has never exceeded 2 percent of all employees who participate in pension plans at small employers (EBRI 2009, Table 10.1c).

Ironically, the most popular type of pension plan currently in the United States in terms of the number of workers participating, the 401(k) plan, was not established to improve coverage. Instead, it was an unexpected outgrowth of a technical amendment expected to have limited consequences. When employers provide a defined benefit plan, workers are automatically covered, but when they provide a 401(k) plan, worker coverage generally depends on the willingness of the worker to contribute to the plan. Thus, the problem of workers not participating in a pension plan is due both to employers not offering plans and workers not always participating when offered.

Automatic enrollment and defaults in 401(k) plans

In recent years, as an outcome of the development of behavioral economics, attention has focused on psychological, rather than economic, reasons for why some workers do not participate in pension plans. This approach has led to the development of the use of defaults to encourage participation in 401(k) plans. With this approach, workers are covered by default, with the option to opt out, rather than the traditional approach, where the default is that workers are not covered unless they take an action to enroll. Once covered, inertia may keep workers covered, though the long-term effects of defaults are not known, and may be considerably less favorable than expected, especially for low-income workers, who tend to cash out their pensions at job change.

In recent years, legislation (the Pension Protection Act of 2006) and regulations have facilitated employers' ability to offer automatic enrollment, where newly hired employees are automatically enrolled but have a period of time in which they can opt out without penalty. While some data for a few firms show a large short-term effect of automatic enrollment increasing the percentage of workers participating, longer term studies taking into account leakage due to cash-outs at job change have not been conducted to analyze the longer term effects. Automatic enrollment may result in some low-wage workers paying tax penalties because they accumulate account balances that they did not really want and that they liquidate at job change.

Recent discussion has focused on requiring that employers offer pension plans and that those plans have automatic enrollment.

Conflicting goals

Other policy goals have conflicted with the goal of raising coverage. The effects of these goals on policy outcomes may account in part for the failure of reforms that were intended to raise coverage.

First, the government has attempted to limit the tax loss (sometimes called tax expenditure) for providing pensions, in particular by limiting contributions to fund defined benefit plans and limiting the generosity of benefits provided to higher income workers, typically high level executives. Because of the limitation applicable to high-income workers in tax-favored defined benefit and defined contribution plans, employers have developed nonqualified plans (plans with more limited tax preferences) for those workers. As a result, company executives have less of a stake in the plan for rank-and-file workers, and the rank-and-file plans may be less generous than they otherwise would be. In an ideal pension system, the interests of the executives of a company with respect to the company pension plan would be aligned with the interests of the rank-and-file workers.

Economists argue that the cost of providing pension benefits is ultimately borne by workers through reduced wages and other nonpension compensation, even if the expense is directly paid for by employers. This concept is viewed with skepticism by many non-economists. While that relationship between wages and pensions is clearly visible in the context of collective bargaining, where negotiators bargain for more generous pensions in exchange for less in other forms of compensation, most economists believe that it also occurs in other labor market contexts as well. Thus, if low-wage workers were covered by a pension, their already low wages would be reduced even further, only constrained by minimum wage laws. Raising the costs of employing workers by providing them with pension benefits could lead to a reduction in employment for low-wage workers to the extent that their wages could not be reduced due to minimum wage laws. It could lead to a reduction in other benefits, such as vacation time or health benefits for those who have those benefits.

To deal with these potential problems, proposals to extend coverage to low-wage workers often involve a government subsidy of the cost of the coverage, so that the cost would not be borne by either the employee or the employer, but by taxpayers. The United States currently has the Saver's Credit for low-wage workers. It is a tax credit that benefits low-wage workers who have a tax liability, but it does not benefit the many low-wage workers who are exempt from paying income taxes because of their low income. For this reason, advocates have long argued for a refundable Saver's Credit that would be paid even to workers who owe no personal income taxes.

In sum, increasing pension coverage in the United States has proven to be difficult. The difficulties arise in part because of the voluntary nature of the U.S. pension system. Conflicting goals have doubtless also played a role. However, the ideal U.S. pension system would have higher coverage than that provided by the current system.

Risk Sharing

Risk is a fundamental aspect of pension systems. Because pension plans promise to pay benefits at a future date, risk is inherent. The risks include financial market risk associated with the investments of the plans, portability risk experienced by job changers and workers who are laid off, interest rate risk associated with converting investments into annuities, longevity risk associated with the length of life after retirement, and inflation risk for the accrual of pension benefits and the value of pension benefits in payment. Also, in the context of a voluntary pension system, participants face risks as to plan terminations or freezes, and other plan amendments by employers.

The policy goal of risk sharing is to allocate risks between workers and plan sponsors in a way so that they are borne by the party best able to do so, taking into account the costs of risk bearing and the degree of risk aversion of workers and employers. Diversification is a fundamental concept in the sharing of risks. By diversifying through combining risks that are not perfectly correlated, risks can be reduced. This applies both for financial market risks and demographic risks.

One aspect of diversification of risks for workers in pension systems is to increase the number of workers who participate in both a defined benefit and defined contribution plan. Workers are subject to different risks in defined benefit and defined contribution plans. In defined benefit plans, they are subject to labor market risks, such as that of being laid off. This is a risk because the wages used to calculate benefits in the United States are not price indexed up to the point of retirement, so they erode in value with inflation. In defined contribution plans, workers are subject to capital market risks on the investments in their account. By participating in both types of plans, they are able to diversify and reduce the total amount of risk that they bear.

Another concept in risk bearing is that risks should be borne by the party who can most easily bear them. Idiosyncratic life expectancy risk is the risk that an individual will live longer than expected. Idiosyncratic life expectancy risk is a major risk for individuals in defined benefit plans that are not indexed for inflation. Sponsors of large defined benefit pension plans, however, can more easily bear this risk through having a pool of many participants.

Cohort life expectancy risk is the risk that on average people in a birth cohort will live longer than expected. Cohort life expectancy risk is expensive for defined benefit plan sponsors to bear because they cannot diversify it away. However, it can relatively easily be borne by individual workers because improvements in life expectancy tend to occur gradually over time and because workers are the prime beneficiaries of the improvements. This risk is not borne by plan sponsors in defined contribution plans because those annuities are determined by taking into account cohort improvements in life expectancy. Cohort life expectancy risk is currently borne by plan sponsors in defined benefit plans, but defined benefit plans could be structured so that it is borne by participants.

In sum, risk sharing is a complex topic involving issues of risk diversification and consideration of which party is best able to bear risks. Policies relating to risk sharing need to take into account the voluntary nature of the U.S. pension system and that shifting nondiversifiable risks to employers reduces specific risks that workers bear but may increase the risk that employers will terminate plans, reduce employment, or decrease wages or other benefits. Arguably, in an ideal pension system, risk sharing could be improved by shifting cohort life expectancy risk to workers in defined benefit plans.

Adequacy

The percentage of old-age individuals living in poverty is high in the United States compared to the levels in many other OECD countries. That result occurs in part because the U.S. Social Security program provides a relatively low replacement rate as compared to that in many other OECD countries.

Replacement rates are a common measure of benefit adequacy, but policy analysts differ as to what level they should be. Many people view a replacement rate of between 70 and 80 percent of preretirement earnings as adequate, but some argue for replacement rates between 80 and 90 percent (Mitchell and Turner 2010), and indeed some argue for even higher replacement rates because of the cost of medical care in old age (VanDerhei 2006). Others, however, argue for a lower replacement rate, noting that workers raising children need a relatively low replacement rate, perhaps 65 percent, to maintain their preretirement standard of living in retirement.

Part of the debate over adequacy is whether the goal should be to maintain the individual's preretirement standard of living or to match the standard of living for a particular cohort group such as current workers in the individual's job or industry. As the U.S. population ages, the question of adequacy becomes intertwined with the intergenerational support issue. If the system of pension support is not prefunded, current workers may demand a greater voice in what constitutes an adequate pension benefit.

Adequacy refers not only to benefits received at the point of retirement, but also to benefits received during the length of retirement. Most policy experts feel that more Americans should annuitize at least part of their 401(k) plan account balances (Iwry and Turner 2009). However, relatively few experts have opted in favor of mandating the annuitization of account balances, though some policy experts favor that approach.

In sum, while the measures for improving coverage and the allocation of risk are relatively straightforward, the issue of adequacy involves determining standards for which there is not agreement among policy experts. This lack of agreement may be partially the result of the need for more research to determine how standards of adequacy would differ among people in different situations, such as childless couples as compared to single parents or couples facing the expenses of raising children. Nonetheless, in the view of many policy experts, the ideal U.S. pension system would involve higher levels of pensions for older Americans, which implies the commitment of greater resources to the pension system, and a lower percentage of older Americans living in poverty.

OTHER GOALS

In addition to the three primary goals of coverage, risk sharing, and adequacy, a number of other goals play a role in the development of the U.S. pension system.

Defined Benefit versus Defined Contribution Plans

An issue in the policy debates is the role of defined benefit plans versus defined contribution plans and hybrids in the ideal pension system. This issue actually may be more about how to reach goals than about the goals themselves, but because of its importance, it is highlighted here. Some analysts appear to consider the decline in defined benefit plans as an inevitable outcome because those plans are dinosaurs that are unable to adapt to changing business and employment conditions. A number of policies could be considered, however, based on the alternative view that the endangered status of defined benefit plans is due in part to policy decisions that have caused changes in their regulatory environment. Further, some people argue that defined benefit plans should form the main part of the private pension system, and that 401(k) plans and other defined contribution plans are not really pension plans but rather are savings plans. Although defined benefit plans currently have few champions, labor unions still tend to favor defined benefit plans.

Others favor 401(k) plans because of the large element of individual responsibility they entail, exactly the reason some people do not like them. Policy experts who favor 401(k) plans argue that managing those plans is not too complex for most people, and investment of financial assets is a skill that people should be expected to have. Others argue that people have busy lives, and they should not be expected to become financial experts. The empirical evidence indicates that many people do a poor job of managing their 401(k) plans in terms of the amount they contribute and the investments they choose (Turner 2003).

A major debate is occurring over the appropriate role for 401(k) plans. There is widespread recognition of the shortcomings of these plans—poor investment choices made by participants, many of whom have the opportunity to participate but do not do so, failure to provide annuitized benefits, and high level of risk placed on participants. A number of commentators have called for the retirement of 401(k) plans.

Opinion differs, however, as to what changes are needed for 401(k) plans. Some favor a focus on fixing these plans, and making them more like defined benefit plans in some respects, for example, by requiring that they provide annuities, have automatic enrollment, and provide appropriate default investment vehicles. Others favor looking for new types of plans, preferably hybrid plans that combine the best features of traditional defined benefit and defined contribution plans.

Distributional Issues

The system of providing tax subsidies for pensions has come under heavy criticism. Because the U.S. tax system is progressive, with higher income persons paying higher marginal tax rates, the tax subsidies for pensions, per dollar contributed, are higher for high-income than for low-income persons. This could be remedied by providing tax rebates that are equal across income classes per dollar contributed, a change many people view would move the U.S. pension system toward an ideal system. Others argue that the higher tax subsidies for individuals with higher marginal tax rates appropriately incentivize those individuals to participate in pension plans. In some plans, such as 401(k) plans, the nondiscrimination rules then require the plan to incentivize sufficient numbers of lower paid employees to participate in the plan to meet the minimum requirements of those rules. Thus the tax subsidies, though unequal, support increased plan participation and align the interests of higher and lower paid employees.

Dealing with Increasing Longevity

Life expectancy has increased in the United States, as in many other countries. However, there has been little discussion of pension policy adjustments that might be made in response to this increase. For example, the idea of encouraging people to work longer and take their pension at a later age has received little attention, other than by a few academics. While Social Security in the United States has raised its Normal Retirement Age from 65 to 67, with the adjustment currently being phased in over a 22-year period, private pension plans are more limited in their ability to make similar adjustments (Muir and Turner 2007). Other adjustments could include an increase in the earliest age at which benefits can be received and an increase in the age at which benefits must be taken.

Financial Literacy

Given the role of individual decision-making in the 401(k) system, where workers generally must decide how to invest the account balance of their individual account from a menu of options, greater emphasis is being placed on financial literacy and on financial education for pension participants.

Some, however, oppose this approach and argue instead that less responsibility be placed on workers when making financial decisions about their pension investments. With this approach, pensions would be collectively managed by professional managers, rather than being managed by individual participants. Economies of scale would result in reduced costs, and professional management would result in better investment choices.

In addition, some argue that financial education is not effective. Although some workers may be helped, financial education often seems to have no effect on the workers' decisions.

POLICY RECOMMENDATIONS

This section discusses policy recommendations for 401(k) plans, which are by far the most prevalent type of defined contribution plan, followed by policy recommendations for defined benefit plans.

Policy Recommendations for 401(k) Plans

Since the 1980s, the role of 401(k) plans has changed from being mainly supplementary plans, offered by employers who also offered a defined benefit plan, to often being the only plan employers provide. However, the regulation of 401(k) plans has lagged in recognizing their increasingly important role.

Regulating 401(k) plans as retirement plans

One approach to regulating 401(k) plans has been called the "DB-ification" of 401(k) plans. This approach calls for changes in 401(k) plans that would make them more like defined benefit plans. These changes include automatic enrollment of employees as the default (with an opt-out option), default investment in life cycle or target date funds, and an automatically increasing contribution rate. Automatic enrollment, however, may result in some low-wage workers paying tax penalties because they accumulate account balances that they did not really want and that they liquidate at job change.

Clear disclosure of costs

Participants in 401(k) plans are frequently unaware of the investment and administrative costs they bear in their 401(k) plans. An underlying premise of the 401(k) system is that workers are capable of making good decisions concerning investments. However, good decisions are not possible if workers do not have easy access to information concerning fees. This information is available for many workers through the prospectuses of the mutual funds they invest in, but research has shown that most people find prospectuses confusing and do not read them when making financial decisions (Turner and Witte 2008).

Increased fee transparency also may encourage employers to offer lower cost investment options in 401(k) plans. If employers seriously consider the more transparent fees when choosing plan options, the resulting competition may drive down fees across the investment industry. Thus, even if participants do not scrutinize fees, increased fee transparency and increased scrutiny by employers in choosing options may lower investment costs.

Some policy experts recommend that the fees participants pay in dollars, as well as the expense ratio for investment expenses, should be disclosed on the annual and quarterly account statements they receive. This type of disclosure is done in Australia for plan administrative fees and by the Janus mutual funds for investment costs. Advocates of increased disclosure believe that the information can be provided in a low-cost way simply by providing a standardized disclosure of the level of fees paid in dollars annually for an account of $10,000. Disclosures should be kept simple, so that they will be understandable to participants.

Opponents argue that many participants will not benefit from such disclosure because they will not take it into account when making decisions. In addition, participants may not understand the implications of the disclosure. Opponents also believe that standardizing fee disclosures for a given account balance may be misleading to individuals with substantially different account balances. This is especially true to the extent flat fees are charged rather than percentage fees based on asset balances. Disclosure advocates respond that, with increasing account balances, more experience with investing, and better financial education, larger numbers of workers would benefit from more extensive disclosure.

In October 2010, the U.S. Department of Labor (DOL) issued new disclosure requirements for 401(k) plans. Plans are required to disclose administrative fees charged to the accounts and charges for individual expenses, such as charges for taking a loan from a plan account. In addition to performance and benchmark information, for investments that do not have a fixed rate of return, plans must report the total annual operating expenses of the investment both as a percentage of assets and as a dollar amount for each $1,000 invested. Thus the DOL appears to believe that, despite the added costs resulting from additional disclosure, the additional disclosure will be of sufficient value to plan participants.

Clear disclosure of benefits

Employees may not understand the relationship between 401(k) account balances and future retirement benefits. This situation could be addressed by requiring employers to report annually to employees how much their current 401(k) balance would provide in monthly payments at retirement age, based on reasonable assumptions. This could be done by providing an example, based on an account of $10,000, a stated life expectancy, and a stated retirement age. This low-cost approach would provide workers an idea of how their account balance would translate into a retirement benefit. Research in behavioral economics has demonstrated the low level of financial knowledge of many Americans, and improved disclosure of this type would help some workers have a better idea of how much they need to save to meet their retirement goals.

Opponents of this type of required reporting of 401(k) account balances are skeptical of the extent to which such increased reporting would affect participant behavior given the strength of the inertia effects that have been reported by behavioral economists. The disclosure of projected monthly benefits also may be misleading and confusing because they will be heavily dependent on assumptions, including life expectancy and interest rates. Those assumptions may create expectations that the lump sum account balance can be annuitized at retirement to achieve the projected monthly benefits. In fact, the assumptions may change over an employee's working career and annuity rates may depend on a variety of factors that are not knowable until retirement.

Leakage

Preretirement disbursements of pension money are particularly a problem in 401(k) plans. Many policy analysts argue that the tax-favored nature of the money means that it should not be available to participants until retirement. Opponents of locking up retirement account balances fear that lack of access to the money would decrease the willingness of employees to make voluntary plan contributions. If some access is permitted in limited circumstances to meet this concern, then at a minimum, account balances over a minimal threshold should not be distributed on job change.

Dealing with market meltdowns

Workers age 50 and older have higher allowed contributions to 401(k) plans than younger workers. These contributions are called "catch up" contributions, based on the idea that older workers may not have saved adequately for retirement. Catch up contributions might be allowed for all workers during an economic downturn, so that they could compensate for the losses in their defined contribution plans. Opponents of permitting such contributions for all workers argue that they could result in a windfall for young workers whose account balances have many years to recover. The increased cost of the tax incentives for all workers also may be politically unacceptable during an economic downturn.

Policy Recommendations for Defined Benefit Plans

Defined benefit plans have declined considerably in their role in the U.S. pension system. Nonetheless, relatively little importance has been placed in policy debates on policies that might reverse this trend. Most people appear to have accepted the decline in defined benefit plans, without considering the role that public policy might have played in that decline. A number of policies could be considered to address this issue.

Equal tax treatment

Differing from most countries with private pension systems, private sector defined benefit plans in the United States are the only major type of pension plan that does not permit employee tax-deductible contributions. Employee tax-deductible contributions are permitted for 401(k) plans and for defined benefit plans for state and local government employees. Non-tax-deductible employee contributions are permitted for private sector defined benefit plans, but those contributions do not make economic sense, and are consequently rare, because of the alternative of relying on employer contributions, which are tax deductible.

Extending tax deductibility of contributions to private sector defined benefit plan participants would help level the playing field between defined benefit plans and 401(k) plans. The tax deductibility of employee contributions appears to be a major reason for the popularity of such contributions in 401(k) plans. Permitting employees to make tax-deductible contributions to defined benefit plans would reduce the direct costs of those plans that are borne by employers and shift costs onto employees. Among countries where defined benefit plans play a major role in their pension system, the United States is practically unique in not permitting tax deductibility of employee contributions. In most countries with defined benefit plan systems, employee contributions play a major role in financing the plans.

Dealing with rising life expectancy

The increase in life expectancy appears to have contributed to the decline in defined benefit plans because defined benefit plans lack the flexibility to deal readily with this continued increase in cost to employers (Muir and Turner 2007). In the United States, some plans have reduced their benefits, but generally this change is only done for new hires and thus has limited effect on the plan sponsor's costs.

A policy innovation, following the example of the Notional Defined Contribution plan in Sweden, would be to permit life expectancy indexing of benefits at retirement. This policy would reduce both costs and risks for employers.

For each new retirement cohort, the generosity of the plan would be adjusted downward to reflect the trend toward greater life expectancy. Under U.S. law, this innovation currently would not be allowed because it would violate the anti-cutback rule, which is defined in terms of annual benefits. If it were redefined to take an economist's perspective and use lifetime benefits as the measure, life expectancy indexing would not constitute a cutback in lifetime benefits. This feature would shift cohort life expectancy risk to workers, who are better able to bear this risk than are employers.

Linking interests of management to workers

The tax system could be used to encourage broader coverage through defined benefit plans. For example, to tie the interests of management to those of workers, the allowable maximum income considered for determining defined benefit plan benefits could be raised in plans that provide coverage to all full-time workers. Another option, possibly in combination with the first, could require that employers provide similar plan features for rank-and-file workers as they provide for executives.

One change to align the interests of management with the interests of the rank-and-file was made in recent years to the funding requirements of defined benefit plans. If a company's defined benefit plan is insufficiently funded and certain other criteria are met, then the company is prohibited from making contributions to non-tax-qualified plans for specified executives.

Funding rules

Volatility in employer contributions to defined benefit plans has increased due to changes in funding rules that restrict the timing of employer contributions. Funding rules prohibit employers from contributing to defined benefit plans in years when plan overfunding exceeds a certain level. Even though employees continue to accrue benefits, plan sponsors cannot contribute toward the increased liabilities of their plans in those years.[1] This prohibition on contributions generally occurs when the stock market and companies are performing well. Because pension plans are long-term commitments and because of the fluctuations in the stock market, plan sponsors then are required to make contributions at a later date. This requirement generally occurs when the stock market and companies are performing poorly. The resulting temporal pattern of contributions not only increases the volatility of contributions, it forces plan sponsors to contribute on a schedule exactly opposite to what they would choose.

To reduce the volatility and timing problem of employer contributions for defined benefit plan funding, both the maximum and minimum contribution requirements can be eased. For example, plans could be allowed to contribute 25 percent of normal cost any year, regardless of funding level, which would permit them to contribute in years when the plan was overfunded. They would still have minimum requirements in years the plan was underfunded, but those requirements should be less onerous and more within the employer's control because of the added funding they could make in years the plan was overfunded.

Volatility could also be reduced by higher target funding levels with longer time periods to reach them. With higher target funding levels, the likelihood that plans would become underfunded would be reduced. An alternative approach would be to use a three-year moving average of funding ratios to smooth changes in funding ratios and thus smooth contributions. This approach has been proposed in Canada.

Lost pensions

The lost pension problem is a problem for workers who are laid off or who change jobs (Blake and Turner 2002). It can be difficult for a worker to track down a pension from a former employer, particularly if that employer has gone out of business. Both the United Kingdom and Australia have made significant efforts to assist people facing this problem.

In the United States, the Pension Benefit Guaranty Corporation (PBGC) maintains a missing participants list for defined benefit plans that the PBGC has acquired and for terminated defined benefit plans. Legislation enacted in 2006 requires the PBGC to extend that program to include former participants in defined contribution plans and in other less common types of plans. The PBGC has not yet issued regulations on the extension of the program. At this time, however, it appears that the program still will not cover some potentially lost participants such as those in non-terminated defined benefit plans.

CONCLUSIONS

Pension policy is an evolving product of social institutions and the economy. With the decline in defined benefit plans and the increasing role of 401(k) plans, improvement is needed in the way pensions are provided to U.S. workers. The regulation of 401(k) plans needs to be updated to recognize that they generally are no longer supplementary plans, perhaps retaining the current, less-stringent regulation, when they are supplementary plans. Policies need to be enacted to strengthen defined benefit plans by making them more flexible and improving the ways they are funded, for example, by allowing employers more flexibility to make contributions to plans during times of high asset values and high interest rates. Such a change could help address the issue of the volatility of employer contributions to defined benefit plans. Improvements in risk sharing could be enabled by legislation, such as permitting plans to shift the risk of improvements in cohort life expectancy to workers.

Note

1. Depending on interest rate movements, plan liabilities might not increase.

References

Blake, David, and John A. Turner. 2002. "Lost Pensions and Lost Pensioners." *Benefits Quarterly* 18(3): 51–64.

Employee Benefit Research Institute (EBRI). 2009. *EBRI Databook on Employee Benefits*. Washington, DC: EBRI. http://www.ebri.org/pdf/publications/books/databook/DB.Chapter%2010.pdf (accessed June 22, 2011).

ERISA Industry Committee (ERIC). 2009. *A New Benefit Platform for Life Security*. Washington, DC: ERISA Industry Committee. http://www.eric.org/forms/uploadFiles/ccea00000007.filename.ERIC_New_Benefit_Platform_FL0614.pdf (accessed June 22, 2011).

Iwry, J. Mark, and John A. Turner. 2009. "New Behavioral Strategies for Expanding Lifetime Income in 401(k)s." In *Automatic: Changing the Way*

America Saves, William G. Gale, J. Mark Iwry, David John, and Lina Walker, eds. Washington, DC: Brookings Institution Press, pp. 151–170.

Mitchell, Olivia S., and John A. Turner. 2010. "Labor Market Uncertainty and Pension System Performance." In *Evaluating the Financial Performance of Pension Funds,* Richard Hinz, Heinz P. Rudolph, Pablo Antolin, and Juan Yermo, eds. Washington, DC: World Bank, pp. 119–158.

Muir, Dana M. 2006. "The U.S. Culture of Employee Ownership and 401(k) Plans." *Elder Law Journal* 14(1): 1–33.

Muir, Dana, and John A. Turner. 2007. "Longevity and Retirement Age in Defined Benefit Pension Plans." In *Work Options for Older Americans*, Teresa Ghilarducci and John A. Turner, eds. South Bend, IN: University of Notre Dame Press, pp. 212–231.

Retirement 20/20. 2011. *Envisioning the Future.* Schaumberg, IL: Society of Actuaries. http://retirement2020.soa.org/ (accessed June 29, 2011).

Retirement USA. 2011. *Working for a Universal, Secure and Adequate Retirement System.* Washington, DC: Pension Rights Center. http://www.retirement-usa.org/steering-committee (accessed June 29, 2011).

Turner, John A. 2003. "Errors Workers Make in Managing 401(k) Investments." *Benefits Quarterly* 19(4): 75–82.

———. 2010. *Pension Policy: The Search for Better Solutions.* Kalamazoo, MI: W.E. Upjohn Institute for Employment Research.

Turner, John A., and Satyendra Verma. 2007. "Why Some Workers Don't Take 401(k) Offers: Inertia versus Economics." CeRP Working Paper 56/07. Moncalieri, Italy: Center for Research on Pensions and Welfare Policies.

Turner, John A., and Hazel A. Witte. 2008. "Fee Disclosure to Pension Participants: Establishing Minimum Standards." Toronto: University of Toronto, Rotman International Centre for Pension Management.

VanDerhei, Jack. 2006. "Measuring Retirement Income Adequacy: Calculating Realistic Income Replacement Rates." *EBRI Issue Brief*, No. 297, September. http://www.ebri.org/pdf/briefspdf/EBRI_IB_09-20061.pdf (accessed June 22, 2011).

3
Imagining the Ideal UK Pension System

Bryn Davies
Union Pension Services Limited

This chapter presents what I imagine to be the ideal pension system for the United Kingdom. It is in the nature of a thought experiment,[1] where the theory or hypothesis to be tested is that it is possible to imagine a pension system that meets a set of desirable objectives, while being constrained as little as possible by politics or the existing structures of pension provision. This contrasts with most discussions on pension provision that focus on these practical constraints. Although a concentration on what is practical is understandable, and perhaps even inevitable, the question is how far it is useful when considering the shape of an "ideal" pension system, given the triple goals of providing socially acceptable benefits, improving coverage, and reducing risks.

Such an exercise faces real constraints. First, ideology still plays some part in whatever is proposed. We all belong to various "epistemic communities" and use our own "conceptual tools" (Ervik 2005). It also determines the language that we use to describe these ideas, and we need to recognize the impact that language has on the outcome of these debates (Davies 2009). None of us is free of ideology, but we can try to control for its impact by being as open as possible about where we stand. Readers can then make the necessary adjustment from their own perspective. The problem comes when ideas are presented as being value-free when, in fact, they are highly subjective.[2]

The second constraint is that the chapter considers only the situation in the United Kingdom, and it is presented entirely as an approach to providing pensions in the United Kingdom. Lessons can be learned from other countries, and it is even possible that other countries can learn from the experience of the United Kingdom. But as Barr and Diamond (2010) point out, when implementing pension reform, "choice is constrained by [a country's] fiscal, political and constitutional capacity." So, as a result, the ideas presented are bound to be shackled, however reluctantly, by existing structures.

The third constraint is that this chapter can only skim the surface of what is really a major exercise, leaving out much of the background and concentrating on the structure of what is ideal, rather than on general principles. However, there are other sources for the background, including a series of reports from the UK's Pensions Commission[3] that were produced from 2004 to 2006. While I do not agree with all of the Commission's analysis and conclusions, there is no point repeating the extensive and detailed work that it undertook in providing the data and setting out the issues that face anyone considering the UK pension system. The Pensions Policy Institute (PPI) has also provided a useful series of reports on UK pensions[4] although, again, I do not agree with all of its conclusions. For an understanding of the principles that should govern pension reform, reference should be made to those laid down in the recent work of Nicholas Barr and Peter Diamond (Barr and Diamond 2009).

Given these constraints, this chapter is structured as follows. First, it briefly explains what is still wrong with the UK pension system, despite some recent reforms. Second, it discusses the elements of pensions that should be provided in a civilized and prosperous society. Third, it considers the role of the State in mandating and/or encouraging these different types of provision. Fourth, it discusses how the required level of retirement income should be provided in practice, setting out a comprehensive approach with appropriate roles for State, employment-based, and personal provision. Fifth, it discusses how the pensions could and should be financed. Conclusions are offered in the final section. Throughout the chapter, I concentrate on the structure of pension provision, rather than on the parameters that should be applied to that structure.

WHAT IS WRONG WITH THE CURRENT UK PENSION SYSTEM?

A short outline of the current UK pension system is provided in Appendix 3A.

The Pensions Commission (2005) concluded that, "The current pension system combined with the current state system will deliver increasingly inadequate and unequal results." The Commission pointed out that while the State had planned to play a reduced role in pension provision for the average pensioner on the assumption that voluntary market-based private provision would increase, such an increase was simply not happening. The reasons identified for this failure were that employers' willingness to provide pensions voluntarily was actually falling and initiatives to stimulate personal pension saving on a voluntary basis had not worked.

In the light of these problems, the Commission recommended two key changes:

1) Reform of the State system (social security) to provide a more generous flat-rate pension that would be less means-tested and closer to a universal benefit with the intention of more effectively preventing poverty while not deterring private pension plans.
2) Automatic enrollment of all employees into a private pension plan, with the right for an individual to opt out, and a default pension savings plan based on compulsory contributions at a minimum 8 percent level from workers and their employers and a low annual management charge.

The Commission's general approach was adopted by the last government, which outlined its proposals in a White Paper in 2006 (Department of Work and Pensions 2006), and the proposals were subsequently incorporated into legislation. Following the General Election held in 2010, the new coalition government indicated that it intended to proceed with the reforms.

Unfortunately, despite the reforms, the UK pension system still falls short of the standards required by an ideal pension system and will continue to do so, even in the longer term when the recent reforms are fully in effect. These shortcomings are explored in more detail later but the main failures can be summarized as follows:

- An overreliance on market-based pension provision, with its inherent inefficiencies, high costs, and excessive risks, which means that many pensioners will still end up with inadequate incomes.
- The right for individuals to choose not to have any pension in addition to the State flat-rate pension (social security) will lead to greater inequalities in retirement between those who belong to an adequate private pension arrangement and those who do not.

It has been frequently suggested that an additional problem is that the Commission's approach means an even more complex pension system than the current one, for example, having two flat-rate pensions with different qualification conditions. However, I am not convinced that having a complex structure is, in itself, a problem, provided that the system delivers adequate pensions without requiring people to make complex decisions. Some level of complexity is inevitable in any system that seeks to protect citizens' accrued rights, and these should not be wished away, however inconvenient they may be.

HOW MUCH PENSION?

The first question that needs to be answered in designing the ideal pension system is how much pension do people need? This amount is typically expressed in terms of the "replacement ratio," that is, the ratio of an individual's income in retirement to that they received at work. The most plausible assumption is that most people will typically expect to have broadly the same standard of living in retirement they enjoyed while working. This is not to say the people would not like a higher income after they retire, and people might need a greater income in retirement than they received while working because, with increased leisure time, they have more opportunities to spend. In any event, there is no doubt that when it comes to income, more is better. Nevertheless, the general objective of the ideal pension system is to allow people to maintain their standard of living into retirement, apart from those with the lowest incomes who, as discussed below, might expect to improve their standard of living.

In practice, research suggests that the standard of living can be maintained in retirement with a lower income than that received while at work and that this will be regarded as adequate by pensioners themselves. A working paper from the Center for Retirement Research (CRR) states that this is because of differences in taxation, a reduction in the need to save, and elimination of work-related expenditures (Munnell and Soto 2005). The working paper concluded that, based on a range of studies that had examined the issue, "middle class people need between 70 and 75 percent of their pre-retirement earnings to maintain their life style once they stop working." The Pensions Commission suggested a lower figure, referring to research that suggests people on average will aspire to a retirement income that is two-thirds of their earnings during their working life (Pensions Commission 2005). A 1994 World Bank report suggested tentatively an even lower figure of "say, 60 percent of the gross average lifetime wage for the average worker" (World Bank 1994).

Such targets are clearly meant to be an average and both individual circumstances and preferences mean that the ideal will vary from person to person. For example, some will need less pension income because they have also accumulated or inherited assets that they are prepared to use to maintain their lifestyle. There are also individual choices to be made about the distribution of consumption over a lifetime. There are also practical difficulties in defining the replacement ratio; for example, the CRR Report points out the difficulty of deciding what should be in the numerator and denominator of the ratio. Should the denominator (work income) be averaged over the working lifetime or only that received in the run up to retirement? Despite these practical and conceptual difficulties, the replacement ratio is too useful a tool to discard when looking at pension systems. It is assumed for the purposes of this chapter, therefore, that the denominator is based on the individual's revalued average lifetime earnings from employment and that the numerator includes state and private pensions but not income from investments and disinvestment of assets, including property.

Given the objective of replacing earnings, the question of whether a pension system creates too great a disparity in retirement incomes is really a question about whether there is too great a disparity in incomes among working people. This suggests that excessive income disparities would be better resolved in the context of the earnings that people receive, rather than their pensions. However, it is generally accepted that there is still a role for some income redistribution within the pension system. The point is particularly significant for the pensions accrued by women who, on average, still receive significantly lower earnings than men.

In practice, this means that people who have lower average incomes while working require higher replacement ratios. The Pensions Commission (2004), for example, states that, "lower income people may need a high consumption replacement rate to be assured of what society considers a minimum acceptable standard of living." The World Bank (1994) similarly suggested that there should be a floor on the replacement rate set at the poverty line for low-income workers. So, if it is assumed that the desirable replacement ratios quoted above of between 60 percent and 75 percent are for people with middle incomes, those with lower incomes should be entitled to a higher ratio, possibly up to 100 percent or more. For example, the Pensions Commission (2004) suggested a range of benchmark replacement ratios, from 80 percent of gross earnings for the lowest earners, to 67 percent for median earners and 50 percent for top earners.

To summarize, while there is obviously scope for disagreement about the precise figures, there is general agreement that the target replacement rate should increase as preretirement earnings decline. Such a structure can be defined in a number of ways, but in the United Kingdom, the practice has been to use a combination of a flat-rate element that is paid regardless of lifetime earnings, plus an earnings-related element that is expressed as a proportion of the individual's revalued lifetime earnings in excess of a minimum, which is referred to as a disregard. On this basis, the general formula that defines the level of pension provision, based on the individual's revalued lifetime earnings, is as follows:

$$P = (FRE + [ARE - D] \times T) \div ARE,$$

where

P = pension (expressed as the replacement ratio),
FRE = flat-rate element (£),

ARE = average revalued earnings (£),

D = disregard from earnings (£) when calculating the earnings-related element, and

T = target ratio for the earnings-related element.

While the pattern is clear, there is still room for considerable discussion about the value of the various parameters and, hence, the overall outcome. However, I suggest that the parameters should be set to meet two objectives:

1) The flat-rate element, which is all those who earn less than the disregard will receive, has to be sufficient to provide an acceptable standard of living in retirement for those with the lowest incomes.
2) The flat-rate and the earnings-related elements taken together should produce a target replacement rate of between 65 and 75 percent for those with median incomes.

What should be regarded as a sufficient flat-rate element for this purpose is obviously open to debate, but it is generally agreed that it should be set at a level that keeps people out of poverty, that is, above the "poverty line." I have assumed for the sake of illustration that it should be 60 percent of the median United Kingdom household income for a single person with no dependents.[5]

The figure leaves out any allowance for housing costs because, as discussed below, it is assumed that these will be met in full for people with the lowest incomes through separate housing benefit arrangements. In current terms, this amounts to a flat-rate element of about £6,500 per year. Coincidentally, this figure is also close to about 60 percent of the annual equivalent of the UK national minimum hourly wage.

The two objectives can be achieved in a number of ways, depending on the relationship between the disregard and the earnings-related target. In the United Kingdom the practice has been to set the disregard at 100 percent of the flat-rate element. This has appeared to work reasonably well, provided the flat-rate element is at or above the poverty line. Given median annual earnings for people in full-time employment of £25,428 per year (Office for National Statistics 2009) and a flat-rate pension of £6,500 per year, the flat-rate element will provide a 25 percent replacement rate for someone with median earnings. So, if the target for the overall replacement rate is 70 percent, the earnings-related element would have to be 45 percent of total earnings or 60 percent of earnings in excess of a disregard that is equal to the flat-rate element. The total income that is produced by the formula previously shown, expressed as the replacement rate, is shown by the line in Figure 3.1.

One possible criticism of this set of outcomes is that individuals with revalued lifetime earnings greater than the median would fall short of the target range. However, the assumption is that people with higher lifetime incomes will typically be able to make up the shortfall from resources other than their pension.

A number of important associated points deserve a fuller treatment but can only be highlighted in this chapter:

- Pensioners should share in the rising living standards of the country as a whole, so the benefit specified above should be indexed to national average earnings.
- It is assumed that the social and medical care required in retirement will be funded separately by the employed population on an insurance basis, which means the National Health Service in the United Kingdom, so such costs do not need to be considered when determining pensioners' regular incomes.
- There are strong arguments for social care for the elderly to be provided on a similar basis, so such costs would also not need to be considered when determining pensioners' regular incomes.
- The target is on a per person basis, with no allowance for the potential savings of living as a couple; that is, all rights should be on an individual basis and there are no derived rights.
- Any additional social payments in regards to children and other dependents for pensioners on low incomes should be covered by the same arrangements as those available to citizens of working age.
- In the same way, support for housing costs for pensioners on low incomes should also be covered by the same arrangements as those available to citizens of working age.
- No account is taken of any additional benefits or concessions, for example, concessionary travel arrangements that are provided for social reasons on the basis of age.

Figure 3.1 Target Replacement Ratio

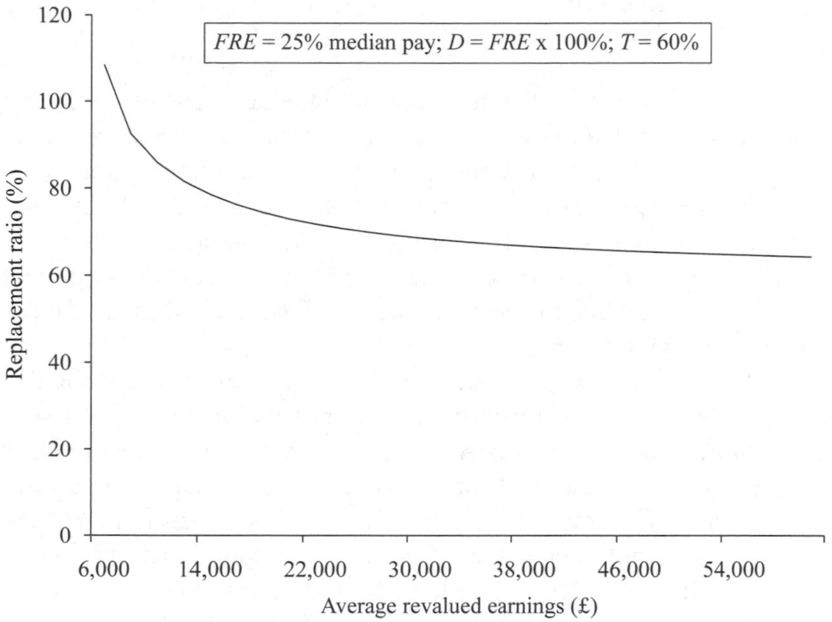

NOTE: *FRE* is the flat-rate element, *D* is the disregard from earnings when calculating the earnings-related element, and *T* is the target for the earnings-related element.

One key issue in designing the ideal pension system is the age at which the pension comes into payment. While not denying the significance of this key parameter in establishing the overall value of a pension system, I do not address this issue in this chapter—the target pension level should apply whatever the pension age. However, it is clear that there is a choice to be made between keeping retirement age down and the level of pension that can be paid. This relationship is clear and direct for funded pension arrangements—the later a person retires the higher the income that can be taken from the accumulated fund—but it is also relevant for unfunded plans, given the resources that are available to pay pensions. The corollary, however, is that an increase in pension age is directly equivalent to a reduction in pension, with the greatest adverse effect on those groups in society with lower life expectancy and poorer health. This raises the issue as to whether and, if so, how pensions should be paid on more favorable terms to such groups.

WHAT IS THE ROLE OF THE STATE IN PROMOTING THIS LEVEL OF PENSION?

Given the answer to the question of how much pension should be provided, the next question is how much of it should the State mandate and how much should it merely encourage? The argument in favor of compulsion is essentially that people can be myopic and lack information, despite the evidence that those with higher incomes in retirement have much higher levels of satisfaction. In the long run, the argument goes, everyone will be pleased that they were compelled to have a decent income in retirement.

In large part I accept the argument for compulsion but recognize that there is still scope for individual choice within the overall suggested target. For example, those who have or anticipate access to other non-pension assets may well prefer to consume current income now, rather than being compelled to put some of it into a pension that they will not enjoy until later in their lifetime. So although there is general agreement that some level of benefits should be compulsory, the issue is determining what that level should be and, in particular, whether it should extend beyond the flat-rate element.

The Pensions Commission approached this topic by identifying four levels of activity for the State in promoting a pension system, as shown in Figure 3.2 (Pensions Commission 2005). In essence, the Pensions Commission's (2005) suggestion was that the State should:

1) Ensure the provision of a minimum income, that is, the flat-rate poverty prevention element.
2) Strongly encourage the provision of half the target earnings-related element through auto-enrollment with opt-out rights.
3) Enable the provision of the other half of the earnings-related element by offering a low-cost option.
4) Facilitate purely voluntary additional provision through tax relief.

This type of setup raises a number of questions, such as what is the difference between "enables" and "facilitates"? There are also questions about the degree of activity at each level, such as whether the provision that the Commission wanted to strongly encourage should, in fact, be compulsory. But the general approach, based on a range of levels of pressure from the State, provides a system that makes the different elements of pension provision work together to produce the desired level of total retirement income, while also offering individuals a reasonable degree of flexibility to exercise their personal preferences about that income.

The pattern of provision illustrated in Figure 3.2, within the overall target replacement ratio shown in Figure 3.1, is illustrated in Figure 3.3. The separate issue of how these pension elements should be provided and by whom is addressed in the next section.

Figure 3.2 Target Pension Income as a Percentage of Earnings for the Median Earner at the Point of Retirement

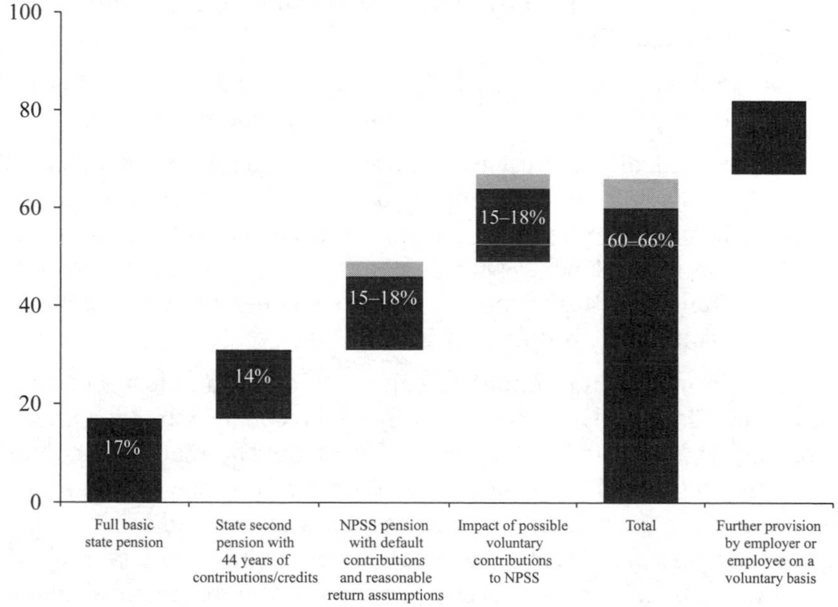

NOTE: NPSS is the National Pension Savings Scheme proposed by the Pensions Commission.

SOURCE: Pensions Commission's Second Report (p. 19); http://www.webarchive.org.uk/wayback/archive/20070801230000/http://www.pensionscommission.org.uk/publications/2005/annrep/main-report.pdf.

This general approach provides the foundation for an ideal pension system, but one significant change is needed to the structure proposed by the Pensions Commission to achieve my ideal. The earnings-related element that the Commission says the State should strongly encourage should be ensured; that is, it should be mandatory. A World Bank (1994) report offers some support for this approach: "the government-mandated replacement should probably be only about half of the gross average lifetime salary for the average worker."

The Pensions Commission (2005) had three arguments against making this element mandatory that can be summarized as follows:

1) Mandatory provision of this element would be on either an unfunded basis that is untenable within the acceptable public expenditure limit and would tend to crowd out adequate flat-rate provision, or on a funded basis that may be seen by many people as taxation by another name and therefore might have the same effect.
2) Individual preferences differ, and there should be scope for different preferences between saving more and retiring later.
3) Individual circumstances differ. An increasing number of people will be able to use housing assets (either accumulated themselves or inherited) to fund at least part of their consumption in retirement, whereas others will not, which means that straightforward compulsion on a significant scale could be against some people's interests.

The arguments for permitting some flexibility are clear, but none of them leads directly or unequivocally to the conclusion that compulsion should be limited to the flat-rate element. The real issue is how much flexibility, and given the general wish for everyone to have an adequate income in retirement (where adequacy is assessed in relation to the individual's preretirement income), there is nothing inevitable about limiting the State's role to poverty prevention. But this is not a technical argument about pensions; it is part of a much broader philosophical debate about the role of the State in a free society. Some more practical points, however, can be made in favor of State involvement with the provision of earnings-related pensions.

Figure 3.3 The Role of State Pension Commission Proposals

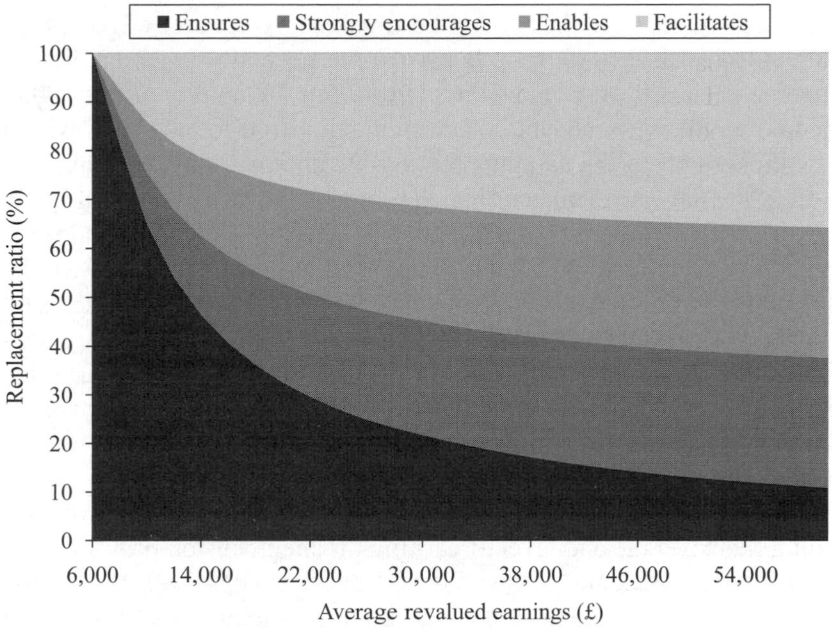

First, requiring a minimum level of earnings-related pension will reduce inequalities in society, for example, between those who work foremployers that provide complementary pensions, including those in the public sector, and those who work for employers that do not. The Labour Party identified the problem of having "two nations in old age" in the ground-breaking report "National Superannuation" (Labour Party 1957). The report identified the "privileged minority," who were entitled to an occupational pension and the "unprivileged majority," who are outside any sort of superannuation plan. The report concluded that everyone should accrue an earnings-related pension, and the following 50 years saw successive efforts to spread the advantages of having such superannuation more widely. But now, as reported by the Pensions Commission, the spread has gone into reverse, both in terms of coverage and benefits provided (Pensions Commission 2004). Put simply, earnings-related pensions for all employees are a reasonable social objective that has not been delivered by a reliance on voluntarism.

Second, at least part of the earnings-related element of the pension needs to be provided on a risk-free basis which, as is explained in the next section, requires the State to be involved. Avoidance of risk is not just an individual preference but a simple necessity when applied to income needed to stay above the poverty line. What this means is that people with low to median incomes cannot afford to take risks with a significant part of the earnings-related income that they need in addition to the flat-rate element. This type of system, however, would only be equitable if the costs and benefits of providing risk-free earnings-related pensions are spread across the working population as a whole. Currently, public service workers in the United Kingdom are often said to be unduly privileged because they have risk-free supplementary pensions, whereas most workers in the private sector do not. Clearly this difference exists, but given the importance of good pension provision, the right answer must be to improve risk-free provision where it is inadequate, not to cut it back where it is adequate.

Third, the only real success in the United Kingdom in terms of widening the coverage and level of earnings-related pension provision has been the little-recognized mandatory State Earnings Related Pension Scheme (SERPS). There were three main problems with SERPS: the perception was that it would become too expensive; it was subjected to a series of cutbacks, which led to the belief that it would offer a poor deal to pensioners; and it was poorly understood, with almost no one willing to promote its advantages. It also suffered because the basic State pension was tied to prices, rather than earnings, so that SERPS (later named the State Second Pension or S2P) was expected more and more to play a poverty prevention role, for which it was ill-suited. Despite all these difficulties, it has resulted in the great majority of new retirees over the last decade receiving worthwhile earnings-related pensions in addition to the flat-rate basic State pension. Unfortunately, this record of success in delivering pensions has largely been ignored.

Even when these arguments are accepted, the question of how much of the total earnings-related target should be provided through a mandatory element and how much should be provided by an element that is encouraged strongly is ultimately a matter of judgment. The ideal might be to have a gradual transition across the whole band of earnings-related provision, passing gradually from "ensures" to "enables," but this is hardly practical. The Pensions Commission for its purposes simply split the target into two equal parts and this does not seem an unreasonable basis to use for the purposes of this discussion.

A summary of what I consider to be the key elements of an ideal pension system and the benefits they should provide is presented in Table 3.1.

HOW SHOULD THESE BENEFITS BE PROVIDED?

Given these key elements of an ideal pension system, this section discusses how they should each be provided.

Flat-Rate Element

There is now general agreement in the United Kingdom that the basic flat-rate pension should be provided by the State on an unfunded basis, without a means-test and financed by the hypothecated (earmarked) payroll tax, known in the United Kingdom as National Insurance. The United Kingdom already has such a benefit in the State basic pension (social security), but at present it falls short of the income replacement target set in the previous section, being only 47 percent rather than the target of 60 percent of median household income after housing costs for a single person. It is envisaged that this shortfall will be made good over the next 20 years by increasing the State basic pension in line with average earnings and transforming the existing earnings-related S2P into a second flat-rate pension, as explained in Appendix 3A.

There is less agreement about what should be the basis of entitlement; that is, should it be based on an individual's contribution record or on the basis of citizenship and/or residence? The Pensions Commission (2005) fudged the issue by suggesting that future accruals of the State basic pension should be on a long-term residence basis (e.g., pro rata to a working life of 45 years), while existing accrued rights to the State basic pension based on an individual's contribution record should be unchanged, except that the benefit could be made universal immediately above a certain age (e.g., 75 or 80). The Commission also proposed that entitlement to the S2P, even after it becomes a flat-rate benefit, should continue to be based on an individual's earnings record.

Table 3.1 Key Elements of an Ideal Pension System

Element	Role of the state	Features	Amount
Flat-rate	Mandates	Poverty prevention and redistribution of income between pensioners	60 percent of median household income for a single person, which is equal to 25 percent of average revalued lifetime earnings for someone with median earnings
Earnings-related minimum	Mandates	Provision of a risk-free element toward an adequate earnings-related income in retirement	30 percent of average revalued lifetime earnings in excess of a disregard equal to the flat-rate element
Earnings-related additional	Encourages	Provision of an element of individual choice in securing an adequate income in retirement	30 percent of average revalued lifetime earnings in excess of a disregard equal to the flat-rate element
Additional personal	Facilitates	Additional income for individuals who desire a retirement income higher than the proposed target	Individual choice

The Government decided that the State basic pension should continue to be on a contributory basis, although the contribution conditions have been eased significantly, with women being the main beneficiaries of the change. For the small minority who fail to meet the conditions for entitlement, a means-tested benefit should continue at a level that would prevent poverty in old age.

While the basis of entitlement is clearly an important issue and my inclination is to support a contributory approach, it would be difficult to do the issue justice in the current chapter and the matter is left for future discussion. In any event, current projections suggest that even on a contributory basis, the great majority of retirees will receive a State pension above the poverty line (Government Actuary's Department 2010). It can be argued, therefore, that this element of the ideal system will come into place over the next 20 years. However, this is achieved at the cost of losing the existing earnings-related pension provided by the State.

Earnings-Related Mandated Element

The United Kingdom has had an earnings-related mandated pension system in place since 1978, initially in the form of the SERPS and in the form of the S2P since 2002. Both of these systems are unfunded, with current benefits paid from current National Insurance contributions. However, as explained above, it is now envisaged that by 2030 the S2P will have been transformed into a second flat-rate pension that is paid in addition to the basic State pension, with the intention that the two flat-rate pensions taken together will exceed the poverty line.

Under the current system, it is proposed that the recognized need for people to have an earnings-related pension in addition to the flat-rate minimum should be met by an approach that "strongly encourages" private pensions by means of the auto-enrollment requirement and the creation of a default low-cost option on a funded basis. The drawbacks of this approach are that the opt-out right will lead to an unknown number of workers that end up with inadequate benefits compared to the target income identified above. They will also be subjected to an unacceptable level of risk and costs for this element of their retirement income, as this is inherent in private market-based provision. The only way these problems can be avoided is for this element of their pension to be compulsory and provided directly by the State.

The UK experience with SERPS/S2P demonstrates that this alternative approach possesses a range of features that are highly desirable, if not essential, for this element of the pension system, including:

- complete protection against any investment risk and the consequent arbitrary fluctuations in the benefits paid on retirement from year to year,
- a lack of complex choices to be made by the individual,
- equity between members, with benefits and contributions based on each member's full earnings record,
- full transferability of rights, with no penalty on switching employment,
- full protection of rights, increasing in line with average earnings up to retirement and inflation thereafter,
- low administration costs, and
- scope for the maturity of the system to be accelerated, compared to the need to wait for a full working lifetime with a fully funded arrangement.

An additional point that, while important, is not considered in this chapter is whether there should be any contracting-out or "carve-out" permitted in place of this element of provision. In other words, should it be possible for private plans that meet defined standards to substitute for the State plan? This type of arrangement is now long established in the United Kingdom, going back to 1961, and was originally proposed because of concern that the expansion of State provision would have an adverse impact on the well-developed system of occupational pension plans that already existed. Such arguments still apply, although the significant reductions that have taken place in recent years in the standard and coverage of such plans suggest that it might not have as much force as in the past. In any event, it is taken as axiomatic that were such contracting-out to be permitted, it would have to be on the basis that the private plan would guarantee to provide at least as much pension as that promised by the State plan.

The conclusion is that this element of provision should be offered entirely or primarily by the State and that it should provide a pension of 30 percent of the individual's revalued lifetime earnings in excess of a disregard equal to the flat-rate pension. There would have to be a joint contribution rate from the employer and employee that would meet the cost of providing such a pension over a normal working lifetime. In other words, I envisage this element of pension being provided on a basis that is cost neutral for society as a whole, with the need for redistribution within the pension system being met principally by the flat-rate element. Redistribution within this element would be limited to arrangements that would provide credits for people who are outside paid employment but have an important social role, for example, those who have full-time caring responsibilities for children or other dependents, most of whom will be women. The cost of such redistribution should be met from general taxation.

The contribution rate that is calculated on this basis would obviously depend on the age at which the pension is payable and underlying actuarial assumptions. Some dispute the appropriate basis upon which such calculations should be made, and such intergenerational judgments are difficult. Nevertheless such decisions have to be made, and to this end, the UK Treasury has set out the policy it wishes to see adopted consistently when making such judgments in the Green Book (HM Treasury 2006).

In essence, for policy decisions that involve a comparison between current and future figures for income or expenditure, the Green Book distinguishes the appropriate discount rate for individuals to use from the one that should be used for society as a whole. One of the key differences is that the former is subject to the exigencies of investment markets, while society as a whole, in the form of the government, is not. As a result, the latter should be judged by using what is termed the social time preference rate, which does not go up and down with movements in markets, but is set for the long term. At present the Treasury considers this to be 3.5 percent per year.

In addition to the assumed discount rate, an assumption has to be made about how long pensions are expected to be in payment, that is, about pensioner mortality. It is now clear that longevity is continuing to improve at a relatively fast rate, and it seems reasonable to assume that this trend will continue for the foreseeable future. Using the discount rate identified above and projected mortality rates for the United Kingdom, Table 3.2 presents the contribution rates, expressed as a percentage of earnings in excess of the earnings disregard, that would be

Table 3.2 Total Contribution Rate for an Earnings-Related 30% Target Pension (% of earnings in excess of disregard)

Retirement age	Contribution rate (%)
65	8.7
66	8.2
67	7.7
68	7.3
69	6.9
70	6.5

SOURCE: Author's calculations.

equivalent in value to the target pension, depending upon the age of retirement. The rates assume a working life equal to the number of years between age 25 and the assumed retirement age.

These contribution rates are broadly consistent with the eight percent proposed by the Pensions Commission (2005) and legislated for by the last government. The important difference is that the pension will be obligatory and provided by the State in this proposal, and hence, it is guaranteed.

Given this general approach to the provision of the earnings-related mandated element, a number of important practical issues still need to be resolved:

- Should the plan be on a notionally funded basis, with the result that the amount of pension accrued each year will decrease with age, or should there be a level rate of accrual? My preference is for a level accrual rate, as this accelerates the payment of benefits, but it also brings the cost forward.
- How should the contributions be divided between employer and employee?
- Because contributions are compulsory, is it necessary for them to give rise to tax relief? If not, what would be the appropriate tax regime?
- Should there be built-in arrangements to deal with changes in circumstances, for example, in expected mortality after retirement?

The last issue is particularly important, but I do not consider it in detail in this chapter. However, it is worth pointing out that, to the extent that such adjustments are necessary, it would be possible to make them by changing the pension system's parameters, for example, by increasing the age at which the pension is received, rather than by making changes to the system itself. Nevertheless, it is important that such adjustments be made automatically on a basis of explicit rules that are determined in advance, rather than being made on an ad hoc basis (Barr and Diamond 2009).

Earnings-Related Encouraged Element

A number of forms of pension provision would be appropriate for the earnings-related encouraged element, but these should preferably be on a collective basis to minimize both costs and risks, while simplifying the choices that might need to be made. The details of these arrangements would be a matter for collective bargaining or individual negotiation and would encompass both defined benefit and defined contribution arrangements.

The role of the State might be limited therefore to offering appropriate incentives and setting minimum prudential standards through a pensions' regulator. Alternatively, the State might have a greater role by allowing individuals and their employers to contribute to the arrangement outlined above for the mandatory element, but on a voluntary basis.

The existing method of encouraging membership in these arrangements is through offering tax incentives on what is described as the "EET" approach—contributions from the employee and the employer are exempt (E) from tax, the fund roll-up is also exempt (E) from tax, but payment of benefits is subject to tax (T). In practice the system is not so simple, with limits on tax-free contributions that are likely to be tightened in the near future, some taxation of equity dividends in the roll-up phase, and the ability to take about 25 percent of the accumulated fund as tax-free cash on retirement. It is not clear whether this is actually the most equitable way of using State resources to encourage this element of pension provision, as greater benefit goes to those with higher levels of income. Consideration should be given, therefore, to the possibility of offering some alternative form of pension support that is not tied so directly to each individual's income.

There are, of course, already well-established plans in the United Kingdom which could meet this particular need. However, the arrangements that are available offer a relatively limited choice between employer-sponsored occupational pension plans on a defined benefit basis on the one hand and funded individual accounts on a defined contribution basis on the other. In other words, the choice is between arrangements that place almost all the risk on the employer and employee, respectively. The former are in significant decline, and it has been suggested that this could be arrested if there were a shift to greater risk-sharing in employer-sponsored plans because employers may be more prepared to offer such plans if they did not face all of the risk. While possible approaches to risk-sharing have been much discussed, including changes in pension legislation, there are relatively few examples of plans where it has been adopted in practice.

Additional Personal Element

As with the earnings-related encouraged element, there are already well-developed arrangements in the United Kingdom whereby individuals who want a pension in addition to that provided by the other elements can provide it for themselves. The only issues for the State in the context of this element are as follows:

- It needs to ensure that these arrangements are properly regulated along broadly the same lines as those that apply to personal investments more generally.
- It needs to determine whether there is the need for and, if so, the extent of any tax advantages that apply to this form of saving that are more advantageous than those available on saving more generally.

HOW CAN IT BE AFFORDED?

The question addressed in this section is whether society can afford the pensions arrangements set out above. This clearly is a political rather than a technical issue, which relates entirely to the earnings-related mandated element. As far as the other elements are concerned, political consensus in the United Kingdom holds that a flat-rate pension that provides an income that keeps pensioners out of poverty can and should be afforded through a hypothecated social security tax. The earnings-related encouraged element and the additional element would ultimately be a matter of individual or collective choice, and the issue of affordability does not arise.

The Pensions Commission's view was that it was untenable for the State to provide an earnings-related element within acceptable public expenditure limits (Pensions Commission 2005). The Commission also suggested that it would crowd out the flat-rate element. However, the pensions that it proposed were broadly the same as those proposed above for the earnings-related mandated element. In other words, the Commission concluded that it was not tenable for pensions at this level to come from an unfunded State plan like that suggested above, whereas it was tenable for pensions of a broadly similar amount to come from funded private plans. So, it is not the size of the pension commitments that the Commission saw as the problem with having a State plan; it is simply the way in which those pension commitments are labeled. That is, the difficulty is political, not financial or technical.

There are, of course, those who argue that funding the pension has a variety of intrinsic advantages, with the 1994 World Bank report being the classic example. Similarly, Hemming (1999) concluded that "theoretical arguments tend to be consistent with the view that funding will be associated with higher saving than pay-as-you-go," although he went on to say that "convincing empirical support is missing." However, Minns (2001) pointed out that, although the proponents of funding suggest that there are a range of advantages, their case depends ultimately on the single argument that funding leads to greater saving and investment, which leads in turn to more economic growth and an enhanced ability to pay higher pensions in future.

The problem for proponents of funding is that there is no sound basis for the argument that the funding of pensions promotes additional growth. For example, Hughes (2000, p. 56) concluded that, "The balance of the evidence . . . does not show that pay-as-you-go state pensions significantly reduce saving or that funded occupational or personal pensions significantly increase it." Similarly, Orszag and Stiglitz (2001) included the idea that (funded) individual accounts raise national saving as one of their 10 myths about (pay-as-you-go) social security systems. Barr (2001) concluded that, "The magnitude of the impact of funding on growth is controversial. Though there is some empirical evidence that funding contributes to higher savings in the USA, there is no robust evidence of a similar effect elsewhere." Barr (2006) also reminds us of the point made by Atkinson (1999), that any analysis that ignores the benefits of the welfare state, while considering its cost, is deficient. In other words, there is no robust evidence in support of the link between greater pension saving and growth and that, even if there is such a link, there is no guarantee about the timing or the extent of any effect.

What all this means is that, if we can afford the pensions proposed by the Pensions Commission on a funded basis, there is no logical reason why they cannot be afforded through the State plan proposed in the previous section. The net effect will be the same, with pensioners receiving higher incomes; the only difference is in the way the cash flows are labeled.

CONCLUSION

This chapter presents a short outline of what I imagine to be the ideal pension system for the United Kingdom. The focus is on the underlying structure, rather than the parameters for such a system, although figures are suggested for the purposes of discussion. In outline, the suggested structure is as follows.

A flat-rate mandatory element aimed at poverty prevention and redistribution of income should be provided by the State on an unfunded basis. This could provide a benefit of 60 percent of the median household income for a single person, which is equal to 25 percent of average revalued lifetime earnings for someone with median earnings.

An earnings-related mandatory element that pays a risk-free minimum level of pension should also be provided by the State on a basis that is unfunded but, in broad terms, cost-neutral to society. The suggested target is to provide an income of 30 percent of the individual's average revalued lifetime earnings in excess of a disregard that is equal to the flat-rate element.

An earnings-related additional element aimed at providing some individual flexibility about the level of pension that is secured could be provided though an occupational pension plan or some form of collective provision. This form of provision should be encouraged by the State, either through tax relief or an alternative more equitable form of support. The suggested target is to provide up to a further 30 percent of an individual's average revalued lifetime earnings in excess of a disregard that is equal to the flat-rate element.

Finally, an additional personal element is proposed to provide further flexibility for those who seek additional pensions. It would be based on personal accounts and is facilitated but not necessarily encouraged by the State.

Such an approach would achieve the triple goal of providing socially acceptable levels of benefit, ensuring the widest practical coverage of such benefits, and reducing the risks and costs to levels that are acceptable across the income range.

Appendix 3A
Outline of the UK Pension System

The UK's pension system has one of the most developed systems of private pension provision in the developed world, but this is coupled with one of the least generous State pension systems. This Appendix provides a short summary of how this works. Table 3A.1 gives a brief summary of the two current State pension systems.

In 2004, the State system was estimated to deliver a gross replacement rate of 37 percent of earnings for current retirees who had enjoyed average earnings throughout their working lives and a replacement rate of 24 percent to those who had twice the average earnings. Since then, there has been some reform of the State system, with a relaxation of qualifying conditions and a move toward indexation of the basic State pension in line with earnings, rather than prices. However, this has been coupled with a move toward the transformation of the S2P into a second flat-rate pension by the year 2030 and an increase in the State pension age to 68, which will be achieved for both men and women by 2046. The key difference between the two elements of the State pension is that the S2P has more restrictive qualifying conditions than the basic pension.

An important feature of the State pension system is that employees who have alternative private pension arrangements that are of an appropriate standard can contract out of the S2P. In doing so, they lose their entitlement to accrue the State earnings-related pension, and in return, they and their employer receive a rebate on their National Insurance contributions. The rebate is designed to be financially neutral to the State system. The conditions for contracting out are currently expressed in terms of either the ultimate benefits or the contributions to be paid, although the latter option is to be abolished by 2012. In the longer term, when S2P becomes a flat-rate pension, it is envisaged that the system of contracting out will be abolished entirely.

Only about two-fifths of those of working age accrue benefits in a private pension system. The rest depend on the inadequate level of State provision for their retirement incomes. This will begin to change from 2012 onward, when the government will start a phased introduction of a new system of personal accounts for employees who are not already in private pensions. Many of the details of this new system have yet to be decided, but it will be on a defined contribution basis, with total contributions of at least 8 percent of pensionable pay. It will also be based on mandatory enrollment, but members will have the right to opt out. Given that it will be on a funded basis and set at a comparatively low level, it will take many years before it will have a significant impact on retirement provision.

Out of the 14 million or so who do have some form of private pension provision, about 4 million workers accrue benefits through an individual arrangement. In some cases, these individual arrangements are sponsored by the employer through what are known as stakeholder plans or group personal pensions. However, these arrangements are almost invariably contract based, are taken out on a voluntary basis through insurance companies, and have little or no employer contributions. The other 10 million or so employees with private pension provision are members of what are termed occupational pension schemes, which are typically plans sponsored by individual employers for their own employees. There are some multi-employer plans (e.g., within a particular industry), but these have limited coverage. Occupational plans are established, invariably by the employer, as part of the employment contract that they offer to employees. Although there is no requirement on employers to offer pension provision, most large employers do so and a significant proportion of medium-sized employers do as well. Few small employers offer this sort of pension arrangement.

Subject to various minimum standards for benefits laid down in legislation, it is up to the employer to decide what the plan provides, although in some cases it is the result of collective bargaining with appropriate trade unions. However, once established, there is a whole range of regulatory provisions that govern how these plans operate. There are also upper limits on benefits and contributions set by the tax authorities, in return for which plans enjoy various tax advantages.

In the private sector, such plans are invariably funded and established on a trust basis, where the assets are held in a trust fund, which is legally separate from the finances of the employer and the members. The great majority of assets are invested by the funds themselves, with the trustees appointing investment managers who make day-to-day investment decisions, within investment policies laid down by the trustees. A minority of assets, mainly in respect of the large number of relatively small plans, is held by insurance companies, although in effect, they are acting in a very similar role as the investment managers.

Some public sector plans, mainly in local government, are also established on a funded basis. However, most public sector plans, including those for civil servants, health workers, the armed forces, and schoolteachers, are run on a pay-as-you-go basis, with benefits being paid out of general taxation.

Table 3A.1 Summary of UK State Pensions

The basic state pension (BSP)	A flat-rate benefit paid from age 65 for men and 60 for women born before April 6, 1950, increasing over a period of years to age 65 for women born after April 5, 1960 and to 68 for men and women born after April 5, 1978.
	Entitlement is based on payment of National Insurance contributions (effectively a payroll tax on employees and employers), with credits for periods of unemployment, sickness, and family responsibility.
	The benefit for someone with a full record of working years is currently £5,078 per year for a single person and £8,120 per year for a married couple (where the partner is not entitled to a full pension in their own right).
	Payments increase at least in line with average earnings.
The state second pension (S2P)	An earnings-related benefit paid at the same age as the BSP.
	Provides a pension of at least 20 percent of revalued average earnings between upper and lower limits, currently £40,040 and £5,044 per year, respectively.
	A higher proportion of earnings is provided for employees with lower levels of earnings, up to 40 percent for those with earnings that are currently less than £14,100.
	Payments are indexed to prices.

Notes

1. A thought experiment is a proposal for an experiment that would test or illuminate a hypothesis, theory, or principle.
2. As Keynes (1936, p. 383) said famously, "Practical men, who believe themselves to be quite exempt from any intellectual influence, are usually the slaves of some defunct economist."
3. See http://www.webarchive.org.uk/wayback/archive/20070801230000/http://www.pensionscommission.org.uk/index.html.
4. See http://www.pensionspolicyinstitute.org.uk/.
5. This rate is sometimes referred to in the United Kingdom as the "official poverty line." The issue is discussed in more detail at http://www.poverty.org.uk/summary/income%20intro.shtml.

References

Atkinson, Anthony B. 1999. *The Economic Consequences of Rolling Back the Welfare State.* Cambridge, MA: MIT Press.

Barr, Nicholas A. 2001. *The Welfare State as Piggy Bank: Information, Risk, Uncertainty, and the Role of the State.* Oxford and New York: Oxford University Press.

———. 2006. "The Economics of Pensions." *Oxford Review of Economic Policy* 22(1): 5–39.

Barr, Nicholas, and Peter Diamond. 2009. "Reforming Pensions: Principles, Analytical Errors, and Policy Directions." *International Social Security Review* 6(2): 5–29.

———. 2010. *Pension Reform: A Short Guide.* Oxford: Oxford University Press.

Davies, Bryn. 2009. "Talking about Pensions: An Analysis of Language Used to Discuss Pensions." In *Personal Provision of Retirement Income: Meeting the Needs of Older People?* Jim Stewart and Gerard Hughes, eds. Cheltenham, UK: Edward Elgar, pp. 253–270.

Department of Work and Pensions. 2006. "Security in Retirement: Towards a New Pension System." London: Her Majesty's Stationery Office (HMSO).

Ervik, Rune. 2005. "The Battle of Future Pensions, Global Accounting Tools, International Organizations, and Pension Reforms." *Global Social Policy* 5(1): 9–54.

Government Actuary's Department. 2010. *Government Actuary's Quinquennial Review of the National Insurance Fund as at April 2005.* London: Her Majesty's Stationery Office (HMSO).

Hemming, Richard. 1999. "Should Public Pensions Be Funded?" *International Social Security Review* 52(2): 3–29.

HM Treasury. 2006. *The Green Book: Appraisal and Evaluation in Central Government.* London: Her Majesty's Stationery Office (HMSO).

Hughes, Gerard. 2000. "Pension Financing, the Substitution Effect, and National Savings." In *Pensions in the European Union: Adapting to Economic and Social Change*, Gerard Hughes and Jim Stewart, eds. Dordrecht and Amsterdam: Kluwer Academic Publishers, pp. 45–62.

Keynes, John Maynard. 1936. *The General Theory of Employment, Interest, and Money.* London: Macmillan.

Labour Party, The. 1957. *National Superannuation.* London: The Labour Party.

Minns, Richard. 2001. *The Cold War in Welfare: Stock Markets versus Pensions.* New York: Verso.

Munnell, Alicia H., and Mauricio Soto. 2005. "What Replacement Rates Do Households Actually Experience in Retirement?" CRR Working Paper 2005-10. Boston: Boston College, Center for Retirement Research.

Office for National Statistics (ONS). 2009. *Annual Survey of Hours and Earnings.* London: ONS.

Orszag, Peter R., and Joseph E. Stiglitz. 2001. "Rethinking Pension Reform: Ten Myths about Social Security Systems." In *New Ideas about Old Age Security: Toward Sustainable Pension Systems in the Twenty-First Century*, Robert Holman and Joseph E. Stiglitz, eds. Washington, DC: World Bank, pp. 17–56.

Pensions Commission. 2004. *Pensions: Challenges and Choices, The First Report of the Pensions Commission.* London: Her Majesty's Stationery Office (HMSO).

———. 2005. *A New Pension Settlement for the Twenty-First Century, The Second Report of the Pensions Commission.* London: Her Majesty's Stationery Office (HMSO).

World Bank. 1994. *Averting the Old Age Crisis: Policies to Protect the Old and Promote Growth.* New York: Oxford University Press.

4
Public and Private Provision of Pensions and the Ideal Pension System for Ireland

Gerard Hughes
Jim Stewart
School of Business, Trinity College Dublin

Pension systems in many countries are far from ideal in terms of equity, efficiency, and viability. Pension reform has moved to center stage in most developed economies, but it is important to recognize that pension reform may not always result in improvement in pension payments or security.[1] Many would dispute the statement in the EU Green Paper on pensions that, "Reforms have underpinned recent increases in effective retirement ages and opened new avenues to delivering adequate incomes in a sustainable manner" (European Commission 2010, p. 5). As shown later, retired persons in Ireland are very dependent on state social security payments. Yet the EU Green Paper assumes "public replacement rates will decline" and that "it is important to provide sufficient opportunities for complementary entitlements" (European Commission 2010, p. 8).

Pension systems need reform, but change is costly for all stakeholders, and hence pension systems have considerable path dependency. Reform that leads to the introduction of new sources of pension income leads to the issue of how the new pension arrangements will be integrated with existing pension arrangements. If there is replacement, there may be considerable administrative costs. A new type of pension arrangement, such as an individual pension, is often introduced in addition to existing arrangements. This has happened in many EU countries (see Stewart and Hughes 2009) and leads to considerable inefficiencies resulting from multiple sources of income, often of relatively small amounts.

Pension systems and government proposals for pension reform are driven by tax relief that disproportionately benefits those with higher incomes. But the main failure is the low level of income given to those in retirement. Although the Irish pension system needs reform, after several reviews and a government Green Paper, proposals for reform remain inadequate in a number of respects.

IDENTIFYING PENSION REFORM ISSUES

Reform must be evidence based, yet there are large data gaps in relation to pension systems and the income and assets of retired persons. This is especially true of the Irish pension system. Three particular data gaps stand out:

1) Despite the enormous cost of tax relief, it is not known whether the relief increases net resources for retirement.
2) Few data are available on the incomes and assets of retired persons. We may surmise that the collapse of bank shares (the "blue chips") has disproportionately affected a certain section of retired persons, but the extent to which this has happened is not known.
3) Despite the encouragement and tax incentives to join funded pension systems, there are no data on the costs in terms of administrative and other charges of running such plans. Instead a government Green Paper on pension reform (Department of Social and Family Affairs 2007a) relied on data from the UK pension system—a very different pension system because of its considerable economies of scale resulting from its larger size. One may surmise that administrative costs are higher in Ireland. The Green Paper refers to a "typical charge" of 1.5 percent per year, but no evidence is offered to support this rate. Indeed, administrative and other charges are a key aspect of pension systems, but they are often ignored. Returns are nearly always given gross of costs, so that a gross return of 4.5 percent becomes a net 3.0 percent after costs. Over time this can have a dramatic effect on accumulating lump sums.

Perhaps the most important data issue is that projections, often for a 40-year period, are treated as facts. One prominent example is that the proportion of those aged 65 and over has been projected to increase, but the age structure of the population and crucially the size of the labor force is uncertain. The only certainty is that past demographic projections for Ireland have been wrong. A second example is that financial market returns are assumed to be constant. The dot com bubble and the recent crash were not forecast—they were assumed to be impossible. This issue is compounded by the false belief that equities will always outperform any other form of investment—that is, there is a positive equity risk premium (Stewart 2011, Table 3). The projected illustrated returns on the proposed auto-enrollment arrangement in the National Pensions Framework document are 7 percent per year real return over a 40-year period (Department of Social and Family Affairs 2010, Table 4.1). This is an important assumption and is crucial to the proposed new pension plan. In contrast, the average return on group-managed pension funds for the 10-year period to April 2010 was 0.5 percent. The latest group-managed pension fund returns are an improvement compared with previous years.

Proposals for an ideal pension system should show how it will solve the problems of the existing system in relation to simplicity, adequacy, cost, equity, coverage, and effectiveness in delivering pensions. We will show how Ireland's current pension system fails to meet many of these criteria and how an ideal system would enable all of them to be met.

THE CONTEXT FOR REFORM

Ireland has a population of about 4 million (see Table 4.1). Home ownership rates are high, with 80 percent of all households and 90 percent of pensioner households owning their own homes. Life expectancy for men and women at age 65 is 15.4 years and 18.7 years, respectively.

Although Ireland is committed to maintaining living standards in old age, the balance, in terms of policy, between public and private provision is struck in favor of private provision. Successive governments have taken the view that the role of the public social security pension

Table 4.1 Key Economic and Demographic Data for Ireland, 2006

Category	
Population (million)	4.2
GDP current prices and current PPPs[a], (US$, billion)	175.1
GDP per capita, current prices and PPPs (US$)	41,300
Home ownership rates: all households (%)	80
Home ownership rates: households aged 65+ (%)	90
Life expectancy in 2001 at age 65: male (years)	15.4
female (years)	18.7

[a] Purchasing power parity.

SOURCE: GDP and GDP per capita: OECD in Figures; home ownership: Department of Social and Family Affairs (2007b, p. 26); life expectancy: Irish Life Table No. 14, 2001–2003.

system is to provide a minimum basic income that will prevent poverty in retirement. As the state social security pension is not sufficient for most people to maintain their living standard in retirement, the private sector pensions market is given generous tax relief on contributions and investment income to encourage individuals to make their own arrangements to top up the flat-rate state pension with an earnings-related supplement from a private pension provider.

The Pension System in Ireland

The structure of the pension system in Ireland reflects successive governments' conceptions about the role of the state. Table 4.2 shows that the structure of the Irish pension system is relatively simple. It is based on a partnership approach between government, employers, and employees. It consists of a compulsory state social insurance system (social security), which levies contributions at a range of proportional rates for different classes of contributors and pays flat-rate benefits, and a voluntary private system, which is subsidized through the tax system. The social insurance system provides a state pension (transition) at age 65 that requires withdrawal from the labor force for one year and a state pension (contributory) at age 66 that does not require withdrawal from the labor force. In addition, a means-tested state pension (non-contributory) is provided for those not covered by the social security system. The amounts paid by the transition and contributory pensions

Table 4.2 Structure of Ireland's Pension System

First tier: Mandatory public pension system—flat-rate social welfare pensions	
Social insurance (employees)	Social assistance (not in workforce or not qualifying for social insurance)
Age 65: state pension (transition)	
Age 66: state pension (contributory)	Age 66: state pension (non-contributory)
Second tier: Voluntary private pension system—occupational and personal pensions	
Occupational (employees)	Personal (self-employed and employees)
Defined benefit	Retirement Annuity Contract (RAC)
Defined contribution	Personal Retirement Savings Account (PRSA)

SOURCE: Department of Social and Family Affairs, http://www.dsfa.ie.

are the same, while the non-contributory pension has usually been about 10 percent less than the social security pension, although the difference is currently just 5 percent. For convenience, these three pensions will be referred to as the social welfare pension where it is not necessary to distinguish among them.

An important feature of the Irish pension system is that the state social security pension is integrated with occupational pension payments for most defined benefit plans, so that both payments combined cannot exceed an agreed replacement rate. This means that an increase in state social security pensions may reduce payments from occupational pension plans. For this reason, employers with defined benefit plans welcome increases in social welfare payments.

The private pension system has two components: occupational pension plans and personal pension plans. Occupational plans are provided on a voluntary basis by employers for groups of employees. Personal pension plans are for employees who are not covered by an occupational plan or individuals who are not employed. Personal plans take the form of Retirement Annuity Contracts (RAC) for the self-employed and Personal Retirement Savings Accounts (PRSA) for everyone else.

In the past, most of the workplace plans were defined benefit pensions. Consequently, they were supposed to provide a guaranteed benefit that would replace up to two-thirds of preretirement earnings for employees who spent their full career with one employer. In the last 10 years or so, many defined benefit pension plans have been closed to new entrants. They have been replaced by defined contribution plans because most employers are no longer willing to guarantee new entrants to the labor force a pension related to length of service and level of final earnings. The benefits that a member of an occupational or individual defined contribution plan can expect will depend on how much is contributed to the plan, how well the plan is managed, and the performance of stocks, shares, and other assets. All of the investment risk in defined contribution plans is borne by employees or the self-employed rather than by employers.

Although the structure of the pension system is relatively simple, operating it has become complex because of the variety of categories of workers contributing to the public social security system and the large buildup of pension and tax law required to regulate private pension funds and the drawdown of pension benefits.

Pensioner Poverty Rates and the Level of State Social Security Pensions

Considerable progress has been made in recent years in reducing poverty among pensioners by increasing the social welfare pension, where poverty is defined as a retirement income of below 60 percent of average earnings. Figure 4.1 shows that the percentage of pensioners at risk of poverty increased from 20 percent in 1997 to over 36 percent in 2003, primarily due to the failure of the social welfare pension to keep pace with increases in average industrial earnings during a period of rapid earnings growth. Since then, however, the social welfare pension has increased faster than workers' earnings and the rate fell to just over 11 percent in 2008.[2]

The increases in the social welfare pension in 2004 and subsequent years have significantly improved Ireland's ranking in international comparisons of pensioner poverty. Using a comparable measure of relative income poverty for all EU27 countries, Figure 4.2 shows that Ireland's pensioner poverty rate of 21 percent in 2008 was a little over the average EU27 rate of 19 percent.[3] Nevertheless, the fact that one-fifth of pensioners were at risk of poverty in 2008 indicates that there

Figure 4.1 Percentage of People Age 65 and Over in Ireland at Risk of Poverty Relative to the 60 Percent Poverty Line, 1987–2008

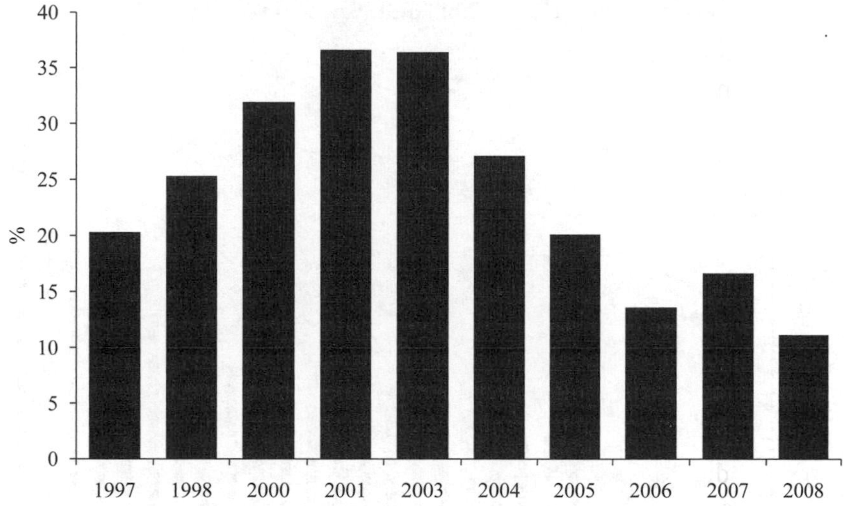

SOURCE: Whelan et al. (2003) and Central Statistics Office (2009).

is some way to go to eliminate pensioner poverty in Ireland. The very low pensioner poverty rate for New Zealand, which has a flat-rate state social security pension similar to the social welfare pension in Ireland, indicates what could be achieved if Ireland were prepared to increase the level of the social welfare pension above the poverty level.

Some progress has been made toward this objective. Figure 4.3 shows that the level of the social security and social assistance pensions for couples relative to average industrial earnings changed little between 1994 and 2000. In 2001, the government began to respond to the large increase in pensioner poverty that had occurred when the economy was booming during the 1997–2000 period by starting to increase pensions faster than earnings. This policy resulted in the gap between social security and social assistance pensions and the 60 percent poverty line for a couple narrowing from about 6 and 10 percentage points, respectively, in 2003 to 4 and 7 percentage points in 2008.

These improvements have, therefore, brought the social security and social assistance pensions to within striking distance of the poverty line of 60 percent of average earnings. It would be perfectly feasible for the Irish government to increase the social welfare pension to a level

Figure 4.2 Percentage of People Age 65 and Over at Risk of Poverty Relative to the 60 Percent Poverty Line for People Age 65 and Over in the EU27 in 2008 and New Zealand in 2009

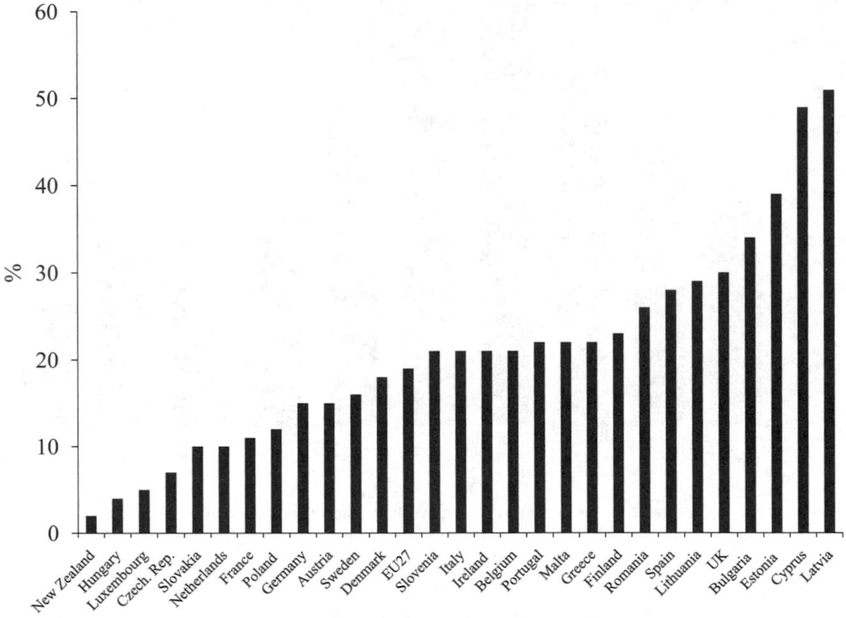

SOURCE: Zaidi (2010) and Ministry of Social Development (2005).

that would virtually eliminate pensioner poverty, as has been done in New Zealand with a similar flat-rate state pension. Callan, Nolan, and Walsh (2007) have shown that an increase in the social welfare pension to bring it above the poverty level would require only 837 ($1,071) million euros (€) of the €1,462 ($1,871) million increase in revenue the Exchequer (government treasury department) could raise by giving tax relief on private pension contributions at the standard rate of tax rather than at the marginal rate of tax.[4]

On its own, increasing the social welfare pension would not resolve the complications resulting from incomplete contribution records for the social security pension, the means test for the social assistance pension, rules about dependency, the retirement condition required for the social security state pension (transition), and the interaction of the social welfare pension with private pensions, which creates uncertainty about

Figure 4.3 Social Insurance, Social Assistance Pension, and the 60 Percent Poverty Line for a Couple Relative to Average Industrial Earnings, 1994–2010

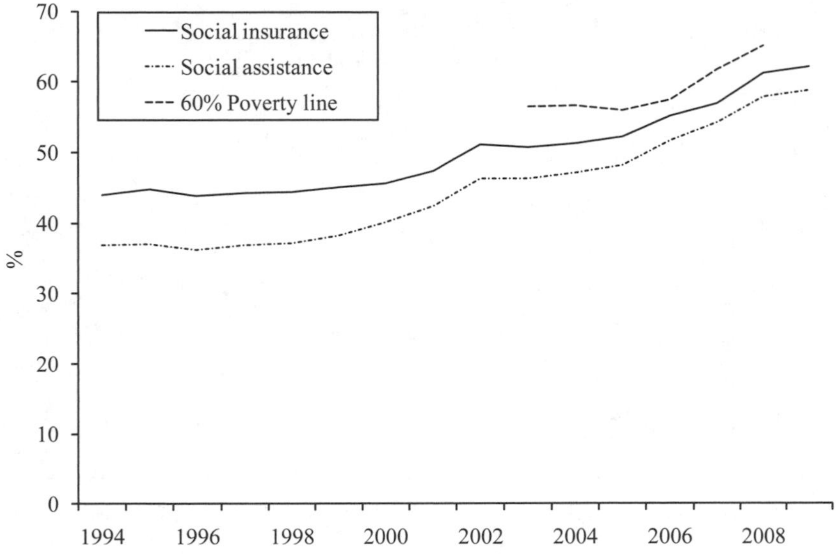

how much to save and results in the loss of private pension benefits for low-paid members of some occupational defined benefit pension plans.

Women in Ireland are particularly disadvantaged by the social security and private pension systems because women provide most of the care required by children and elderly relatives. Consequently, their work histories are more irregular than those of men, and it is more difficult for women to qualify for either a social welfare or a private pension. As the purpose of Ireland's flat-rate social welfare pension is to prevent poverty in old age, these problems could ideally be addressed by introducing a universal state social security pension to eliminate the means test and differential payments to pensioners whose needs are the same.

The introduction of a universal pension would require an increase in public expenditure. This is the primary reason why a universal state social security pension was ruled out in the Green Paper on Pensions (Department of Social and Family Affairs 2007a). However, as already noted, there is some scope for increasing current expenditure on pensions because Ireland has operated a very favorable tax regime for

Figure 4.4 Actual Expenditures on Social Welfare Pensions and Tax Expenditures on Pensions, 1980–2007

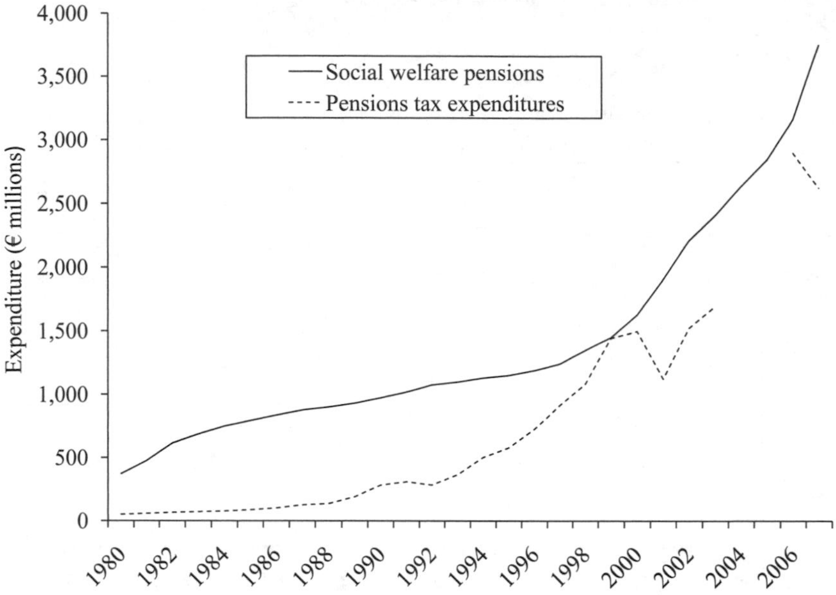

NOTE: There is a break in the tax expenditure series in 2004 and 2005, and the figures for 2006 and 2007 are not comparable with those for previous years because of a change in the method of estimation.

SOURCE: Social welfare pensions: Hughes (1985, Table A4) and Statistical Reports of the Department of Social and Family Affairs. Pensions tax expenditure: Statistical Reports of the Revenue Commissioners.

pensions to encourage the development of the private pension system. Figure 4.4 indicates that the cost of tax relief was initially fairly modest, but it has grown rapidly over the last three decades. As argued later, reducing tax relief would enable the payment of higher social welfare pensions.

In 1980, the earliest year for which the Revenue Commissioners estimated the cost of the tax relief for occupational pensions, it amounted to about €51 ($64) million. By 1990, its cost had increased more than five times to €283 ($362) million. In the year 2000, just before the dot com bubble burst, the Exchequer was forgoing about the same amount in tax revenue, €1.5 ($1.92) billion, as it was spending on state social

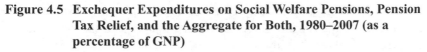

Figure 4.5 Exchequer Expenditures on Social Welfare Pensions, Pension Tax Relief, and the Aggregate for Both, 1980–2007 (as a percentage of GNP)

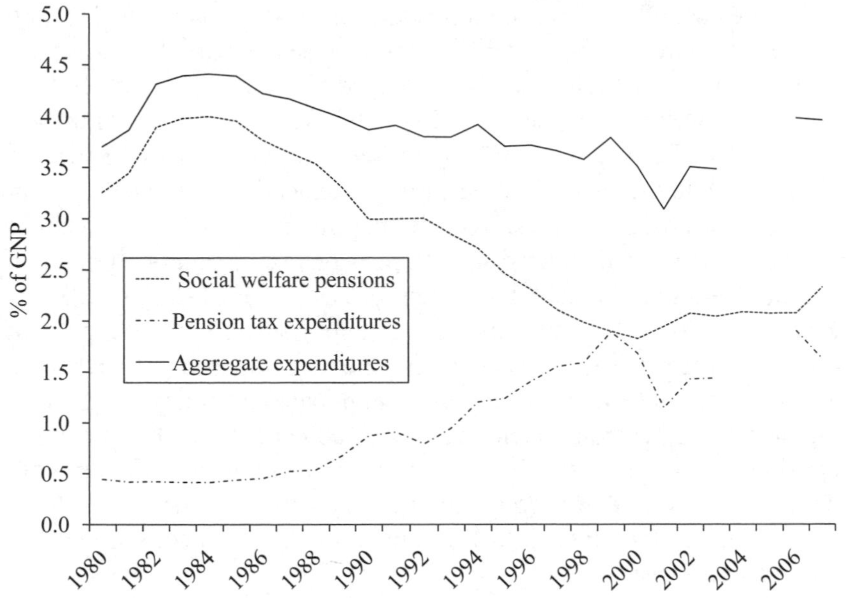

NOTE: There is a break in the tax expenditure series in 2004 and 2005, and the figures for 2006 and 2007 are not comparable with those for previous years because of a change in the method of estimation.
SOURCE: Annual Statistical Reports of the Department of Social and Family Affairs and the Revenue Commissioners.

security pensions, €1.6 ($2.05) billion, for those aged 65 and over. In the Finance Act of 2004, steps were taken to improve the quality of data on pension contributions by requiring employers to provide details in their annual P35 tax return form of aggregate employer and employee contributions to pension plans. When the results of the new method of estimation were published in the Green Paper on Pensions (Department of Social and Family Affairs 2007a), they showed that the cost of tax relief for private pensions was significantly higher than had been shown by previous estimates. In 2006, the cost of the tax relief amounted to €2.9 ($3.7) billion—almost the same as the amount the Exchequer spent, €3.2 ($4.1) billion, on state pensions for older people. In 2007, the cost of the tax relief fell to €2.6 ($3.3) billion as a consequence of the financial crisis, while the cost of state social security pensions increased to €3.9 ($5.0) billion.

If the cost of tax forgone on private pensions is taken into account, we get a different perspective on pension costs. Figure 4.5 shows the cost of public expenditure and tax expenditure on pensions in Ireland relative to GNP over the period 1980–2007. At the beginning of the period in 1980, the cost of the state social security pension was 3.3 percent of GNP, while the cost of the pension tax expenditure was 0.4 percent of GNP. The cost of the social security pension increased to 4 percent of GNP up to 1985, while the cost of the pension tax expenditure remained around one-tenth of that at 0.4 percent of GNP. From 1985 to 2003, the cost of the social security pension fell continuously to about 2 percent of GNP while the cost of the pension tax expenditure more than tripled to 1.4 percent of GNP as the government pursued its policy of developing the private pension system. Between 2000 and 2001, the cost of the pension tax expenditure fell as a result of the collapse of the dot com bubble. However, it recovered quickly and it rose to 1.9 percent of GNP in 2006 before falling back to 1.6 percent in 2007 as a consequence of the financial crisis.

Adding the cost of the tax relief for private pensions in Ireland to the cost of public social security expenditure on pensions provides a different perspective on the issue of the affordability of a universal state pension in Ireland. The addition of the tax expenditure on the private pension system in Ireland indicates that the resource cost of supporting the public social security and private pension systems has fluctuated around 4 percent between 1980 and 2007. There is scope, therefore, for reallocating resources between the public and private components of the pension system.

PROBLEMS WITH THE PRIVATE PENSION SYSTEM

The way in which pension tax relief is allocated to members of occupational and individual pension plans is inequitable. Figure 4.6 shows the distribution by income quintile of the tax relief on self-employed in 1999–2000 and employee contributions to occupational pension funds

Figure 4.6 Distribution by Income Quintile of Tax Relief on Pension Contributions by Employees in 2000 and Self-Employed Workers in 1999–2000

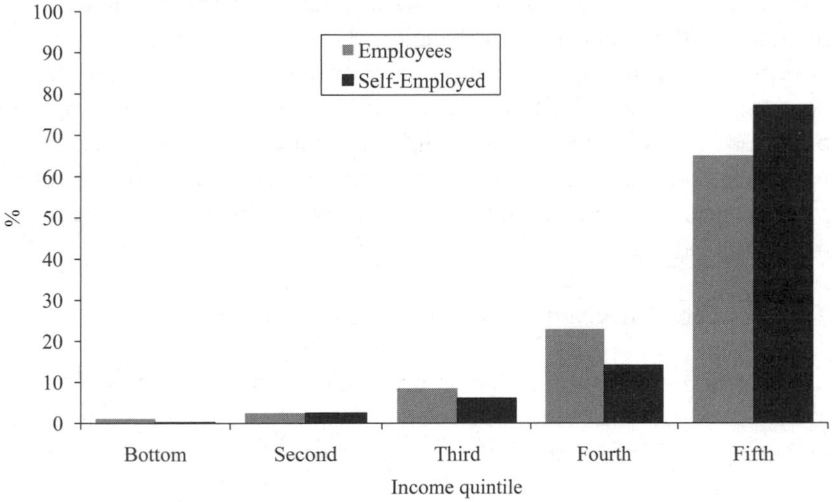

SOURCE: Hughes (2007, Figure 3.12).

in the year 2000. The distribution for both employment groups is much the same—the bulk of the tax relief accrues to the top 20 percent of earners (quintile 5 in Figure 4.6), while the bottom 20 percent receive virtually nothing. Two-thirds of the tax relief for employees and three-quarters of the relief for the self-employed accrued to people in the highest income quintile. The bottom 20 percent of employees and the self-employed received only 1.1 percent and 0.2 percent, respectively, of the tax relief. The distribution of the tax relief for the self-employed is more concentrated than it is for employees because the pension coverage rate for the self-employed is significantly lower than it is for employees.

The distribution of tax relief is concentrated at the top end of the earnings distribution because the effective limits on employee contributions in Ireland were largely determined by the maximum pension permitted under Revenue Commissioners rules that would attract tax relief, rather than by a maximum contribution. In Ireland, the pension benefit could not exceed two-thirds of pensionable salary, so this put an upper bound on how much could be contributed, although it varied with age and level of earnings.

Pension tax relief in Ireland is intended to increase the coverage of the private pension system and to provide an earnings-related supplement to the social welfare pension. Hence, one would expect the coverage of occupational pension plans to have risen over the last 20 years and the social welfare pension to be less important than private pensions in delivering an income in retirement. Let us consider, therefore, what has happened to private pension coverage and how effective public and private provision are in delivering retirement income to the older population.

Trends in the Coverage of Occupational Pensions

Figure 4.7 shows that the occupational pension coverage rate declined by 8 percentage points from 1985 to 1999. From 2000 to 2009, however, much of the ground lost was recovered so that the coverage rate was just under 45 percent at the start and end of the period shown in

Figure 4.7 Occupational Pension Coverage Rates, 1985–2009 (%)

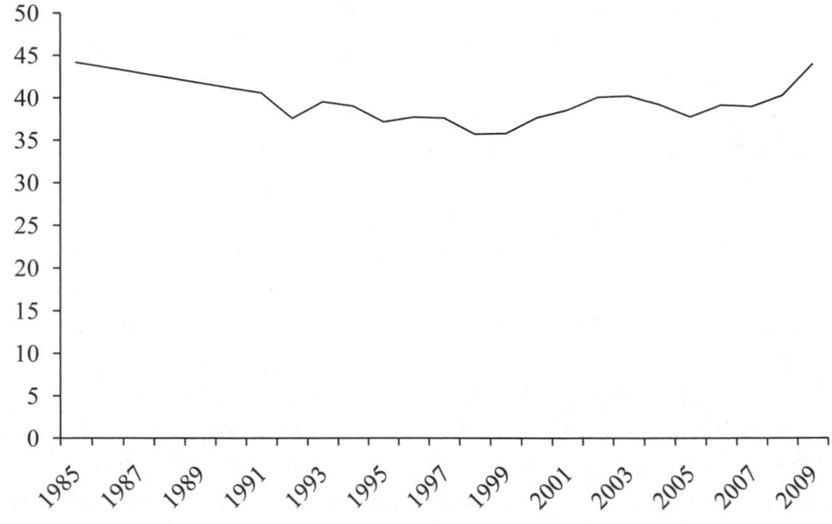

SOURCE: Hughes (2007, Figure 3.13) and authors' estimates.

Figure 4.7. A factor that may have contributed to this recovery was the very strong employment growth experienced between 1995 and 2006 when Ireland's economy grew at rates that were unprecedented since Independence in 1921.

It is evident, therefore, that the policy of providing generous tax relief to encourage the growth of occupational pension plans has not been effective in increasing pension coverage over the last 25 years. This failure has been compounded by a switch in coverage from occupational defined benefit plans to defined contribution plans, as Figure 4.8 shows. The switch to defined contribution plans places a big obstacle in the path to the achievement of the Pensions Board target of replacing 50 percent of preretirement income because the difference between the target for the social insurance pension (34 percent of average earnings) and the overall target has to be made up by a private pension.[5] The decision by employers to replace defined benefit with defined contribution

Figure 4.8 Percentage of Workers Covered by Defined Benefit (DB) and Defined Contribution (DC) Occupational Pension Schemes, 1985–2006

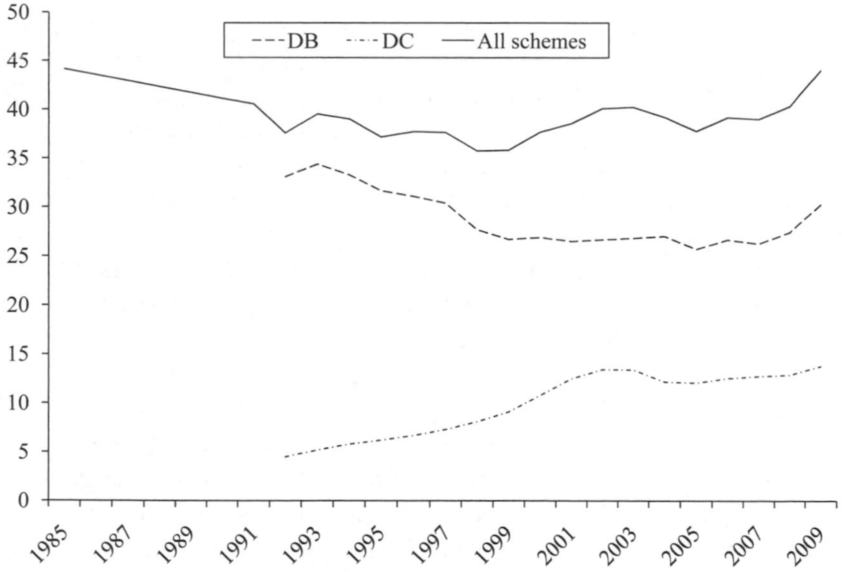

SOURCE: Pensions Board Annual Reports.

plans for most new entrants to the labor force means that there can be no certainty about what average level of pension the private sector can deliver.

Despite the uncertainty surrounding the average level of pension that can now be delivered by the private pension system, Ireland has put a lot of effort during the last 10 years into the development of a personal pension option in the hope that it would help to increase the pension coverage rate. The government's advisory body on pensions, the Pensions Board, identified a number of barriers to improving pension coverage (see Pensions Board 1998). It recommended that a standardized, low-cost personal retirement savings option should be made widely available irrespective of employment status.

The government accepted the Board's recommendation, and it introduced the PRSA in 2003 for employees and others not covered by an occupational plan or an RAC. The government made it mandatory for employers to designate a PRSA provider, but it did not require the employer to make a contribution on behalf of employees. Age-related tax incentives were provided to encourage people to start saving for retirement. Anyone under the age of 30 taking out a PRSA is allowed to claim tax relief on contributions of up to 15 percent of earnings. The percentage of earnings on which tax relief can be claimed increases with age until it reaches 40 percent for those aged 60 and over.

PRSAs operate like defined contribution pension plans, but their charges are considerably higher than those for occupational plans as they do not benefit from the economies of scale accruing to group plans. It was hoped that tax relief, and the mandatory requirement for employers to provide access to a PRSA, would result in a significant increase in pension coverage within five years of the introduction of the PRSA. This expectation has not been met. Seven years after the introduction of PRSAs, coverage had increased by only 2 percentage points, from 52 percent in the first quarter of 2002 to 54 percent in first quarter of 2008.

The failure of a voluntary approach to increasing pension coverage has resulted in the publication of a National Pensions Framework (Department of Social and Family Affairs 2010) in which the government proposes to increase coverage by introducing an auto-enrollment plan for employees who are not covered by their employer's plan. Very few details are provided about how this plan will work. It is worth noting that the option of a quasi-mandatory addition to the Irish pension system was considered in the Green Paper on Pensions and a decision was deferred because "It would be useful, perhaps, to allow time for more evidence on performance of soft mandatory schemes elsewhere to emerge, particularly from New Zealand" (Department of Social and Family Affairs 2007a, par. 8.54). To date, the government has not produced any evaluation of how the auto-enrollment plan has worked in New Zealand, but St John, Littlewood, and Dale (2010) have shown that the New Zealand plan has required significant subsidies from the government to achieve the large number of enrollments that have occurred to date.

EFFECTIVENESS OF PENSION DELIVERY

A key issue in designing an ideal pension system is determining how effective the public and private components are in delivering pensions. One way to look at this issue is in terms of what proportion of the target population actually receives income from each component.

Despite all the tax relief, the long-term existence of occupational pensions, and various government initiatives, state welfare pensions and other transfer payments provide the bulk of income to retired persons. These and other points can be deduced from Household Budget survey data for the 2004–2005 period. The data consist of a randomly chosen cross-section survey of 6,884 households. Because the raw data are based on households,[6] they were converted into a per capita equivalent basis using standard adjustment techniques. Table 4.3 shows the numbers of those aged 65 and over reporting income from various sources. Not all of those aged 65 and over report pension income, but the number of people reporting occupational pension income is less than half of those included in the survey. Over 70 percent of respondents report income from the state social security pension; slightly over 50 percent report financial income and just under 30 percent report earned income.

Table 4.4 shows income per capita broken down by various sources. The main features of Table 4.4 are as follows:

- Mean and median gross income decline with age, except for income from state welfare pensions.

- Income from various state welfare pensions accounts for 38 percent of total income for those aged 65–74 and 53 percent of income for those aged over 75.
- Mean income from occupational pension coverage is low, and median values are zero, indicating that most of those included in the survey do not receive an occupational pension.
- Financial sources of income are low and highly skewed; the median values are zero.
- Non-pension income accounts for 28 percent of mean income for those aged 65–74 and 13 percent of those aged 75+. This represents a significant reliance of retired persons on sources of retirement income other than pension income, mostly representing paid work.

The small number of those with occupational pensions is surprising, but it is of interest to examine incomes for those reporting occupational pension income. Table 4.5 shows income data for those with pensions from state employment. Even for those with occupational pensions from state employment, state social welfare payments are important, accounting for 30 percent of mean pension income for those aged 75+, or 38 percent of median pension income. Mean income from financial assets is higher than for the entire survey group but still low. Non-pension income is lower than for retired persons as a group in the survey, at 18 percent of mean income.

Table 4.5 also shows the same data for those who report pension income from non-state employment. The gross income and pension income are lower for all age groups compared with those who report pension income from state employment. For example, for those 75 and older, median pension income is almost 30 percent lower than those reporting pension income from state employment. The gap is even larger for those aged 65–74 (35 percent). However, gross incomes are closer, at about 81 percent of the level of those with a pension from state employment because financial income and income from paid work are higher.

Table 4.5 also shows an inequality in pension income (and gross income) between those groups reporting pension income from state employment as compared with those reporting pension income from non-state employment. The median pension income as a percentage of

Table 4.3 Numbers of Those Aged 65 and Over Reporting Income from Various Sources

Age	Gross household income (€)	Total pension income from all sources (€)	Income from state employment pension	Income from other employment pension	Income from all state social security pensions[a]	Financial income	Earned and other income
65–74	871	831	138	257	630	475	314
75+	573	557	81	136	440	251	107
Total	1,444	1,388	219	393	1,070	726	421

NOTE: The cells do not sum to the number of respondents in the survey because some people reported income from multiple sources.

[a] State old-age pension, state retirement pension, widows' pensions, and blind person's pension.

Table 4.4 Sources of Pension Income (€ per week)

		Total gross household income[a]		Total pension income from all sources		Income from state employment pension		Income from other employment pensions		Income from all state social security pensions[a]		Total other financial income		Earned and other income	
Age	*N*	Mean	Med.	Mean	Med.	Mean	Med.	Mean	Med.	Mean	Med.	Mean	Med.	Mean	Med.
65–74	871	339	242	221	185	43.2	0	48.4	0	129	166	10.5	0.4	83.7	0
75+	573	276	203	219	187	35.1	0	37.8	0	146	176	9.6	0.0	27.3	0
Total	1,444	314	216	220	187	40.0	0	44.2	0	136	173	11.0	0.1	61.3	0

NOTE: Not all income is shown by source. Hence the individual rows do not sum to total gross mean income.

[a] State old-age pension, state retirement pension, widows' pensions, and blind person's pension.

Table 4.5 **Income for Those Reporting Pension Income from State Employment Pensions, Non-State Employment Pensions, and No Occupational Pensions (€ per week)**

		Total gross household income[a]		Total pension income from all sources		Income from state employment pension		Income from other employment pensions		Income from all state social security pensions[a]		Total other financial income		Total earned income	
Age	*N*	Mean	Med.	Mean	Med.	Mean	Med.	Mean	Med.	Mean	Med.	Mean	Med.	Mean	Med.
State employment pension															
65–74	138	465	413	377	370	273	238	12	0	92	101	14	6	61	0
75+	81	444	387	378	356	248	214	15	0	115	135	19	2	28	0
Total	219	457	403	377	359	264	230	13	0	100	105	16	4	49	0
Non-state employment pension															
65–74	257	424	334	295	242	16	0	164	0	115	132	19	2	91	0
75+	136	355	293	289	252	15	0	159	0	114	138	14	0	25	0
Total	393	400	326	293	244	16	0	162	0	115	132	17	1	68	0
No occupational pension															
65–74	498	267	193	145	174	0	0	0	0	145	174	4	0	88	0
75+	367	218	193	163	180	0	0	0	0	163	180	5	0	29	0
Total	865	246	193	153	175	0	0	0	0	153	175	4	0	63	0

NOTE: Not all income is shown by source. Hence the individual rows do not sum to total gross mean income.

[a] State old-age pension, state retirement pension, widows' pensions, and blind person's pension.

Table 4.6 Gender of People with and without Occupational Pensions for Single-Person Households

Age	Without occupational pension	Male	Female	With occupational pension	Male	Female
65–75	235	87	148	125	54	71
75+	222	69	153	98	38	60
Total	457	156	301	223	92	131

average income varies between 73 and 87 percent for those reporting pension income from non-state employment, compared with 94 to 98 percent for those reporting income from state employment.

Gross income and pension incomes of those with pension income from non-state employment, while lower than those with pension income from state employment, is still higher than the average pension income of all retired persons in the survey. The reason for this is the much lower pension income of those with no occupational pension income, as shown in Table 4.5. The gap between median pension income and median gross income is not large, but the gap between mean gross income and mean pension income is the largest in percentage terms of the separate groups examined. This reflects the relatively higher contribution to income from paid work for this group

Apart from considerable differences in pension income between those who report occupational pension income as compared with those who do not, there are also large differences in pension income by gender. Table 4.6 shows the gender of those reporting no occupational incomes for single-person households only. People without an occupational pension are predominantly female. There are nearly twice as many single females as males living alone without any occupational pension. Although not shown in the table, their incomes are one-third to one-half of those with occupational pensions. Females also make up the majority (60 percent) of those living alone with an occupational pension.

Table 4.7 shows occupational pension income broken down by state employment pension, non-state employment pension, and gender for single-person households (hence the numbers of respondents are smaller). Median pension income is highest for females with a state occupational pension, and there is also less dispersion in female pension

Table 4.7 Occupational Pension Income (€ per week) by Gender

	State pension income						Non-state pension income					
	Male			Female			Male			Female		
Age	*N*	Mean	Median	*N*	Mean	Median	*N*	Mean	Median	*N*	Mean	Median
65–74	19	272	217	31	304	333	35	219	140	40	168	154
75+	11	375	214	22	230	239	29	182	144	39	151	120
Total	30	310	215	53	274	268	64	202	142	79	159	125

NOTE: Not all income is shown by source. Hence the individual rows do not sum to total gross mean income.

[a] State old-age pension, state retirement pension, widows' pensions, and blind person's pension.

Figure 4.9 Value of All Pension Unit Incomes by Source and Income Quintile

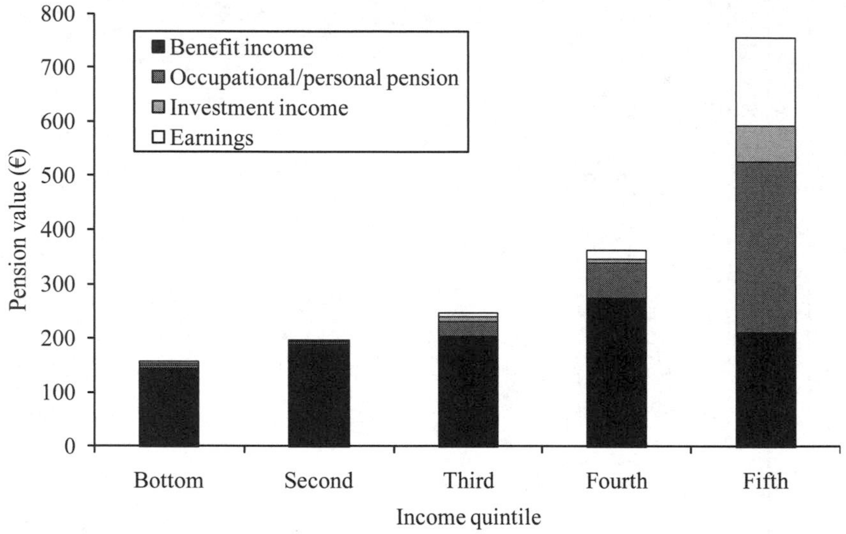

SOURCE: Department of Social and Family Affairs (2007a, Table 4.4).

income—the mean and median values are much closer in all cases. For those reporting non-state occupational pension income, the median income is higher for males aged 75+ but not for those aged 65–74.

Finally, the minor role that the private pension system and other sources of income play in providing retirement incomes in Ireland becomes even more evident when the data are disaggregated by income quintile to show how much income pensioners in different quintiles receive from each income source (Figure 4.9). State pensions account for almost all of the income received by pensioners in the first four quintiles. Private pensions and other income provide a significant part of total income only to the group at the top of the income distribution. Private pensions, investments, and earnings provide around three-quarters of the total income of pensioners with the highest incomes. This is hardly surprising given the skewed distribution of pension tax relief in favor of the highest earners.

THE FAILURES AND SUCCESSES OF IRELAND'S PENSION SYSTEM

Our evaluation of the pension system in Ireland in terms of simplicity, adequacy, cost, equity, coverage, and effectiveness in delivering pensions leads to a number of conclusions. The main defect of the Irish public pension system is that it has failed to eliminate pensioner poverty. Successive governments' preferences for a public system that provides only a subsistence income in retirement and for a private system that is supposed to provide an earnings-related top-up has focused attention on the cost of the public social security system while the cost of Exchequer support for private pensions has been largely ignored. The cost of the tax expenditure for private pensions in Ireland is now nearly as great as the cost of direct expenditure on the public social security system. Consequently, when the cost of the tax expenditure is factored in, the aggregate cost of pension provision has fluctuated around 4 percent of GNP for the last 30 years.

Contrary to expectations, the provision of generous tax relief for private pensions has not increased the coverage of occupational pensions. Most of the benefits of the tax relief for private pensions have been appropriated by the very highest earners. This occurs at the expense of taxpayers, most of whom generally receive little benefit from the favorable tax treatment of private pensions.

PROPOSED REFORMS: NATIONAL PENSIONS FRAMEWORK

The recently published National Pensions Framework (Department of Social and Family Affairs 2010) sets out the government strategy on pensions. It states that the government "will seek to sustain" the state social security pension at 35 percent of average weekly earnings. It is currently at 32 percent. It will also become easier for some groups to qualify. There will be tax reform, but rather than granting all relief at the standard 20 percent rate, relief will be granted at a 33 percent rate, and rather than eliminating the tax exemption from lump sum payments, the maximum tax-free lump sum will be reduced to €200,000 ($256,000), which exempts from tax the lump sum payable to the most senior civil servants.

The National Pensions Framework proposes an individual pension plan in addition to those already in existence (Additional Voluntary Contribution, PRSA, Approved Retirement Fund, and others) but only for those without pension coverage (Department of Social and Family Affairs 2010, pp. 29–31). This proposed plan has all the signs of an initiative led by the pension industry. There will be auto-enrollment (with an opt-out option), funds will be invested, and as noted above there is the typical industry analysis of returns assuming a constant 7 percent per year, in real terms, for 40 years (Department of Social and Family Affairs 2010, Table 4.1, p. 32).

It is most unlikely that this plan will succeed in providing adequate retirement income. The contribution periods of workers will be less than forecast, given periods of unemployment, working abroad, or caring for children and other family members. Financial market returns will certainly not be as forecast. In addition, the proposed contribution level as a proportion of salary is too low (8 percent) to provide retirement income as forecast in government proposals. In addition, the proposals do not attempt to quantify the extra risk borne by members of the new plan.

There is a danger that employers will see this new plan as a cheaper alternative to existing plans because they may contribute 2 percent of salary to the new plan, whereas contributions to existing defined contribution plans have been reported to be 11 percent of salary and contributions to defined benefit plans are 16 percent of salary. More recently a figure of 6 percent has been cited as the average contribution rate to defined contribution plans. Thus employers may seek to switch employees from an existing defined benefit, or more likely defined contribution plan, to the new cheaper plan. A similar trend has occurred in the United States with 401(k) plans.

The cost of the new plan (managing funds, a tracking mechanism to keep track of mobile workers, and managing dormant accounts) will be expensive, as has been shown to be true in Australia. For small accounts, fees over time could reduce sums considerably.

Government proposals also involve reform of pensions in relation to state employment. The main proposed reforms for new entrants involve increasing the retirement age to 66 and basing pensions on career average earnings. The main proposal in relation to existing and future public service employees is that the consumer price index rather than final salary will be used as the basis for post-retirement pension increases.

The new government proposals have nothing to say about the National Pension Reserve Fund. Perhaps this is because the reserve fund is now essentially a vehicle to provide finance to the Irish banking system. Originally it was intended to partially prefund future state employee and social welfare pensions and was hailed by some commentators as the most important initiative in a decade.

The government-proposed reforms have little to offer to members of defined benefit plans in actuarial deficit. A particular concern for many employees is that their employer may be unprofitable or insolvent as a result of property speculation, over-borrowing, and extraordinarily poor management.

The government proposals, however, devote some space to advocating programs of financial education for individuals relating to retirement planning and summarizing the considerable state effort at financial education for individuals. However, financial education is not the key to successful retirement planning or financial decision making, as Ghillarducci (2008, p. 137) notes.

Finally, there is a proposal that the earliest age at which the state social security pension can be received will increase to 68 starting in 2014. There is no discussion of enhanced benefits as a result. Increasing the retirement age may be welcome by some groups with particular skills, for example, professional groups such as lawyers. But for those working in hazardous or physically demanding employment, increasing the retirement age could substantially reduce the period of retirement. It is therefore regressive, representing a transfer from those who are less well off and with lower life expectancies to those who are better off and with higher life expectancies.

These proposed reforms do not address the issues of equity and efficiency. The ultimate viability of any pension system depends on the future productivity of an economy. Unless issues of equity and efficiency are addressed, future productivity will be adversely affected.

THE KEY TO DEVELOPING AN IDEAL PENSION SYSTEM FOR IRELAND

Despite the poor performance of private pensions, the National Pensions Framework proposals for the future development of the pension system aim to maintain the social welfare pension at a subsistence level of about one-third of average earnings and to try to increase the coverage of the private pension system. It is hoped this can be done by automatically enrolling employees who are not covered by an occupational plan in individual pension accounts that would be managed by the private sector. This proposal flies in the face of the evidence that the social security public pension system is far more effective than the private system in delivering pensions and in providing the bulk of retirement income. Only a small minority of pensioners at the top of the income distribution receive significant benefits from the private pension system.

The evidence on the performance of the two components of Ireland's pension system strongly suggests that the opposite should be done in an ideal system. There should be a larger role for the public component rather than for the private component of the pension system.

The current system could be developed in ways that draw on the strengths of the public component and begin to correct the inequitable treatment of taxpayers who gain little from tax relief for private pensions. Ireland is not, of course, starting with a clean slate. Pension systems are to some extent path dependent, so it is not being suggested that Ireland should ignore what has been done in the past. What would be possible is to change the balance of pension provision in favor of the social security public system.

Elements of an Ideal Pension System for Ireland

The evidence presented above shows that the public component of the pension system is doing a far better job of delivering an income in retirement than the private component, that it is currently providing retirement income for over 90 percent of pensioners, and that its benefits are not high enough to prevent poverty in old age. To build on the strengths of the social security public pension system and to address its weaknesses, the TCD Pension Policy Research Group (see Hughes 2007; McCashin 2005; Stewart 2005) proposed that the tax incentives for private pensions should be at the standard rate of tax rather than the marginal rate; the flat-rate social welfare pension should be increased to 40 percent of earnings to bring it above the poverty level; it should become a universal benefit, similar to New Zealand's superannuation, which would be payable to every pensioner on the basis of residence in the country for a specific period of years; and a second-tier social security pension should be introduced to top up the universal pension to 50 percent of earnings.

A universal social security pension funded out of general taxation would be distinctively redistributive, it would ensure pensions as of right for men and women, and it would abolish the means test for pensions. The transformation of the current social security system into a second-tier earnings-related pension recognizes the strong social and political attachment to work-based pensions in Ireland. The social security pension would not require dependents' additions because dependents would be entitled to a pension in their own right under the proposal for a universal state social security pension. This would strengthen the role of social security as a benefit derived from participation in the labor force. The pension could be flat rate, as it is now, or it could be related to earnings. This design "recognises the fact that a pensions system, of necessity, must incorporate a number of competing values, that reform must build to some extent on existing provisions and expectations, and command broad public support" (McCashin 2005, p. 117).

At present, Ireland is using social security pensions to try to achieve a number of different objectives: the prevention of poverty in old age; the provision of support for pensioners' dependents; the maintenance of contribution records during periods of unemployment, illness, or temporary withdrawal from the labor force; and the provision of adequate income during retirement. It is difficult to achieve this multiplicity of objectives with just one instrument. The introduction of a universal state social security pension and a state earnings-related pension would separate the goal of poverty prevention from that of income maintenance and permit the development of policies that would have a better chance of achieving each objective.

The increase in the state basic social security pension would be paid for by giving tax relief for private pensions at the standard rate of

Table 4.8 Distribution of Gains and Losses from Using the Standard Tax Rate for Pension Tax Relief and Increasing the Social Welfare Pension Above the Poverty Level and Percentage Change in Income by Income Decile, 2005

Income decile	Gain or loss (€ million)	Percentage change in income
1	10.80	0.6
2	160.10	6.4
3	264.80	10.0
4	122.80	3.3
5	26.40	0.5
6	−18.70	−0.3
7	−58.10	−0.8
8	−137.60	−1.7
9	−299.90	−3.1
10	−435.60	−3.1
All	−365.00	−0.6

NOTE: The Social Welfare Pension is assumed to increase by €38 per week.
SOURCE: Callan, Keane, and Walsh (2009, Tables 5.1 and 5.4).

tax. The earnings-related component would be paid for by increasing employer and employee Pay Related Social Insurance Contributions (PRSI) and using some of the revenue released by standard rating the tax relief of private pensions. This approach would enable Ireland to eliminate pensioner poverty at a cost it could afford and at the same time contribute to the long-term sustainability of the public social security pension system. This approach also has the very considerable advantage that it is the only one that would improve the position of existing pensioners. Policies that rely on the private pension system to improve pensions will do nothing for existing pensioners because a long period of time is required for assets to build up to a level that could provide even a modest improvement in living standards.

Is the Ideal Pension System for Ireland Affordable?

The proposals for the ideal pension system for Ireland pose a key question: are they affordable? Researchers at the Economic and Social Research Institute (ESRI) in Dublin have used a micro-simulation model to estimate the cost of implementing this policy (see Callan, Keane, and Walsh 2009). They simulated what would have been the cost in 2005 of increasing the social welfare pension by €38 ($48) per week, which would have brought it just above the poverty level, and financing the increase in the pension by giving tax relief on private pension contributions at the standard rate of tax rather than the marginal rate. The outcome of this exercise is shown in Table 4.8. The effect of using the standard rate of tax relief on pension contributions would be to release almost €950 ($1,216) million in tax revenue forgone from taxpayers in the sixth to the tenth deciles. Just over three-fifths of this sum, or €585 ($749) million, would be required to bring nearly all pensioners above the poverty level (i.e., by increasing all social security and social assistance pensions by €38 [$48] per week). The losses for taxpayers in the top five income deciles would range from −0.3 percent to −3.1 percent of income, while the gains for those in the bottom half of the income distribution would range from 0.5 percent to 10 percent of income. The biggest losses would be borne by taxpayers in the top two income deciles who would contribute to the Exchequer almost 80 percent of the additional revenue that would be raised by using the standard tax rate for tax relief on pension contributions, a result that is hardly surprising in view of the evidence presented previously showing that the bulk of pension tax relief accrues to taxpayers at the top of the income distribution.

Callan, Keane, and Walsh (2009) also calculated the effect of using the standard rate for tax relief and raising the social welfare pension on the "at risk of poverty" measure for pensioners. They found that the pensioner poverty rate would fall by almost 90 percent, from 25.9 percent of households headed by a pensioner to 2.8 percent.

If the state social security pension were brought up to 40 percent of earnings, a 10 percent gap would remain between the first-tier pension and the replacement rate target of 50 percent of preretirement income set by the Pensions Board for the average worker. The objective of the proposal for a second-tier social security pension is to close this gap. Estimating how much it would cost to do so would necessitate complex simulations requiring access to a long-term projection model that is not available to us. However, in its *National Pensions Review*, the Pensions Board (2005) considered a mandatory state social security earnings-related system (Alternative 4) that would provide a flat-rate pension of 34 percent of average industrial earnings and a supplementary social security earnings-related payment that would provide a benefit close to the 50 percent target for a substantial additional number of workers. The earnings-related component would provide a benefit of 1 percent of annual pensionable earnings between the minimum income for PRSI payment and twice average industrial earnings. Annual earnings would be revalued at retirement to take account of inflation and the benefit would be based on career average earnings. Projected retirement income replacement rates under Alternative 4 range from 68 percent for those with half average earnings, to 55 percent for those with average earnings, and 47 percent for those with twice average earnings.

The additional contributions required to pay for an earnings-related social insurance pension would be equivalent to about 5 percent of labor force earnings. To meet the full cost of the existing flat-rate social welfare pension and the Alternative 4 earnings-related component, the contribution rate required for a new entrant to the labor force would be 26.5 percent of pensionable earnings within the limits described above. Although we differ with some of the assumptions underlying this alternative, it is the closest in spirit to our proposal and it gives a broad indication of the long-term costs and benefits of the proposal.

If Alternative 4 were operated on a pay-as-you-go basis, rather than funded as the Pensions Board prefers, it would result in a substantial improvement to the Exchequer finances in the first decade of its operation and no increase in cost through 2056 over the current system of flat-rate state social security pensions and tax relief for private pensions. The Pensions Board (2005, p. 253) describes this outcome as "illusory" because it assumes costs would increase after 2056. However, it is worth noting that even if Alternative 4 were funded, it would cost just 1.6 percent of GNP more now than the current system and 0.3 percent more in 2056. On average in the period up to 2026, it would cost 1.3 percent of GNP, or 0.3 percent more than the annual contribution to the National Pension Reserve Fund.

CONCLUSION

The proposal to introduce a universal social security pension and to reduce the tax relief for retirement saving is not as dramatic as it might seem at first sight (see McCashin 2005). The state social security pension system is already providing the bulk of retirement income for the great majority of pensioners in Ireland. The tax relief for retirement saving has not succeeded in increasing coverage of occupational pension plans, and the tax incentives for personal pensions (PRSAs) have had little effect on coverage, especially at the lower end of the income distribution. The cost of expenditure on the public social security pension system and the tax expenditure on the private pension system in Ireland are now almost the same. Consequently, there is scope for a reallocation of resources between the public and private components of Ireland's pension system.

An important advantage of the proposed strategy is that it would provide a secure framework for people who wish to save to maintain a reasonable relationship between their income from work and their income in retirement. It would improve the living standards of current pensioners, contribute to the elimination of pensioner poverty, improve the equity of the tax system, provide equal treatment for men and women, and contribute to the long-term sustainability of Ireland's public pension system. Finally, it would strengthen the public social security component of the pension system which is already nationally established, politically accountable, and enjoys public credibility and legitimacy.

Notes

1. For example, the introduction of 401(k) plans in the United States has been associated with a collapse in retirement income. See Ghilarducci (2008, pp. 56–57).
2. Although governments in Ireland have never committed themselves to formally indexing pensions, they have maintained a close relationship with average industrial earnings since the contributory old-age pension was introduced in 1961. Over the period 1961–1998, the average personal rate of the contributory pension was about 25 percent of average industrial earnings. Following a recommendation in 1998 by the Pensions Board (1998) that the personal contributory pension be increased to 34 percent of average industrial earnings, it increased to about 30 per-

cent of average industrial earnings in the period 1998–2007. In 2007 it reached the 34 percent target set in the Pensions Board report (see Hughes and Watson 2005).

3. The at risk of poverty rates for Ireland in Figures 4.1 and 4.2 differ because the rate in Figure 4.1 is primarily based on a national definition that includes income from private pensions whereas Figure 4.2 is based on an EU definition that excludes such income. For further information, see Central Statistics Office (2009).
4. The exchange rate on June 30, 2006, was €1 = $1.28, and this rate is used throughout the paper to convert euros into U.S. dollars.
5. The Pensions Board replacement rate targets of 34 percent and 50 percent are modest. Munnell and Quinby (2009, p. 3) point out that "as a general benchmark, retirement income equal to 65 to 80 percent of pre-retirement earnings should be more or less adequate."
6. The accuracy of the data depends on the accuracy of information given by independent households. For example, the Household Budget Survey notes (Central Statistics Office 1997, p. 6) that, "no adjustment is made for the understatement of expenditure, for example [on] alcoholic drink which is a traditional national and international phenomenon in household expenditure surveys of this type." In addition, the Central Statistics Office (2001, p. 5) comments that, "some categories of income tend to be underestimated in surveys of this nature."

References

Callan, Tim, Claire Keane, and John R. Walsh. 2009. "Pension Policy: New Evidence on Key Issues." Policy Research Series no. 14. Dublin: Economic and Social Research Institute.

Callan, Tim, Brian Nolan, and John R. Walsh. 2007. "Pension Priorities: Getting the Balance Right?" In *Budget Perspectives 2008*, Tim Callan, ed. Dublin: Economic and Social Research Institute, pp. 27–43.

Central Statistics Office. 1997. *Household Budget Survey 1994–95*. Pn. 3934. Dublin: Stationery Office.

———. 2001. *Household Budget Survey 1999–00, Preliminary Results*. Pn. 10623. Dublin: Stationery Office.

———. 2009. *Survey on Income and Living Conditions (SILC) 2008*. Dublin: Stationery Office.

Department of Social and Family Affairs. 2007a. *Green Paper on Pensions.* Dublin: Stationery Office.

———. 2007b. *A Social Portrait of Older People in Ireland.* Dublin: Stationery Office.

———. 2010. *National Pensions Framework.* Dublin: Stationery Office.

European Commission. 2010. "Towards Adequate, Sustainable, and Safe European Pension Systems." Green Paper. SEC (20100)830. Brussels: European Commission.

Ghilarducci, Teresa. 2008. *When I'm Sixty-Four: The Plot against Pensions and the Plan to Save Them*. Princeton, NJ: Princeton University Press.

Hughes, Gerard. 1985. "Payroll Tax Incidence, the Direct Tax Burden and the Rate of Return on State Pension Contributions in Ireland." Paper no. 120. Dublin: Economic and Social Research Institute.

———. 2007. "Delivering Pensions: The Performance of Public and Private Providers and the National Pensions Review." In *Choosing Your Future: How to Reform Ireland's Pension System*, Gerard Hughes and Jim Stewart, eds. Dublin: Tasc at New Island Press, pp. 61–101.

Hughes, Gerard, and Dorothy Watson. 2005. "Pensioners' Incomes and Replacement Rates in 2000." Policy Research Series no. 54. Dublin: Economic and Social Research Institute.

Ireland. 1976. "A National Income Related Pensions Scheme: A Discussion Document." Dublin: Stationery Office.

McCashin, Anthony. 2005. "The State Pension—Towards a Basic Income for the Elderly?" In *For Richer, for Poorer: An Investigation of the Irish Pension System*, Jim Stewart, ed. Dublin: Tasc at New Island Press, pp. 94–128.

Ministry of Social Development. 2005. "Social Report Indicators for Low Incomes and Inequality: Update from the 2004 Household Economic Survey." Wellington, New Zealand: Ministry of Social Development.

Munnell, Alicia H., and Laura Quinby. 2009. "Pension Coverage and Retirement Security." Issue Brief no. 9-26. Boston College, Center for Retirement Research.

Pensions Board. 1998. "Securing Retirement Income: National Pensions Policy Initiative Report of the Pensions Board." Dublin: Pensions Board.

———. 2005. *National Pensions Review*. Dublin: Pensions Board.

Stewart, Jim. 2005. *For Richer, For Poorer: An Investigation of the Irish Pension System*, Jim Stewart, ed. Dublin: Tasc at New Island Press.

———. 2011. "The Financial Crisis and Pension Funds in Ireland." In *Protecting Pension Rights in Times of Economic Turmoil*, Yves Stephens, ed. Antwerp: Intersentia, pp. 169–182.

Stewart, Jim, and Gerard Hughes, eds. 2009. *Personal Provision of Retirement Income, Meeting the Needs of Older People?* Cheltenham, UK: Edward Elgar.

St John, Susan, Michael Littlewood, and M. Claire Dale. 2010. "KiwiSaver: The First Three Years: Lessons for Ireland?" Working Paper no. 2010/2. University of Auckland, Retirement Policy and Research Centre.

Whelan, Christopher, Richard Layte, Bertrand Maitre, Brenda Gannon, Brian Nolan, Dorothy Watson, and James Williams. 2003. "Monitoring Poverty Trends in Ireland: Results from the 2001 Living in Ireland Survey." Policy Research Series no. 51. Dublin: Economic and Social Research Institute.

Zaidi, Ashgar. 2010. "Poverty Risks for Older People in EU Countries: An Update." Policy Brief. Vienna: European Centre for Social Welfare Policy and Research.

5
The Optimal Pension System

Is Denmark Best?

Finn Østrup
Center for Financial Law, Copenhagen Business School

In its report *Averting the Old Age Crisis: Policies to Protect the Old and Promote Growth*, the World Bank (1994) recommended that countries set up a multifaceted pension system based on three pillars:

1) a public old-age pension that covers the basic needs of older people,
2) mandatory pension plans that are fully funded, and
3) personal pension plans.

The Danish pension system closely resembles this type of system. A basic flat-rate pension benefit (social security benefit) is provided to all residents in Denmark through the government budget. On top of this, persons are covered by labor market systems, which are negotiated between employees and employers at the level of the individual firm or profession. Third, persons may derive an income from tax-subsidized personal pension arrangements that can be established with banks and life insurance companies.

This chapter first discusses the main characteristics in the design of a pension system. It then discusses how the pension system affects a number of different policy objectives. The chapter finally turns to the Danish experience and describes some of the problems that have been encountered in this multifaceted pension system. A major finding from the chapter is that no universal formula can be found for an optimal pension system. The optimality of a national pension system depends on the goals that the pension system is supposed to achieve, which may vary between countries. Based on the Danish experience, it is shown that a multifaceted pension system such as that recommended by the World Bank may give rise to a range of problems.

POSSIBILITIES OF DESIGNING A PENSION SYSTEM

The main goal of pension systems is to provide a certain standard of living for people who no longer receive a labor income after a certain age. If people without a labor income are to maintain a certain standard of living, consumption possibilities must be transferred from people who are active in the labor market. This can take place in two ways.

One possibility is to directly transfer money from employed people to pensioners. These types of payments take place in pay-as-you-go systems, which have various forms. A levy may, for example, be charged on individuals who are actively working, the proceeds of which are then used to finance benefits for pensioners. Payments can also be made by an enterprise to its former employees. A third possibility is that the retirees receive benefits through the government budget. In pay-as-you-go systems, the criteria for the size of pensions may change. A person may, for example, receive a pension income that is determined as a certain percentage of the person's final salary in the firm in which he or she worked. People may also receive a flat-rate pension, for example, one financed through the government budget.

Pay-as-you-go plans are usually defined benefit plans, implying that the amounts used to finance the pensions are determined by the size of benefits. Pay-as-you-go systems may, however, also be defined contribution plans. A government or an enterprise may, for example, set aside a certain sum that is then shared among the retirees. In practice, such a system has, however, not been implemented, possibly due to the large amount of uncertainty that would result with respect to the pension to be received by individual retirees.

Another possibility for organizing a pension system is that persons save for their old age while they are employed. The type of pension system is said to be prefunded. The saving can be managed either by the individual or it may be placed in an institution, for example, a pension fund or life insurance company. Pensions are later paid from the institution in which the saving was placed.

A second way to classify pension systems is to consider the institutional level at which the plans are organized. A broad distinction can be made between three institutional levels:

1) pensions are organized at the individual level, implying that it is the decision of each individual how to provide for his or her living in old age;
2) pensions are organized at the level of an enterprise or collective group (e.g., employees in a certain sector or persons with a similar educational background), implying that it is left for enterprises or collective groups to organize pension plans; or
3) pensions are organized at the societal level, implying that pensions are organized by, for example, the government, which establishes a universal pension system for all residents or for all persons who fulfill certain socioeconomic criteria.

Classifying pension systems on the basis of these two criteria—on the basis of financing (pay-as-you-go vs. prefunded) and institutional level at which pensions are organized (individual, enterprise/sector, and society)—we can derive six different ways to organize pension systems (Table 5.1).

Examples of systems organized at the level of society based on pay-as-you-go finance include the public old-age pensions that are widespread in the United Kingdom and in the Scandinavian countries (Denmark, Norway, and Sweden). One example is the Danish basic old-age pension, which is financed through the government budget. The Danish government pays a basic pension benefit to every person aged 65 or older who has been a resident in Denmark for a certain minimum period. The benefit is calculated based on criteria stipulated in legislation adopted by the Danish Parliament. All persons above the age of 65 receive a uniform basic benefit, but supplementary benefits are paid to people with low incomes. The general labor market system in Sweden is an example of society-wide systems that are based on prefunding. This system has been legislatively established and covers all employees. Employees are required to pay a certain percentage of their wage income to a pension fund that determines benefits based on the savings and accrued earnings. Examples of pension plans organized at the sector level with pay-as-you-go financing are the various sector plans that constitute the basis of pension systems in Continental Europe (e.g., Belgium, France, and Germany). Employees belonging to specific sectors pay contributions to a sector-wide plan that finances pensions out of its

Table 5.1 Categories of Pension Systems

System organization	Pay-as-you-go finance	Prefunded finance
The society level	Public old-age pensions	General systems financed through taxes
The enterprise or sector level	Pensions based on pension promises from firms	Sector systems with prefunded saving (pension funds, etc.)
	Pension systems for public servants financed through the public budget	
The individual level	Old-age provision through family members	Individual pension savings (e.g., in life insurance companies)

revenue. Benefits are determined on the basis of the retiree's previous labor income.

As an example of prefunded pension systems organized at the level of the firm are those negotiated between firms and either single employees or labor unions. Such pension plans are common in Denmark. In many Danish enterprises, part of the company policy is that a certain percentage of the employee's wage income is paid to an individual pension account in a pension fund or in a life insurance company, which manages the funds. The employee's pension benefit is subsequently calculated on the basis of past contributions and investment earnings. In most plans, the pension participant is guaranteed a minimum rate of return. For certain groups of employees, mostly in the public sector, pensions are part of a general wage agreement that is negotiated by a trade union on behalf of its members. Persons covered by the wage agreement make contributions to the pension fund, and pensions are determined on the basis of past contributions with accrued returns. The pension funds guarantee a certain minimum rate of return.

An example of pensions organized at the individual level with prefunding is personal pension plans established by individuals in life insurance companies or other pension institutions. The agreement entered into between the individual and the pension institution stipulates that the policy holder is entitled to certain benefits after a specified age either in the form of a lump sum or an annuity. In Denmark, tax-subsidized personal pension plans are widespread. Pension savings can be undertaken not only in life insurance companies but also in banks.

Finally, pension plans organized at the individual level based on pay-as-you-go financing include plans under which a group of people contribute to a retired person out of their income. Such pension provision is known in non-industrial societies. Family-based pensions, in which members of a family contribute to older family members, belong in this category.

POLICY OBJECTIVES IN DESIGNING A PENSION SYSTEM

The pension system serves or affects a range of goals, which are seen as valuable from the point of view of society in a variety of ways. Below we discuss how the pension system affects

- the desire to bring about a desired standard of living for persons who have retired from the labor market,
- the reduction of uncertainty concerning the postretirement standard of living,
- the level of national saving,
- the size of the labor force and the efficiency of labor markets, and
- the efficiency of financial markets.

The Desired Standard of Living after Retirement

Individuals have preferences with respect to the standard of living that they desire after retirement from the labor market. A main goal of pension arrangements is to bring about this desired standard of living.

Complications arise in the design of a pension system because different conceptions exist, both among individuals and in society, concerning the standard of living that pension systems should provide. Here we distinguish three possibilities. One possibility is that individuals may wish to achieve a certain level of consumption. After retirement, a person may, for example, desire to realize certain goals with respect to travel, the purchase of a holiday cottage, or providing other family members with gifts. In the case of such preferences, the goal of pension systems should be to ensure that persons have acquired the financial resources that make it possible to realize the desired level of consumption during retirement.

Another possibility is that people wish to maintain a certain standard of living relative to a reference group, for example, people with the same educational background or who have worked in the same sector or enterprise. They may also want to maintain a certain standard of living relative to the general standard of living in the population.

Finally, a third possibility is that individuals may wish to maintain a certain standard of living relative to the standard of living that they enjoyed when they were active in the labor market, for example, with respect to housing or leisure activities. Some people may want to maintain the same standard of living, whereas others may accept limited downsizing.

Individuals may have views regarding their postretirement standard of living that differ from the level that is regarded as reasonable from the perspective of society. From the point of view of society, it may, for example, be seen as unacceptable if older people have a standard of living that is markedly different from that which is enjoyed by the rest of the population. If the standard of living among older people falls markedly below that of the rest of the population, political pressures may build up to improve the living standard among the pensioners. It may also be seen as unacceptable from a societal point of view if pensioners enjoy a living standard that is markedly above that of the rest of the population. In this case, political pressures may arise for making pensioners shoulder a larger part of the "societal" burden.

If the goal of the pension system is to maintain a certain standard of living relative to other societal groups, it is preferable that the pension system be organized on a defined benefit basis. Thus, in defined benefit plans, pensions can be adjusted in such a way that individuals realize a certain standard of living relative to other groups. If defined benefit plans are organized at the level of society, older people will normally receive a pension that makes it possible to maintain a certain standard of living relative to the rest of the population. The level of public old-age benefits is often adjusted on the basis of the general wage level. In the case of defined benefit plans organized at the level of an enterprise or a sector, the pension is often tied to the wages of people who currently work in the enterprise or sector. In enterprise plans, pensioners may, for example, receive extra benefits if wages rise in the enterprise.

In defined contribution plans, pensions depend on past savings and on the return that can be achieved on this saving. The return on investments may follow a development that is different from the development in wages. In defined contribution plans, it may therefore be difficult to realize a certain standard of living relative to the groups who are active in the labor market. If, however, it is the goal to achieve a certain level of consumption in old age, defined contribution plans organized at the individual level may be seen as most desirable because this gives individuals the opportunity to adjust contributions in such a way that a certain sum will be available at a certain age. If the goal is to bring about a desired standard of living relative to other pensioners, it may be desirable to have defined contribution plans organized at the level of the group with which the individuals want to make comparisons. If, for example, the goal of economists is to maintain a certain living standard relative to other retired economists, it can be seen as appropriate if economists join together and organize their own pension plan.

Reduction of Uncertainty in the Level of Pensions

A desirable goal of pension systems is to reduce the risks that are related to reaching a desired standard of living. Below we discuss the different risks that arise in different types of pension systems. Pension systems should be assessed in terms of the likelihood that these different risks will arise and of the weight that is attached to risk minimization.

Pay-as-you-go pension systems

In pay-as-you-go pension plans organized at the enterprise level, pledges regarding the future level of pensions usually result from employment contracts. Enterprises are legally bound to keep these pledges. The fulfillment of the pension pledge is conditioned on the survival of the enterprise. In the case of bankruptcy, the pension pledge will no longer be met. Pensions in pay-as-you-go plans organized at the enterprise level are therefore subjected to the risk that the company may go bankrupt.

In the case of pay-as-you-go plans organized at the societal or sector level, the level of pensions will depend on decisions made by those who make the pension possible by agreeing to transfer consumption possibilities to the pensioners. At any time, contributors can change the rules of the game, thereby changing the size of the benefits. In a public old-age system, for example, legislators may decide to change the level of pensions. In plans organized at the sector level, the employed members of the plan may find that the economic burden related to contributions is too big and decide on reductions in pensions. Legislative rules may make such changes at the sector level difficult or impossible, but legislators may also take the view that the burden related to pension contributions is too heavy and decide on changes in legislation that will make it possible to cut back on pensions.

Various shifts in the economic or political environment may bring about situations that may either cause enterprises to go bankrupt, thus being unable to meet pension pledges in enterprise-based pension plans, or may lead to decisions about a reduction in the level of pensions in plans organized at the sector level or the level of society. An overview of different types of risk is found in Table 5.2.

One risk arising for pay-as-you-go pension systems is related to negative macroeconomic shocks that cause a lowering of wage incomes. It may be seen as "fair" if retirees share in these types of economic downturns. Thus, in the case that there is a reduction in after-tax wage incomes caused by an economic downturn, it is likely that a decision will be made also to reduce pensions. Thus, the consumption possibilities for pensioners will be cut back in line with a reduction in the purchasing power that has taken place for wage earners. In the most extreme example, in pay-as-you-go systems organized at the enterprise level, negative macroeconomic shocks may lead to the bankruptcy of an enterprise, which will then be unable to meet pension pledges.

In addition to macroeconomic shocks, pay-as-you-go systems organized at the enterprise level or at the sector level are exposed to shifts in the demand for the product that is produced by the sector. A decline in demand may, for example, reduce the number of workers in a particular sector and thus make it more burdensome to finance pensions. One example is the financial difficulties experienced by pension systems that are organized for workers in coal or steel industries. A shift in the composition of demand may also bring about the bankruptcy of single enterprises.

Table 5.2 Overview of Risks Related to Pension Plans Based on Pay-As-You-Go Finance

Level of organization for the pension plan	Possibility of changing the pension level	Types of risk
Enterprise	Bankruptcy risk	Macroeconomic at the national level affecting the survival of the company Sector-specific economic risks Enterprise-specific economic risks Demographic shifts
Sector	Change in underlying pension agreement	Macroeconomic risks related to changes in real wages (national level) Sector-specific economic risks Demographic shifts Change in preferences regarding level of pension
Society	Change in legislation	Macroeconomic risks related to changes in real wages (national level) Demographic shifts Change in preferences regarding level of pension

Other factors also affect pay-as-you-go plans organized at the enterprise level. A firm may go bankrupt because of factors that are specific to the enterprise in question. There may, for example, be a reduction in the demand for the products produced by the particular firm. Inefficient management may also bring the enterprise down.

For pay-as-you-go plans organized at the sector or society level, a further risk arises in connection with changes in the attitude toward the level of pension considered to be "fair." Younger generations may not support the "generation pact" that implies they should support a certain living standard for older generations.

Pay-as-you-go plans are also exposed to demographic shifts. If, for example, as a result of a reduction in the birth rate, there is a reduction in the number of younger people relative to older people, it will be more burdensome for the young to support a certain living standard for the old. In plans organized at the sector level or at the level of society, this may cause a decision to change the level of pensions. The same risk exists in plans organized at the enterprise level. A larger share of older people relative to workers means that the burden for the enterprise associated with the financing of pensions will increase, increasing the risk that the enterprise may go bankrupt and thus be unable to meet pension pledges.

Prefunded pension systems

Four types of risk arise with respect to the level of the pensions in prefunded pension systems: risks related to

1) fluctuations in the return on the pension savings,
2) the sale of assets in the pension system,
3) political intervention that may change the standard of living of future pensioners, and
4) mismanagement of the pension arrangement. An overview is given in Table 5.3.

Pension plans will be exposed to changes in the various economic factors that may cause a reduction in the earnings of companies in which the pension plan has placed its investments, either in the form of equities or debt instruments (e.g., corporate bonds). In the case of equities, the pension arrangement will be exposed to the losses that occur in

Table 5.3 Overview of Risks in Prefunded Pension Plans

Level of organization for the pension plan	Possibility of changing the pension level	Types of risk
Individual	Changes in return on pension savings	Macroeconomic risks which affect capital income (global level)
	Policy changes that reduce after-tax real income	Change in preferences regarding level of pensions Demographic shifts Inefficient management of pension plan
Enterprise	Changes in return on pension savings	Macroeconomic risks which affect capital income (global level)
	Policy changes that reduce after-tax real income	Change in preferences regarding level of pensions Demographic shifts Inefficient management of pension plan
Sector	Changes in return on pension savings	Macroeconomic risks which affect capital income (global level)
	Policy changes that reduce after-tax real income	Change in preferences regarding level of pensions Demographic shifts Inefficient management of pension plan
Society	Changes in return on pension savings	Macroeconomic risks which affect capital income (global level)
	Policy changes that reduce after-tax real income	Change in preferences regarding level of pensions Demographic shifts Inefficient management of pension plan

connection with a fall in earnings and thus also in the stock price. In the case that the pension plan invests in debt securities issued by companies, it will be exposed to the risk of bankruptcy in the enterprise. One may assume that pension plans will try to diversify their investments, including globally. This will cause the plans only to be exposed to the nondiversifiable (systemic) macroeconomic risks that occur in connection with changes in capital income at the global level.

Pension plans will further be affected by the risk related to the sale of assets in the pension plan, which will depend on demographic shifts. At the time when pensioners need to use their pension savings for consumption, pensioners will have to sell assets (e.g., equities) in the pension plans. The purchasers of these assets will primarily be employed people. If there is a large number of retired older people relative to employed younger people, the outcome will be a fall in the price of the assets the pension plans want to sell. In this case, we may see a fall in share prices or in the price of fixed property. This fall in asset prices will reduce the purchasing power of the older generation.

A third type of risk is that the performance of pension plans will be affected by political intervention. Several possible policy changes would benefit the working generation. One is the pursuit of inflationary macroeconomic policies, which will erode the real value of fixed-income assets in the pension plans. Another possibility is the taxation of the pension savings, either in the form of higher taxes on capital income in general or in the form of taxes levied specifically on pension savings. An exchange-rate policy directed toward a real depreciation of the domestic currency works to reduce the purchasing power of the older generation insofar as pension plans have invested in financial assets denominated in foreign currencies. A further policy intervention to reduce the purchasing power of the older generation is to raise prices on government services used by that generation, for example, fees related to health care or higher prices on medicine.

Finally, policymakers can reduce the purchasing power of pensions through a low interest rate policy. The big losers from the pursuit of low interest rate policies pursued after 2001 and again since 2008 have been the pension savers who have experienced a large reduction in the return on their savings. It may be asked whether this policy would have been politically feasible if the saving had been undertaken by private individuals and not by pension institutions, which are distanced from the savers and which the savers, due to a lack of transparency, find it difficult to assess.

Policy changes that reduce the after-tax real income of pensioners may be caused by shifts in preferences concerning the standard of living for the older generation. Concepts with respect to what is regarded as a "fair" living standard may change. Policy changes aimed at lowering real incomes for pensioners may also be caused by macroeconomic shifts that reduce real wages for the younger generation. One may further expect the working generation to be less inclined to maintain the living standard of the old generation and thus more likely to undertake legislative changes that reduce the purchasing power of pensioners, if demographic shifts reduce the number of young people.

An additional risk for prefunded pension plans arises in connection with inefficient management of the plan. In attempts to attract customers, managers of life insurance companies may, for example, promise pensions that are too high. A recent example of this is the British life insurer Equitable Life. Plans may also be managed by incompetent managers who derive a low return on assets. The risk of mismanagement is exacerbated by corporate governance problems that arise particularly in relation to pension institutions.

IS THE DANISH SYSTEM BEST?

As mentioned previously, the World Bank (1994) advocated a pension system based on three pillars. The basic idea is that the first pillar—the mandatory public plan (social security)—will provide individuals with a guarantee of a minimum standard of living in old age. The goal of this first pillar is to redistribute income toward those who have a need for additional income in old age. The goal of the second pillar—mandatory privately managed plans—is to shift income from the active working years to retirement years. According to the World Bank (1994, p. 9), this shall be done "avoiding perverse intragenerational redistributions and unintended intergenerational redistributions." The second pillar is further seen as promoting saving and as facilitating the development of financial markets. Finally, the goal of the third pillar—the voluntary personal or occupational plans—is to facilitate individuals' efforts to achieve a higher income in old age.

Denmark has a pension system that closely resembles the system recommended by the World Bank. As its first pillar, Denmark has a basic flat-rate public pension (social security) that is tax financed. This pension provides all residents with a basic income when they reach age 65, presently (2010) about €9,000, with a possibility of as much as about €18,000 if the individual has no additional income. In addition to this basic public old-age pension, nearly all Danish workers are covered by fully funded occupational systems in which benefits are determined on the basis of contributions and investment returns on pension savings. Finally, many Danish citizens have personal saving plans that are subsidized through the tax system and withdrawals can be made only after a certain age.

The question is, however, whether this organization of pensions is in fact the best system. In the discussion above, questions have been raised concerning some of the basic assumptions that underlie the recommendations in the World Bank report.

The main portion of pensions will, according to the World Bank recommendations, come from the mandatory fully funded private pension plans (the second pillar). A main argument against such fully funded pension plans is that they provide less certainty concerning the living standard in old age than defined benefit plans. Thus, in fully funded pension plans based on defined contributions, the size of pensions depends on the share of production that goes to capital income. In contrast, under defined benefit systems, it comes from development in wage incomes. Because the profit share of capital income in production varies more than the wage share, fully funded pension plans based on past contributions will cause more uncertainty in terms of the standard of living in old age than will defined benefit plans. This is a serious objection against such a pension system. After all, a major goal of a pension system is to provide individuals with a certain real income in old age.

It may be argued that the benefit rate in defined benefit plans is exposed to the uncertainty that results from the benefit rate being determined in a political process in which decisions are made about a proper standard of living for the retirees. This is, however, also the case in defined contribution plans. Thus, the consumption possibilities for old people under defined contribution plans are determined by decisions made concerning the taxation of pensions and capital income. Policymakers may also decide that pensioners will have to pay more for the services that they use. Working-age people may also reduce the living standard of the retirees through macroeconomic policies that may erode the purchasing power of saving (e.g., inflation). Thus, defined contribution plans are exposed to basically the same political uncertainty as defined benefit plans.

The case of Denmark demonstrates that fully funded plans, in addition to being subjected to economic uncertainty, are exposed to political uncertainty. Following lengthy political discussions, Denmark introduced in 1982 a tax on the investment returns in pension plans. The goal was to reduce the real return in pension plans to reduce the real income of future pensioners. It was widely argued that the high real return earned on funded pensions would lead to an unbalanced social situation in which an excessive share of national income would accrue to pensioners. In recent years, there has been much discussion in Denmark on cutting back on the free services offered to wealthy pensioners through the government budget. In 1980, the Social-Democratic government had plans to force Danish pension funds and life insurance companies to earmark part of their investments to finance enterprises with a growth potential. Similar plans have recently (August 2010) been proposed by the current Liberal-Conservative government. The plan is to establish a fund financed by pension institutions with the aim of providing finance for small- and medium-sized enterprises with a growth potential. In September 2010, at the height of the financial crisis, the government initiated discussions with the pension institutions to encourage them to invest in and thus rescue problem banks. The plan was abandoned after resistance from the pension industry.

These different examples show that the existence of a large pool of savings in pension institutions represents a temptation for policymakers. They may want to use the funds for purposes that, for political or financial reasons, are difficult to pursue through the government budget. These episodes raise doubt whether it is possible to efficiently manage the savings in prefunded pension plans.

Another basic objection to fully funded pension plans with defined contribution benefits is that such plans are unable to provide pensioners with a desired standard of living relative to the working population.

Thus, if the goal of a pension system is to provide pensioners with a certain living standard relative to the rest of the population, funded defined contribution pension plans can be seen as inferior relative to defined benefit plans in which explicit political decisions are made regarding the proper living standard for pensioners.

During the recent decade, interest rates have fallen to very low levels. The prefunded Danish plans are guaranteed so that the rate of return cannot fall below a set minimum rate. For plans established before 1994, the promised minimum rate of return was 4.5 percent. It was then lowered to 2.5 percent, and for plans established since 1999, the rate has been 1.5 percent. Due to the low interest rates that have prevailed during the past decade, the Danish pension industry wants to abolish the minimum rate guarantees. This has met with fierce resistance from many of the members. One argument is that the pension institutions will evolve into mutual funds with some cover against life risk if the minimum return guarantees are abolished.

A basic challenge for pension systems is to handle a future larger share of older people in the population. This implies that funded pension plans will have to sell their assets to a shrinking share of working-age people, which would result in downward pressure on asset prices, for example, a fall in prices of shares and of long-term fixed-rate bonds. The implication is that the losers in the intergenerational conflict over resources will be the future pensioners who will experience a fall in the value of their investments. Seen from the perspective of securing pensioners a certain living standard, fully funded pension plans can be viewed as especially deficient in situations in which there is a rising share of older people in the population.

To some extent, pension plans can dispose of assets that can be used immediately for consumption without the need to effectuate sales in markets. Pension plans may, for example, hold bank deposits or debt securities that mature at the time when proceeds are needed for pension payments. In this case, the outcome could be inflation because the pensioners are competing with workers to lay hold of production for consumption. An upward price pressure may be expected in particular on goods and services that are used by older people, for example, health services and medicine. If the monetary authorities in this type of situation try to maintain price stability through a strict monetary policy, the outcome will be a rise in unemployment. In this case, the losers in the intergenerational conflict will be workers who face a higher unemployment risk. If the monetary authorities allow inflation to take place, the losers will be pensioners who see the real value of their assets diminished. In either case, social tensions are to be expected.

Similarly, a reduction in a country's production resulting from a smaller labor force will imply an upward pressure on prices of the national production, implying that the country will experience a real appreciation and thus a reduction in the purchasing power of pensioners, as discussed above.

The World Bank report stresses the positive effects on saving as a point in favor of mandatory defined contribution–funded pension plans. It is, however, uncertain to what extent funded pension plans increase saving. In spite of the expansion of prefunded pension plans, Denmark has one of the lowest household saving rates among the industrialized countries. The same is true in the United States and the United Kingdom. As argued above, prefunded plans organized at the society level or at the sector level may harm saving because they lack transparency and thus make it difficult for households to make correct decisions concerning saving. Surveys regarding the saving behavior of Danish households show that there are considerable differences between households with the same age and income regarding saving behavior (see Hansen, Meding, and Østrup 2009). A large number of people in their fifties have no savings except for that in their pension plans. This seems to confirm that it may be particularly difficult to make informed savings decisions with prefunded plans.

The World Bank report finally views funded pension plans as a positive contribution to the development of financial markets. It is, however, uncertain to what extent this is the case. If pension plans diversify internationally, they will not help to develop domestic financial markets, and the experience from Denmark shows that pension institutions are increasingly diversifying internationally. Furthermore, it seems reasonable to ask whether the goal of high saving could not be reached more suitably through a strict fiscal policy that creates a budgetary surplus or through credit restrictions that make it more difficult to take out positive equity in houses.

A wider choice of financial instruments may, on one hand, be seen as positive as it may help the diversification of risk and alleviate the financing of investments. The recent financial crisis has, however, demonstrated that a wider choice of financial instruments also works to reduce transparency and encourage excessive risk taking.

CONCLUSIONS

Contrary to the recommendations of the World Bank, we conclude that no universal formula can be found for an optimal pension system. The optimality of a pension system should be seen in the light of the goals that the pension system is supposed to pursue. While the main goal of a pension system is to provide persons with a desired standard of living after retirement, the pension system affects, however, a number of other policy goals, for example, the labor supply and the efficiency of financial markets. The optimality of a pension system depends on the extent to which the pension system meets this range of policy goals. Because policy goals may differ among countries and change over time, no universal answer can be derived as to what is the optimal pension system. The Danish experience with a pension system that closely resembles the recommendations in the World Bank report is not unambiguously positive. Among industrial countries, Denmark has, for example, experienced one of the lowest saving rates for households. The accumulation of savings in pension institutions has acted as an invitation to political intervention through which changing governments have sought to use the pension saving for purposes that are unrelated to securing the living standard of older people. Moreover, a main topic of discussion in Denmark has been the complexity of the pension system, which has caused a lack of transparency.

References

Hansen, Hans, Frederik Meding, and Finn Østrup. 2009. *Debt and Consumption*. Copenhagen: Thomson Reuters.

World Bank. 1994. *Averting the Old Age Crisis: Policies to Protect the Old and Promote Growth*. New York: Oxford University Press.

6
German Private Pension Law

Current State and Future Directions

Markus Roth
University of Marburg

PRIVATE PENSIONS AT THE CROSSROADS OF SECURITY AND PERSONAL RESPONSIBILITY

Shifting demographics and increased globalization are challenging the pension systems of industrialized nations worldwide. Given the structural problems of Germany's social insurance and state-funded social security programs, the privately funded pension sector needs to be strengthened (Börsch-Supan 2004).[1] A comprehensive analysis and doctrinal foundation for private pensions must be developed with due regard of the opportunities and risks associated with private pensions, both of which result from the asset funding of private pensions. Despite the general economic downturn during the recent financial crisis, the expected rate of return of private pensions constitutes a major opportunity. Key risks lie in the failure to achieve expected rates of return and in the possibility of capital loss. In developing a legal framework of a system of private pensions and its individual products, appropriate consideration needs to be given to such opportunities and risks.

Whereas the German social security plan, the cornerstone of the German public pension system, generates an expected nominal return on employee and employer contributions of 0 to 2 percent,[2] a return of 4 to 8 percent is possible for private pensions. In the past, these levels of real returns have been achieved on capital markets, at least over significant time periods. This is particularly true of long-term investment in equity securities.[3] The risks associated with private pensions must be understood against the background of a long contractual period.[4] The financial security of citizens does not depend on a low rate of return volatility alone; other factors may well have to be considered in assessing the suitability of an investment vehicle for retirement. The guarantees granted by private pension providers ought to be reviewed according to their long-term feasibility and economic profitability.

The opportunities and risks associated with the investment in capital raise the question of the underlying model of modern private pensions. While traditional legal thinking in Germany focuses on nominal security, the modern view, as well as international thinking, attaches greater importance to personal responsibility. Looking at the concepts of security and personal responsibility, it is necessary to balance the tension between them in private pensions. First steps were undertaken by the 65th German Jurists Forum of 2004, which addressed issues of financial security and personal responsibility in both occupational and individual pensions (Steinmeyer 2004). The international prevailing model of the responsible and informed citizen focuses on the possibilities rather than the risks of private pensions. The model further underpins the freedom of choice through disclosure duties.

UNDERSTANDING PRIVATE PENSION LAW

Links between Branches of Private Pension Law

Analyzing the system of private pensions in an integrated fashion departs from the traditional approach, which separates the treatment of investment products of individual pensions, such as life insurance and investment funds. The systems of occupational and individual pensions have also been analyzed separately. However, the products of individual and occupational retirement provision are frequently interlinked and functionally interchangeable. For individual citizens, it makes no difference whether they receive an occupational pension or payments from an individual pension in addition to their social security pension. Furthermore, the law of occupational pensions utilizes investment vehicles of individual pensions. According to the German Occupational Pensions Act, this is the case for occupational pension plans managed through external institutions, provided the external institution is a life insurance company; retirement funds and pension funds are also used, albeit to a lesser extent. If the use of defined contribution plans (in which employers make no pension payment guarantees) were accepted by the German Occupational Pensions Act, then all investment vehicles of individual pensions would also be possible in occupational pensions.

A comprehensive analysis of German laws on occupational and individual pensions facilitates the identification of similarities in legal instruments of private pensions and sets a basis for developing principles protecting participants spanning all legal forms of private pensions. At the same time, these protective principles could serve to further develop the existing law on private pensions. This is of particular relevance for disclosure requirements and, more generally, for occupational pension law. Only when provided with adequate information is the beneficiary able to make an informed decision on a preferred pension product. Because private pension products are interchangeable, the required information needs to be delivered in a consistent format.

To develop occupational pension law in Germany, key issues are the creation of a separate pool of assets for funding occupational retirement plans and the introduction of defined contribution plans.[5] The Occupational Pensions Act does not require external funding of defined benefit plans. Many German employers fund pension obligations internally, by means of a book reserve recorded on the company's balance sheet (book reserve funding). Corresponding with the international standard of external funding and encouraged by international accounting standards (IAS 19), large listed stock corporations in Germany already deviate from this practice and cover (direct) pension obligations with internal or external trusts. The Accounting Law Modernization Act (Bilanzrechtsmodernisierungsgesetz)[6] recently reformed German accounting law, and companies subject to the accounting standards of the Commercial Code (Handelsgesetzbuch) are expected to follow international practice in the future.

Again departing from international standards, German occupational pension law does not provide for true defined contribution plans; instead, it requires the employer to serve as a guarantor of payments during the disbursement period. According to the Federal Labor Court (Bundesarbeitsgericht), general labor law applies in this regard. In concrete terms, this means that the system of protective principles applicable to occupational pension law, rather than the Occupational Pensions Act, serves as the legal basis for defined contribution pensions. True defined contribution pensions could be transferred into the scope of the Occupational Pensions Act by making the protective principles prescribed by the Act applicable to them. A further point of concern is that the Occupational Pensions Act does not give employees the choice between various pension products. In the interest of affording employees more personal responsibility, this should be rectified in the future.

Interdisciplinary Approach

The importance of private pensions in general, and the position of the capitalization (advance funding) principle as an autonomous field of law in particular call for an interdisciplinary and comparative analysis. The fact that asset funding of private pensions necessarily involves capital markets[7] highlights the need for an interdisciplinary treatment of the topic. To understand capital markets properly, and to evaluate the investment decisions, requires consideration of both legal and economic academic literature.

An analysis of private pensions is not possible without using economic concepts and theories, including questions relating to the economic advantages of funding private pensions,[8] as well as debating whether to favor the efficient financial market hypothesis or behavioral finance theory. Taking account also of the financial crisis and its effects, economic theories might serve as a guiding principle for appropriately developing private pension law, provided the theories are substantiated by empirical data. The contribution of private pensions to intergenerational justice is of general significance. Every generation is responsible to provide for its retirement (Leinert and Esche 2000). This highlights the need for a funded pension plan for the baby boom generation's old age. Failing to develop funded pensions would unfairly burden the next generation in providing for a much larger older generation through traditional pension systems (Börsch-Supan 2004).

The societal importance of private pensions also requires consideration of social sciences. Of significance are demographics (thus far showing a constant trend toward rising life expectancy), actuarial sciences, and behavioral sciences. Retirement provision is a topic frequently ignored by society in general. Private retirement provision has thus far been practiced mainly by those who have higher incomes and are better educated, but those who have lower incomes or education

levels are particularly in need of private pensions. Because it can be difficult to interest the latter social classes in private pension plans, setting incentives for intermediaries and especially employers ought to be considered.[9]

CONTRACTUAL AND INSTITUTIONAL FOUNDATIONS

Defined Benefit, Defined Contribution, and Hybrid Pensions

German law on private pensions is in need of systematization. This can be done typologically according to the service content of a particular individual pension contract. Based on internationally acknowledged labor law terminology, private pension contracts can be divided into three categories: defined benefit pensions, defined contribution pensions, and hybrid pensions.

For individual pensions, fully guaranteed (defined benefit) retirement income in the form of an annuity is rarely provided; whereas for occupational pensions, defined benefit pensions in the form of so-called direct obligations funded internally by a book reserve on an employer's balance sheet are still common German practice. Trust administration, management by power of attorney, investment funds, and defined contribution pensions depend entirely on the asset management's outcome. Hybrid pensions are of particular importance. Insurance-based pension contracts, which have traditionally dominated individual pensions in Germany, belong to this group. Retirement funds (Pensionskassen), life insurance contracts in occupational pensions, pension funds, and investment funds with warranty certificates typically are also hybrid pensions.

As previously stated, defined contribution pensions do not fall under the Occupational Pensions Act; rather, their regulation is derived from general principles of German labor law, subject to further development by the courts and academia.[10] The development of employee protection for defined contribution pensions should, however, be modeled after the Occupational Pensions Act. Such an approach would imply a restriction on forfeiture, increased portability, and the allocation of the profits from asset management. Because they bear the risk of investment, employees

are no less in need of the legal protection granted to people with classical benefits under the Occupational Pensions Act. As in other countries, defined contribution pensions in Germany ought to be conceptually understood as occupational pensions.

Institutions in Private Pensions

The term "private pension" is a generalized term encompassing the provision of individual and occupational retirement provision. Individual pensions are frequently managed through insurance companies and sometimes through investment funds and annuities. The term "occupational retirement provision" covers defined contribution pensions and conceptually also occupational pensions falling under the Occupational Pensions Act. The Occupational Pensions Act focuses on guarantees of the employer and therefore on the disbursement period. Until 2001, it was called the Act for Improved Retirement Provision. Internationally, the focus is more on the period of accumulation, in which the investment decisions are made. In this period, an institution is chosen through which the private pension plan is to be managed.

The choice of a pension product is determined by German tax law, which is relatively restrictive in international comparison. Particularly for individual retirement plans, the scope of fiscal promotion is limited when compared to the state-funded social security pension. In addition, the guarantee offered for the deposited contributions restricts the beneficiary's freedom of choice. The tax law's reference to the Occupational Pensions Act effectively makes the occupational retirement provision less flexible because only occupational pension plans as defined by the Occupational Pensions Act are promoted. The Act also does not grant the employee freedom of choice and requires a guarantee by the employer.

Employees' restricted freedom of choice follows from the synchronization of control and liability in the Occupational Pensions Act. Mandatory defined benefit pensions lead employers to select a risk structure. Employers' choice for the risk structure neglects the individual interests of employees especially in defined contribution plans in which the employees bear the investment risks. Following the practice in the United States, greater freedom of choice should be granted to employees. An insurance-based pension could also be offered.

When comparing the risk structures of various types of private pensions, the specific risks of defined benefit pensions need to be taken into account. This is especially true of the risk of insolvency, which is partially borne by the employee, and the lack of inflation adjustment of pension promises for workers leaving employment prior to being eligible to receive a pension. Overall, the generalized statement that defined benefit pensions are more beneficial for employees than defined contribution pensions must be rejected. Each plan carries risks and benefits that must be examined in light of potentially unstable and changing political and economic environments, subject to shifting demographics and climate change.

PRINCIPLES OF PROTECTION FOR PRIVATE PENSIONS

Principles of protection for private pensions include the pension protection triangle and the loyally administered separate fund. To focus on one to the exclusion of the other neglects the particular nature of private pensions and the tension between security and responsibility.

Termination (exit), consultation (voice), and guarantees taken together form the pension protection triangle. The triangle relaxes the traditional German focus on guarantees in private pensions. The inclusion of exit (i.e., the termination of contract) and voice (i.e., consultation) applies the general concepts of protection in private law to pension contracts. Extending protection from nominal guarantees takes into account the tension between security and responsibility; while guarantees are associated with security, exit and voice are legal rules providing for self-responsibility. Not all components of the protection triangle need to be contained in each pension contract. Guarantees for defined benefit pensions in particular and the possibility of termination for asset management are sufficient. Alteration of the contract is a less severe measure than termination of insurance contracts and occupational pensions.

To the extent that occupational pensions are subject to supervision by a general financial market authority, this supervision could be transferred to a specific regulatory authority, as is done in the United Kingdom. This would take account not only of the distinctive features of occupational pensions but also of the fact that insurance-based investments are not the only means of obtaining financial security. Pursuant to the Pension Funds Directive, contractual trust agreements (CTAs) could also be placed under supervision, but this has not yet been done in Germany. Establishing a specific regulatory authority to oversee CTAs would be an appropriate measure. Germany's insurance supervision is particularly rigid and should be developed on the basis of the British model. Such a development is expected in the coming years due to European solvency requirements.

The model of the loyally administered separate fund is applicable to private pension plans managed through life insurance companies and investment funds. However, the model has thus far not featured prominently in Germany's occupational pension laws, which have traditionally been premised on an occupational pension promise covered solely by a book reserve recorded on the sponsoring company's balance sheet. Yet, according to the German Federal Court, book reserves covering direct obligations constitute a quasi-separate fund. In practice, the model of the loyally administered separate fund already applies to companies bound by internationally accepted accounting principles. The pension promises of about two-thirds of the 30 largest German companies listed on the Frankfurt stock exchange (the DAX 30) are already covered by separate assets, particularly through CTAs. CTAs and separate funds in general are important for insolvency protection. Due to the possibility of netting pension obligations and internal or external trusts pursuant to the Accounting Law Modernization Act, CTAs can newly be used by companies subject to the accounting standards of the Commercial Code.

In regard to occupational pensions, both the Pension Funds Directive in Europe and the ERISA pension law in the United States stipulate that separate funds be managed solely in the interests of the beneficiaries. Private pension institutions are subject to fiduciary duties, and investments should also be managed in the sole interest of beneficiaries. The principle of precautionary investments, which is the prudent person rule based on portfolio theory, should apply. The focus should be on the investment risk of the entire portfolio, not on particular classes of investment. The principles of diversification and long-term investment should also be adhered to.

The legal concept demanding a prompt allocation of surplus funds in life insurance policies, which the Federal Financial Supervisory Authority inherited from the previous federal Supervisory Office for the Insurance Industry, is not compatible with long-term investment practice. By contrast, accumulation of unallocated reserves enables investments in both high-risk and long-term investment forms, promising higher returns. Investment in shares is particularly effective in this regard.

PENSION CONTRACTS

Establishment of Pension Contracts

Occupational pension contracts can be established individually or collectively and should contain the essential contractual elements. All pension contracts should also specify whether they provide for defined benefit, defined contribution, or hybrid pensions.

In terms of the revised law on standard business terms, pension contracts are now subject to the tests on standard form clauses prescribed by the German Civil Code. This is also true of insurance contracts, investment contracts, and since the reform of the law of obligation, pension promises under the Occupational Pensions Act. Even clauses reciting legislation trigger the tests of standard business terms, and transparency requirements are also applicable. Further attention should be paid to equal treatment requirements, upon which the validity of pension contracts in occupational pension plans can depend.

Pension contracts are often integrated into a web of various persons' contractual obligations. Contractual arrangements, particularly for occupational pension plans managed through an external institution, can be described as a nexus of contracts. This legal concept can be used especially for the allocation of contractual obligations. Thereby an overlap in duties of both an employer and an external private pension institution can be avoided. This enables disclosure duties to be assigned to the external occupational pension institution.

To date, private pension institutions' duties to provide information at the stage of contract conclusion are still arranged heterogeneously.

Disclosure duties for private pension institutions even before contract establishment are based on fiduciary duties. At the same time, disclosure duties should be understood as correlating to the participation of private pension products in the marketplace. This enables the disclosure duties to be harmonized. It is highly recommended to require insurance companies, in addition to investment funds and pension funds, to disclose the principles of their investment policy to beneficiaries. Such a requirement exists in the United Kingdom. To make an informed decision on entering into an insurance contract, the insured party has to be made aware not only of the role of the investment income but also of the manner in which it was earned.

The Period of Pension Accrual

In the period of pension accrual, the beneficiary is obliged to provide capital and remunerate the private pension institution pursuant to contractual specifications. The remuneration must be explicitly disclosed in the pension contract, failing which, the usual remuneration is payable. If the pension contract lacks such disclosure, the remuneration is to be set by the courts at the lowest margin of the remuneration range used in the market. Forfeiture of pension plans is a special feature, and the respective provisions in the Occupational Pensions Act apply to defined contribution pensions. In Germany, employers have no obligation to fund occupational pension promises. Yet such an obligation can be imposed if distributions to shareholders would disproportionately increase the risk of insolvency, thereby protecting employees from bearing the associated risk that the adjustment of pensions would be cancelled in the disbursement period. This is especially the case in debt-financed company takeovers.

Private pension institutions are frequently subject to investment requirements. One such requirement is imposed by the Pension Funds Directive to develop and implement investment guidelines. Insurance companies are also subject to this requirement. Deriving from the principle of precautionary investment, the requirement of diversifying investments of the separate fund can only be dispensed with for direct pension obligations covered by a book reserve in the balance sheet.

In fulfilling the standards of investments of assets, the possibility of the employer's contingent liability should be considered. Imposition of contingent liability on the employer allows a riskier investment of assets bundled together in a separate fund. Contingent liability is also relevant for a temporary deficit, and this is specifically regulated in pension funds. The mandatory contingent liability of employers in CTAs releases the trustee both of his duties to diversify and of the limits on the amount he is permitted to invest in the employer's company.

There is a further correlation between guarantees and investment behavior regarding life insurance policies. Allocation of surplus funds increases the guarantees. The currently prescribed solvency requirement, ensuring the ability to fulfill pension guarantees and the instant allocation of profits generated particularly from asset management, ought to be viewed with circumspection. In the international context, the common practice in the United Kingdom demonstrates that merely allocating profits from the surplus on maturity of the policy makes long-term investment in shares possible. The British model is largely based on the famous British economist John Maynard Keynes, who encouraged long-term investment in shares as a safeguard against inflation risks in his capacity as advisor of life insurance companies in the 1920s (Keynes 1927).

For life insurance policies, having a greater share of the final allocation of surplus funds in relation to the overall entitlement tends to increase profits. An appropriate innovation is that insurance contract law now facilitates the possibility of agreements in each individual contract on how to deal with surplus funds on maturity. The disclosure requirements of furnishing appropriate information on the product's performance and the guaranteed value of an individual pension contract are sufficient in this regard. German insurance contract law now stipulates the above disclosure duties. Furthermore, Germany should follow the British practice of obliging life insurance companies to point out the secondary market in cases where the beneficiary considers terminating his or her life insurance contract.

The model of the loyally administered separate fund and the pension protection triangle are characterized by security and the possibility of contract modification. Both in the insurance industry and in occupational pensions, beneficiaries are secured by setting up a separate fund and special security plans. Yet the Pensions Securities Association for occupational pensions ultimately guarantees only nominal interest, with the employee thus effectively bearing the inflation risk. Where occupational pension promises are covered externally, a guarantee, even of minimal interest, would be possible. For the purposes of funding the Pensions Securities Association, external coverage through CTAs should be considered.

A key protective mechanism for individual pensions is the beneficiary's right to terminate the contract. This is the only possible way for the beneficiary to react to long-term poor results in asset management. In the event of the contractual terms being modified, particularly where contractual parties are replaced, consideration must be given to the transfer of the pension contract's entire value. The German Insurance Contract Act was recently changed to improve consumer protection in this respect. The portability principle in the law of occupational pensions also applies to defined contribution pensions.

Employees are in special need of protection of annuity benefits in cases where the employer reorganizes. Following the employer's reorganization, the new legal entity must have sufficient funds irrespective of other security mechanisms, so that pensions in the disbursement period can be adequately adjusted. However, insurance-based funding or absolute security should not be required.

The Disbursement Period

The beneficiary should be able to choose between annuity payments and lump-sum payments in the disbursement period. Except for tax-favored individual pension plans, annuities are not mandatory, with lump sum payments and withdrawal rights as possible alternatives. Such alternatives are desirable considering the high costs associated with annuities and the possible need of funds for nursing home care. These principles apply in German occupational pensions.

When a beneficiary chooses annuity payments, consideration must be given to adjusting the payment in the disbursement period, failing which, the beneficiary will bear all of the inflation risk. In the disbursement period, for many pension products German pension law requires, at least in principle, a guaranteed interest rate. Where the beneficiary has an additional retirement plan, the allocation of the proceeds resulting from asset management meets the parties' interests in principle. Thus the freedom of the beneficiary to select an appropriate pension product corresponding with his individual risk preferences would be advisable in this respect.

DEVELOPING GERMAN PRIVATE PENSION LAW

Implementing Defined Contribution Pensions in the German Occupational Pensions Act

The doctrinal foundation for defined contribution plans ought to be laid in the German law of occupational pensions. Defined contribution pensions can be developed from common legal principles applicable to private defined benefit pensions. Except for the employer's obligation to meet claims (guarantee) and protection against insolvency, the essential protective elements of the Occupational Pensions Act can be applied to defined contribution pensions. Restrictions on forfeiture, portability, and retention of profits in the disbursement period also apply to defined contribution pensions. The previous employer duties of guaranteeing claims and providing for nominal insolvency protection (without adjusting inflation) could to a great extent functionally be replaced by a requirement to establish a separate fund, the principles of precautionary investment, encapsulation of the requirement of diversification, and stringent requirements regarding encroachments on the employee's contractual position.

Against conventional German wisdom, a proposition that defined contribution plans are more risky than defined benefit pensions or hybrid pensions does not hold true. When properly managed, defined contribution pensions provide better protection against inflation risk than defined benefit pensions. Employees and employers both can benefit from the use of tax-advantaged defined contribution pensions, which will shorten the period for vesting in occupational pensions, decrease the uncertainties surrounding the EU provisions stipulating equal treatment and anti-discrimination, and improve both personal choice and mobility.

Against the background of an aging society and particularly in light of low-income workers' reservations toward entering into private pension contracts, automatic enrollment in occupational pensions should be provided, giving employees the possibility to opt out. The 65th German Jurists Forum proposed automatic enrollment as early as 2004, and international studies on behavioral science have substantiated the positive effects of automatic enrollment in occupational pension plans (Steinmeyer 2004).[11] For automatic enrollment provisions, defined contribution schemes are best suited. Since employees lack a guaranteed income in defined contribution plans, employers should offer sufficient investment choices, accommodating the fact that the employees bear the investment risk. The United States Pension Protection Act of 2006 requires a choice between at least three investment products for defined contribution pensions. Other countries, such as Switzerland, require mandatory guarantees by external private pension institutions. Following these examples, German law should also allow workers a choice of investments in defined contribution pension plans.

Information Provided to Beneficiaries

The information required to be provided to beneficiaries and retirees should and can be based on general principles. The duties of private pension institutions to provide information are linked to participation in the private pension market. These duties follow from the fiduciary duties of the private pension institutions. Disclosure duties for life insurance companies still also need to be developed in spite of the reform of insurance contract law. Disclosure of investment principles, allocation policies, and security of relevant guarantees are necessary in general, whether in a defined contribution pension or in life insurance contracts. In Germany, disclosure of investment principles is provided by explicit regulations for pension funds and investment companies. Such disclosure duties for life insurance companies should be introduced, building on the British supervisory practice of the Financial Services Authority.

Disclosure of investment principles enables the participant in individual accounts and defined contribution pensions to assess the investment risks of different options. It allows the participant to make a decision corresponding with his or her individual risk preferences. Special importance should be attached to the full transparency of costs. Disclosure of costs and performance of fund products should be supervised by an independent office and perhaps even by the government, similar to the British and Swedish models. For life insurance policies, the British model of requiring companies to inform their clients about the secondary market should be followed.

Special disclosure duties exist at the conclusion of pension contracts and before the disbursement period. Product information in individual pensions should always be given prior to the establishment of the pension contract. In occupational pensions, the fact that the pension is frequently attached to the initiation of the employment contract needs to be taken into account. Thus, providing information of the existence of a pension before contract finalization is sufficient. Detailed information only needs to be given after the finalization of the employment contract. Where information is provided externally, for example, by pension funds, retirement funds, and direct life insurance companies, essential disclosure duties can be assigned solely to the external occupational pension institution.

Before the disbursement period commences, the beneficiary should be informed about payment options, including plans of disbursement or annuity payments. Special emphasis should be placed on information regarding indexation of pension benefits. Choosing an indexed pension plan is advisable; failing this, the beneficiary will bear the entire risk of inflation. Participation in the outcome of asset management principally meets the interests of the parties, e.g., the employer, the beneficiary, and the external pension provider. This is particularly the case if a minimum payment is guaranteed.

CONCLUSION

Germany's occupational pension system should provide employees with investment choices and encourage higher participation rates. The latter goal should be realized through automatic enrollment in occupational pension schemes, giving employees the possibility to opt out. Incentives for automatic enrollment should be set by the Occupation Pensions Act or by tax law, at least with regard to large employers. Cost-effective individual choices for employees should be promoted through including defined contribution pensions in the German Occupational Pensions Act. Offering investment alternatives with different risk profiles would allow employees to find solutions corresponding with their individual risk preferences. In light of typical German saving behavior and the corresponding expectations of beneficiaries, a traditional insurance product should be chosen as the default investment product.

Notes

Text is derived from my German habilitation thesis *Private Altersvorsorge: Betriebsrentenrecht und individuelle Vorsorge* (Private pensions: occupational and individual pensions), *Max-Planck-Instituts für ausländisches und internationales Privatrecht* (Max Planck Institute for Comparative and International Private Law), *Beiträge zum ausländischen und internationale Privatrecht* (Contributions to Comparative and International Private Law), Mohr Siebeck, 2009. I thank Martin Wilhelm, LL.M., for preparing the English translation.

1. See Steinmeyer (2004) for an account of the reduced performance of state-funded pension plans.
2. These are the figures currently reported in the yearly pension information provided by the German state pension system.
3. Poterba, Shoven, and Sialm (2004) report a nominal return for 12 investment funds for the period 1962–1998 of 12.7 percent at an inflation rate of 4.7 percent. Munnell and Sundén (2004), referring to Ibbotson, put the real return for United States shares at 7.1 percent for the period 1926–2008; Hopp (2008) puts the equivalent figure for German shares at 4.9 percent for the period 1960–2007.
4. According to Dimson, Marsh, and Staunton (2008), among the largest industrialized nations for the period 1990–2007, German shares have been the most volatile, and German bonds have had the lowest real returns (−1.8 percent). In addition, losses on the German share market were the highest worldwide in the periods immediately following World War I and the bursting of the Internet bubble.
5. For an earlier account of true defined contributions, see Arbeitsgemeinschaft für betriebliche Altersversorgung e.V. (1997).
6. Gesetz zur Modernisierung des Bilanzrechts (Bilanzrechtsmodernisierungsgesetz – BilMoG) (Accounting Law Modernization Act), 25.5.2009, BGBl (Federal Gazette) I 1102.
7. For an instructive review on the impact of private pensions on capital markets, see Kübler (1991); see Buxbaum (1991) for the basic conditions set by occupational pension law and tax law.
8. For the United Kingdom, see Myners (2001, p. 1), which states that "strong funded pension system[s] [are] . . . key national asset[s]."
9. For a discussion of the employer's position as an intermediary, see Köndgen (2004).
10. Federal Labor Court, BAGE 112, 1, 7. The Federal Labor Court builds on the German legal position up to the end of the Weimar Republic in 1933.

11. For the United States, see Akerlof (2002), Lucas (2005), Madrian and Shea (2001), Orszag and Orszag (2005), Poterba (2005), Thaler and Bernartzi (2004), and Turner (2006). See also Munnell and Sundén (2005). For the United Kingdom, see Department for Work and Pensions (2008).

References

Akerlof, George A. 2002. "Behavioral Macroeconomics and Macroeconomic Behavior." *American Economic Review* 92(3): 411–433.

Arbeitsgemeinschaft für betriebliche Altersversorgung e.V. 1997. "Thesen zur Integration von Beitragszusagen in das Gesetz zur Verbesserung der betrieblichen Altersversorgung." Arbeitsgemeinschaft für betriebliche Altersversorgung e.V., pp. 318–320.

Börsch-Supan, Axel. 2004. "Zur Reform der Altersvorsorge in Deutschland: Einschätzung und Empfehlung eines Ökonomen." Presentation at the 65th German Jurists Forum held in Bonn, Q 11–23.

Buxbaum, Richard M. 1991. "Institutional Owners and Corporate Managers: A Comparative Perspective." *Brooklyn Law Review* 57(Spring): 1–53.

Department for Work and Pensions. 2008. "Pensions Bill Impact Assessment." April 24. London: Department for Work and Pensions. http://www.dwp.gov.uk/docs/impact-assessment-240408.pdf (accessed June 23, 2011).

Dimson, Elroy, Paul Marsh, and Mike Staunton. 2008. *Global Investment Returns Yearbook 2008: Synopsis*. London: ABN AMRO Bank NV in association with The Royal Bank of Scotland and London Business School.

Hopp, Frank-Peter. 2008. "Kaufen und Liegenlassen erlebt eine Renaissance." *Frankfurter Allgemeine Zeitung*, June 3, p. 21.

Keynes, John Maynard. 1927. "Kapitalanlagepolitik der Lebensversicherungsgesellschaften nach englischer Auffassung." *Zeitschrift für die gesamte Versicherungswissenschaft* 27: 32–38.

Köndgen, Johannes. 2004. "Die Neuordnung der Altersvorsorge: Vom Sozialrecht zum Vorsorgemarktrecht." Presentation at the 65th German Jurists Forum in Bonn, Q 25–56.

Kübler, Friedrich K. 1991. "Institutional Owners and Corporate Manager: A German Dilemma." *Brooklyn Law Review* 57(Spring): 97–111.

Leinert, Johannes, and Andreas Esche. 2000. "Advance Funding of Pensions." *International Reform Monitor*. Special Issue. Gütersloh, Germany: Bertelsmann Foundation Publishers.

Lucas, Lori. 2005. "Individual Responsibility and the Imperfect Investor: The Need for Automating the 401(k) Plan." *Benefits Quarterly* 21(4): 34–40.

Madrian, Brigitte C., and Dennis F. Shea. 2001. "The Power of Suggestion: Inertia in 401(k) Participation and Savings Behaviour." *Quarterly Journal of Economics* 116(4): 1149–1187.

Munnell, Alicia H., and Annika Sundén. 2004. *Coming Up Short: The Challenge of 401(k) Plans*. Washington, DC: Brookings Institution Press.

Myners, Paul. 2001. "Institutional Investment in the United Kingdom: A Review." A report to HM Treasury ("Myners Report"). London: HM Treasury.

Orszag, J. Michael, and Peter R. Orszag. 2005. "Individual Accounts: Lessons from International Experience." *Science Magazine* 309(5732): 250–251.

Poterba, James M. 2005. "Individual Decision Making and Risk in Defined Contribution Plans." *Elder Law Journal* 13(1): 285–308.

Poterba, James M., John B. Shoven, and Clemens Sialm. 2004. "Asset Location for Retirement Savers." In *Private Pensions and Public Policies*, William G. Gale, John B. Shoven, and Mark J. Warshawsky, eds. Washington, DC: Brookings Institution Press, pp. 290–325.

Steinmeyer, Heinz-Dietrich. 2004. "Private und betriebliche Altersvorsorge zwischen Sicherheit und Selbstverantwortung." Report F on the 65th German Jurists Forum in Bonn: Association of German Jurists.

Thaler, Richard, and Shlomo Bernartzi. 2004. "Saving More Tomorrow: Using Behavioral Economics to Increase Employee Saving." *Journal of Political Economy* 112(1): 164–187.

Turner, John A. 2006. "Designing 401(k) Plans That Encourage Retirement Savings: Lessons from Behavioral Finance." *Benefits Quarterly* 22(4): 24–36.

7
The Ideal Pension System for Belgium

Kim De Witte
University of Leuven

This chapter discusses the ideal pension system for Belgium. Currently, the Belgian pension system is a subject of debate. Political and social actors have proposed substantial reforms. To get a good picture of the necessary reforms, value judgments and technical analyses have to be taken into account. Sometimes deep changes in the pension system are advocated as if they were technically unavoidable, but this is obviously wrong. Not only are there different reform options available, the choice between them is based on ideological background and value judgments. In this chapter, I develop a clear set of evaluation criteria for pension reforms. The main reform proposals are then evaluated in the light of these criteria.

First, I give an overview of the Belgian pension system. The structure, adequacy, and financing of the different types of pension plans are explained. Then I present the pension reform proposals of the main social and political actors in Belgium, where there is a consensus with respect to the necessity of a pension reform but no consensus with respect to concrete reform proposals. After evaluating the various pension reform proposals, I present my personal vision on the ideal pension system for Belgium.

OVERVIEW OF THE BELGIAN PENSION SYSTEM

In this first section, the structure, adequacy, and financing of the Belgian pension system are presented. The Belgian pension system consists mainly of statutory pension plans, supplemented by occupational and individual pension plans. This is a variant of the well-known three-pillar model. The statutory pension plans are pay-as-you-go defined benefit arrangements, the occupational pension plans are funded defined benefit or defined contribution arrangements, and the individual pension plans are funded defined contribution arrangements.

Structure of the Belgian Pension System

Statutory pension plans

In Belgium, employees (both public and private), self-employed workers, and civil servants (a special class of public employee in Belgium) are compulsorily insured under three different statutory pension plans.

Pension plan for employees. The statutory old-age pension for employees depends on annual earnings, length of career, and marital status. The formula for the pension accrual of employees in a given year is as follows: the pension accrual for year *X* is the wage of year *X* (capped) divided by 45 (the length of a full career) and multiplied by either 60 percent or 75 percent. The wage of year *X* is the gross salary during that year up to a certain ceiling (€47,282 in 2009, adjusted annually to current prices). The pension is computed as 60 percent of the capped wage for a single person or 75 percent for the head of a household (persons with a dependent spouse). At retirement, a statutory pension is paid as an annuity equal to the result of this formula.[1] Pension coverage is continued during unemployment or other forms of involuntary inactivity (illness, pregnancy, disability, etc.). These periods of inactivity are valued at the last corresponding salary. To claim an old-age pension, an employee must have reached the age of 65 and stopped working.[2] Pensions are paid monthly by direct deposit into the pensioner's bank account. Pension benefits are automatically adjusted to a price index and partially adjusted to average wage increases.

Pension plan for the self-employed. The statutory pension plan for the self-employed is similar to the employee plan, except for a reduction coefficient. The reduction coefficient reflects the discrepancy between the contributions paid by employees and by self-employed workers. Because there were no social security contributions by the self-employed prior to 1984, statutory pension rights were calculated based on a fixed income. The formula for the old-age pension accrual for self-employed individuals is basically the same as the employee plan except the amount is also multiplied by the reduction coefficient. There are also some other minor differences with respect to the employee plan.[3]

Pension plan for civil servants. The formula for determining the old-age and disability pensions for civil servants is different. The pension is equal to the average wage of the last 5 years multiplied by the length of the career (maximum of 45 years) divided by 60 (the retirement factor). To receive a pension benefit, a civil service career of at least 5 years is required.[4] At the maximum career length of 45 years, a replacement rate of 75 percent of the average wage of the last 5 years is obtained. Some occupations have a preferential retirement factor (55 for teachers and less for other specific categories such as magistrates and academic services). People in these areas therefore reach the maximum replacement rate of 75 percent in less than 45 years.

With some exceptions, the legal retirement age is 65 for men and women, and retirement with pension benefits is possible from the age of 60. The pension benefit is biannually adjusted to the consumer price index (CPI) and to the real wage increase of working civil servants. To benefit from a minimum pension, a career of 20 years is required. In addition, the survivor's pension is calculated as 60 percent of the average wage of the last 5 years of the deceased person.

Early retirement pension. An early retirement plan (the so-called prepension) is embedded in the unemployment plan, but only for employees. The full prepension consists of an unemployment benefit, paid by the public authorities (the National Employment Office), which amounts to 60 percent of the last gross wage earned, limited by a ceiling, which is different from that used in the pension plan. The beneficiaries also receive an allowance, paid by the employer. Since 2008, the legal age to receive the prepension is 60, provided the career length as an employee was at least 30 years for men (35 years as of 2012) and 26 years for women (after 2008, this age increases by 2 years every 4 years until it reaches 35 years). Exemptions (for those who have reached at least age 58) are still possible for those who have worked in physically demanding jobs. The prepension benefit is automatically adjusted to the CPI and partially adjusted to average wage increases.

Disability. If a person's disability prevents him or her from working for more than one year, a disability benefit is paid. In the employee plan, disability benefits are calculated at 65 percent of the limited lost remuneration for beneficiaries who are a head of a household, 53 percent for single persons, and 40 percent for cohabitants. In the self-employed workers' plan, the disability benefits are fixed but differ according to whether the beneficiary is a head of household. The disability benefit is automatically adjusted to the CPI and partially adjusted to average wage increases.

Guaranteed income for elders. Every person 65 or older whose pension plus other income is below a certain threshold is entitled to a means-tested guaranteed income for the elderly (GIE). In 2009, the GIE was €892.92 per month for a single person and €595.33 per month for cohabitants (for each person). The GIE benefit is automatically adjusted to the CPI and partially adjusted to average wage increases.

Occupational pension plans

In general, occupational pensions in Belgium are not mandatory, and only a few branches of industry have a mandatory occupational pension plan. The occupational pension must be externally funded by either group insurance companies or pension funds.[5] About 70 percent of pension plan members are covered under an insurance contract. Hence, the Belgian occupational pension landscape is dominated by insurance companies.

Legal framework. The legal framework for occupational pension plans was implemented at the beginning of 2004. The "Vandenbroucke Law" was enacted in 2003 to strengthen occupational pensions and regulate industry-wide pension plans. It covers occupational pensions, a tax plan for those pensions, and some related social security benefits.

Industry-wide pensions. Industry-wide pension plans are the result of collective bargaining agreements between social partners, for example, employer associations and trade unions.[6] Employers of a given branch of industry are obliged to join the industry-wide plan, unless the collective bargaining agreement allows them to opt out of the plan. Opting out is only possible if the employer offers an occupational pension plan at the company level providing benefits equivalent to the industry-wide plan.

Tax treatment. Belgium has enacted tax legislation improving the tax-exempt status of occupational pension contributions. The tax treatment of occupational pensions is based on the so-called exempt-exempt-taxed system, meaning that contributions and investment earnings are almost exempt from taxes, but benefit payments are taxed. However, instead of the normal social security tax of approximately 35 percent of gross salary, a special social security tax of 8.86 percent and an insurance tax of 4.4 percent are imposed on contributions to occupational pension plans.

For the employer, contributions to occupational pension plans are tax-deductible to a certain amount. This deductibility is linked to the condition that the expected sum of statutory and occupational pensions does not exceed 80 percent of gross salary in the given year. For the employee, contributions to occupational pensions are not part of the employees' taxable income. Income tax is only paid on the benefits received at retirement. If the benefit is paid as a lump sum, it is subject to a flat-rate tax (10 or 16 percent). If the benefit is paid as an annuity, the annuity is taxed as normal income, but the actual tax is lowered by a special tax credit for retirees.

Social plans. So-called social plans can be set up, either at the company or the industry level. Contrary to ordinary occupational pension plans, social plans are required to offer benefits for risks such as death, disability, or unemployment. In order to finance these risks, part of the contributions must be allocated in a "solidarity" fund. These so-called solidarity payments have to amount to at least 4.4 percent of contributions. Other requirements include joint management, cost reduction, and profit sharing. Social plans are encouraged through special tax advantages, such as relief from the 4.4 percent insurance tax.

Guaranteed investment return. From 2004 onward, Belgium has required a minimum rate of return guarantee for defined contribution pensions. The minimum guaranteed rate is 3.25 percent for contributions by employers and 3.75 percent for contributions paid by employees. These rates are considered to be set for an indefinite period, presumably lasting many years. If the employment contract ends, the employee can transfer his accrued reserves either to the occupational pension plan of his new employer or to a freely chosen insurance company. He can also opt for a further accrual within the occupational pension plan of his former employer. If the employee decides to leave the plan, the company is responsible for complying with the guaranteed investment return. If there is an accrual deficit, the gap has to be bridged immediately.

Minimum retirement age. A beneficiary is prohibited from cashing in accrued reserves or getting his or her benefits paid out before reaching the age of 60. Benefits can be paid out as an annuity or as a lump sum. The vast majority of occupational pensions are paid out as a lump sum. Therefore, indexation of occupational pension benefits is not an issue in Belgium.

Individual pension plans

Different forms of individual voluntary pension provision exist in Belgium. The main forms are life insurance, pension saving, individual pension commitments, and voluntary pensions for the self-employed. The common features of these different forms are the voluntary character of participation, the contributory character of funding, and the management of the assets by private actors, such as insurance companies or financial institutions (De Witte, Roels, and Stevens 2009).

Individual life insurance. The main characteristic of individual life insurance agreements is the provision of an annuity or lump sum payment at the moment the insured person reaches a certain age or dies. Individual life insurance is accessible for everybody, irrespective of professional status. An individual life insurance agreement is financed by premiums paid by the subscriber. The level of the premiums is agreed upon and stated in the insurance contract. The premiums are invested in insurance contracts that guarantee a capital value based on a fixed interest rate. The subscriber can also choose investment in real estate through a tax incentive based on a mortgage loan and debt insurance that is linked to the mortgage loan.

Pension saving. Pension saving is the generic term for three forms of tax-advantaged long-term savings that are accessible to everybody: 1) pension saving insurance, 2) collective pension saving, and 3) individual pension saving. Pension savings are accessible to everybody. Pension savings accounts and individual pension savings are offered by financial institutions (mainly banks). Contributions to pension savings accounts are used to buy units in investment funds. These funds are popular because they allow a wide choice of assets and risks. Contributions to individual pension savings are invested in shares chosen by the individual.

Individual (occupational) pension commitments. Individual pension commitments are strictly regulated. Individual pension commitments are only permitted in companies that have a collective occupational pension plan for all employees. This implies that a commitment can only be granted in addition to such a collective occupational plan. Measures to protect employees are included, such as the obligation to conclude a pension agreement, to finance it externally with a pension provider, and to obtain the explicit approval of the employee for personal contributions.

Voluntary pensions for the self-employed. A specific individual voluntary pension provision for the self-employed was introduced in Belgium because statutory pensions for the self-employed are low (see below). Voluntary pension plans for the self-employed are very similar to individual life insurance.

Adequacy of the Belgian Pension System

In this section, we review the adequacy of the Belgian pension system by focusing on three aspects: 1) coverage, 2) risk sharing, and 3) benefits.

Coverage

Statutory pension plans. In Belgium, employees, the self-employed, and civil servants are all compulsorily covered under statutory public pension plans. These plans are part of the Belgian social security system. The payments are deducted from the employees' regular pay, and the self-employed pay obligatory contributions on a quarterly basis.

Occupational pension plans. According to the most recent figures, approximately 60 percent of employees are members of an occupational pension plan. Approximately the same number of white and blue collar workers are members of occupational pension plans (AON Consulting 2007; Assuralia 2009; Belgian Parliament 2009; de Dessus les Moustier and Masy 2007). The majority of occupational pension plans are organized at the company level, and these plans provide higher pension contributions than industry-wide pension plans. They involve primarily white collar workers and impose no solidarity mechanisms (Pierreux 2009). In 2009, the 27 existing industry-wide plans covered 740,485 plan members (83 percent were men and 81 percent were blue collar workers, CBFA 2009). The number of industry-wide plans is increasing. Higher income workers benefit more from occupational pensions and the tax relief they offer than lower income workers.[7]

Individual pension plans. According to Wuyts et al. (2007), participation in individual pension plans rose strongly during the last decade. In 2006, 37 percent of the people in Belgium between the ages of 15 and 64 participated in one or more individual pension plans. Unsurprisingly, income is a very important factor for participation. The average income of individual pension plan members was €24,410 in 2003. Only 9.1 percent of single people with a monthly income less than €750 participate in individual pension plans, whereas almost 50% of single people with a monthly income above €2,000 participate (De Witte, Roels, and Stevens 2009). Persons who participate in occupational pensions also participate markedly more frequently in individual pensions (Gieselink et al. 2003). Self-employed persons participate in and contribute more to individual pension plans, which in part could be due to their lower statutory pension (see below).

Benefits

Statutory pension benefits. The GIE is €892.98 per month for singles and €595.33 per month for cohabitants (in 2009). Every person who meets the requirement of a defined link to Belgium and is at least 65 years old is eligible for the GIE. The financial means of an individual is checked, and if the individual's total income is lower than the guaranteed amount, the difference is paid monthly.

Unlike the GIE, which has no link whatsoever with the contributions paid in the past, statutory pension benefits for employees, the self-employed, and civil servants are related to contributions (up to a certain level). Table 7.1 presents the average monthly statutory pension benefits.

The average statutory pension benefit for employees is €891.42 per month for a single male and €631.47 per month for a single woman (assuming both have been employees during their entire careers). These benefits are considerably lower for the self-employed and considerably higher for civil servants.[8] The average gross monthly wage in Belgium was €2,837 in 2007 (NIS 2007), so the difference between statutory pension benefits and average salary is considerable. Table 7.1 presents the average replacement rates in 2008,[9] which are quite low, except for civil servants.

Table 7.1 Average Statutory Old-Age Pension Benefits and Average Replacement Rates (in Parentheses) for Single Persons (Gross Amounts, € and %)[a]

	Men	Women
Employees	891 (47)	631 (56)
Self-employed workers	676 (48)	331 (62)
Civil servants	1,980 (64)	1,488 (62)

[a] National Pension Administration, monthly statistics, November 2009 (for civil servants: 2005).

Occupational pension benefits. Occupational pension benefits increase statutory pension income by an average of 16 percent for men and 13 percent for women (Belgian Secretary of Pensions 2010). However, this average has to be put in perspective. Amounts spent for plans covering the highest income workers are four to five times higher than amounts spent for pension plans for lower income workers: 6.3 percent of salary is spent on the top plans, 3.4 percent on plans for white collar workers, and only 1.4 percent on plans for blue collar workers (AON Consulting 2007). Industry-wide pension plans in Belgium cover many employees, but the benefits paid out are exceedingly marginal (between 0.75 and 1.75 percent of actual salary).[10]

Individual pension benefits. The benefit amounts paid out by individual pension plans are unknown because of a lack of necessary data. Data concerning the accrued reserves in individual pension plans do exist, but they are incomplete because they do not take into account the investments of households in real estate, which is stimulated with the same tax incentives as individual life insurance plans.

Table 7.2 presents the evolution of accrued reserves in individual and occupational pension plans during the last decade. For the individual pension plans, the value of real estate accrued with tax-driven incentives is not taken into account. Even without taking the investments in real estate into account, the reserves of individual pension plans have increased greatly since 1998. These reserves have tripled, whereas the reserves of occupational pension plans only doubled.

Table 7.2 Evolution of Occupational and Individual Pension Reserves (€ billion)

	Pension reserves										
	1998	1999	2000	2001	2002	2003	2004	2005	2006	2007	2008
Occupational pensions	30	35	37	36	38	42	44	46	48	53	58
Individual pensions	45	53	58	62	68	80	96	116	135	142	147

SOURCE: Belgian Secretary of Pensions (2010, p. 234).

Risk sharing

Pension accrual often takes place over a period of decades. Therefore, risk control is a key issue. The main risks that threaten pension accrual are: longevity, inflation, financial, bankruptcy of the pension provider, and political. These risks cannot be entirely avoided, but they can be shared within smaller or larger groups. Four different levels of risk sharing can be distinguished: 1) no risk sharing (the individual plan or plan member bears the risk), 2) risk sharing within a company, 3) risk sharing within the branch of industry, and 4) nationwide risk sharing. An overview of the scope of risk sharing within the different forms of pension accrual in Belgium is presented in Table 7.3.

Risk sharing in statutory pension plans. Risk pooling in the statutory pension plans is based on a nationwide separation of employees, the self-employed, and civil servants (which have several different pools). Except for a few minor exceptions, the statutory pension plans are organized on a pay-as-you-go basis. The risk of inflation and financial turbulence in pay-as-you-go systems is very restricted. The other risks are present, but they are shared within a nationwide pool. Given the fact that statutory pension benefits are required to be paid out as annuities, the longevity risk is shared within each nationwide pool. The risk of bankruptcy of the pension provider (i.e., the Belgian state) is not completely unimaginable, but the risk is also shared within each nationwide pool. Finally, statutory pensions are subject to the risk of changes in pension or social security regulations (i.e., political risk). However, retroactive changes are difficult to enforce, given the protection as property of state and social security pensions.

Risk sharing in occupational pension plans. The longevity risk in occupational pension plans is borne by the individual plan member because occupational pension benefits are almost always paid out as lump sums. The inflation risk during the period of pension accrual is shared at the company level for defined benefit plans and borne by the individual plan member for defined contribution plans. The risk of financial crises and bankruptcy of the pension provider are real and reside at the company level. Moreover, the law fixes a minimum guaranteed return on occupational pension contributions. This means that the employer

Table 7.3 Scope of Risk Sharing within the Different Forms of Pension Accrual in Belgium

		Individual pension plans		Occupational pension plans				Statutory pension plans	
Scope of risk sharing		Pension saving	Individual life insurance	Company plan (DC)	Company plan (DB)	Industry-wide plan (DC)	Social industry-wide plan (DC)	Statutory pensions	GIE
Longevity	No risk sharing	X	X	X	X	X	X		
	Company								
	Branch of industry								
	Nationwide							X	X
Inflation	No risk sharing	X	X	X		X	X		
	Company				X				
	Branch of industry								
	Nationwide							X	X
Financial risks	No risk sharing	X	X						
	Company			X	X				
	Branch of industry					X	X		
	Nationwide							X	X
Bankruptcy of the pension provider	No risk sharing	X	X						
	Company			X	X				
	Branch of industry					X	X		
	Nationwide							X	X

NOTE: DB = defined benefit; DC = defined contribution.

remains liable to the individual plan members concerning the payments of the pension benefits, including a minimum return, when the pension fund or insurance company fails to fulfill its obligations. With respect to the investment of pension funds, Belgium applies the prudent person principle, with some quantitative limits that are mainly diversification requirements. With respect to group insurance, the reserves are invested in the general investment portfolio of the insurance company, and the insurance company determines the investment policy. The effect of political changes on occupational pension promises seems very small.

Risk sharing in individual pension plans. In individual pension plans, the longevity and inflation risks are borne by the individual plan member. The risks of financial crises and bankruptcy are shared at the company level. However, contrary to occupational pensions, the law does not require a guaranteed minimum return. The bankruptcy of the pension provider will mean the loss, in whole or part, of the pension reserves.[11] The effect of political changes on individual pensions seems very small.

Financing and Expenditure

Financing

Statutory pension plans. All employees and self-employed persons in Belgium pay compulsory contributions for the statutory pension plans. Contributions for employees are just over 16 percent of gross salary. Self-employed persons pay much less.[12] General government revenues subsidize approximately 10 percent of annual costs (Dellis, Jousten, and Perelman 2001).

Occupational pension plans. In occupational pension plans, the contribution rate in percentage of annual salary is usually established in the plan rules. Most plans are predominantly employer financed with contribution rates usually ranging from 0.5 to 1 percent for lower income workers and 4 to 5 percent for higher income workers. The total contributions paid in Belgium for occupational pension plans amounted to €5.1 billion in 2007. Total occupational pension reserves in Belgium amounted to €48.74 billion in 2007.[13]

Individual pension plans. No one knows exactly how important individual pension plans are in Belgium because of the previously mentioned lack of data for this form of pension accrual. According to the Social Policy Centre of the University of Leuven (CeSo), 2.63 million residents participated in pension saving or life insurance in 2006. The total contributions and premiums paid amounted to €2.1 billion (Berghman 2009). However, considerable differences can be found depending on whether or not long-term savings linked to mortgage loans for investment in real estate are taken into account. As mentioned above, similar tax relief applies to the reimbursement of a mortgage loan for a dwelling as to the payment of premiums for an individual life insurance policy. Therefore, certain researchers classify this form of saving as an individual pension. According to Gieselink et al. (2003), total premiums and contributions to individual pension plans amounted to €10 billion in 2000 (i.e., 4.2 percent of GDP). Following the same approach as Gieselink, we calculated that total premiums and contributions to individual pension plans amounted to €16 billion in 2006 (i.e., 5.4 percent of GDP).[14]

Expenditure

To compare the expenditures for the different types of pension accrual, Table 7.4 presents an overview of the weight of the various pension plans in Belgium from two perspectives. First, pension spending for the statutory pension plans is compared with pension provisions for the occupational and individual pension plans (statutory pensions are pay as you go and occupational and individual pensions are funded). Second, statutory pension entitlements are compared with occupational and individual pension reserves.

In 2007, statutory pension spending (including prepensions and disability allowances) amounted to 10 percent of GDP.[15] In the same year, occupational pension accrual amounted to 1.52 percent of GDP. In 2006, individual pension accrual amounted to 0.66 percent or 5.1 percent of GDP, depending on whether or not pension accrual linked to a mortgage is taken into account.

In 2007, statutory pension entitlements amounted to 250 percent of GDP, and occupational pension reserves amounted to about 14.5 percent of GDP. Individual pension reserves amounted to 45.1 percent of

GDP in 2006 (pension accrual linked to a mortgage was not taken into account). No exact data are available concerning the real estate property of the elderly, but the macroeconomic wealth of the country is well known. It grew from €200 billion in 1970 to €1,300 billion in 2002. Approximately half of this wealth (€650 billion) is estimated to be linked to real estate, mainly dwellings (Belgian Secretary of Pensions 2010). This represented 240 percent of GDP in 2002.

Although the comparison is simplified and exact figures are lacking in some categories, the overview gives an idea of the proportion of investment in the different forms of pension accrual in Belgium. The financial assets invested in statutory pensions are the most important (250 percent of GDP in 2007), whereas the financial assets invested in occupational pensions are clearly less important (14.5 percent of GDP in 2007). The financial assets invested in individual pensions are considerable (45.1 percent of GDP in 2006), even more so if tax-driven investments in real estate are taken into account (up to 240 percent of GDP in 2002).

Projections

In 2007, Belgium had 1.8 million residents older than 65. This number will increase to 2.2 million in 2020 (i.e., 20.6 percent of the total population), 2.65 million in 2030 (24.3 percent), 2.86 million in 2040 (26.1 percent), and 2.90 million in 2050 (26.5 percent). In 1990, for every person older than 65, Belgium had four persons between 20 and 65. In 2020, for every person older than 65, there will only be three persons between 20 and 65. By 2040, this proportion will be two persons between 20 and 65 for every person older than 65.[16]

Projections of the impact of demographic changes on pension spending are only available for statutory pensions. There are no projections for occupational and individual pensions because they are not mandatory (except for a few branches of industry, where an industry-wide plan is installed). Table 7.5 presents the results of projections for expenditure for statutory pensions, as well as an estimate of the tax incomes on statutory pensions, both expressed as percentage of GDP.

Expenditure for statutory pensions increases by 3.9 percent of GDP between 2007 and 2030. Then, between 2030 and 2060, pension expenditure is projected to increase by another 0.8 percent of GDP. Employee

Table 7.4 Relative Weight of the Various Pensions in 2007 (2006 for Individual Pension Plans)[a]

		Pension spending/provisions[b]		Pension entitlements/reserves		Plan members	
		€ billion	% GDP	€ billion	% GDP	Number	%
Statutory pensions	Total	33.51[c]	10.00	837.75	250.00[d]	4,681,394	100% of active population
Occupational pensions	Total	5.10[e]	1.52	48.47	14.46	2,492,679[f]	60% of employees
	Insurance companies	4.13	1.23	NA	NA	1,794,728	43% of employees
	Pension funds	0.97	0.29	NA	NA	697,950	17% of employees
Individual pensions	Total (excl. mortgage)	2.10[g]	0.66	142.50	45.10	2,626,000[g]	37% of population aged 15–64
	Total (incl. mortgage)	16.00[h]	5.10	NA	NA	NA	NA
	Individual life insurance	0.91	0.27	NA	NA	1,465,000	20.1% of population aged 15–64
	Pension saving	1.20	0.35	NA	NA	1,859,000	26.4% of population aged 15–64

NOTE: NA = not available.

[a] In 2007 in Belgium, GDP was €335 billion, total population was 10,584,534, total population between 15 and 64 years of age was 7,046,685, and the active population (people working plus people searching for a job) was 4,681,394. The activity rate (i.e. percentage of working population plus the unemployed) was 67.1 percent. In 2006 Belgian GDP was equal to €316 billion.

[b] More recent figures concerning costs of the statutory pensions in Belgium are available. In 2010 the total costs of statutory pensions were €33.7 billion, broken down as follows: civil servants plan, €9.9 billion; employees plan, €18.2 billion; self-employed plan, €2.7 billion; GIE, €0.4 billion; and others, €2.5 billion (Belgian Secretary of Pensions 2010, p. 124).

[c] Belgian Secretary of Pensions (2010).

[d] Capretta (2007), OECD (2006), and Dellis, Jousten, and Perelman (2001, p. 3).

[e] Belgian Secretary of Pensions (2010), Hannes (2009), Sommerijns and De Bilderling (2009), and Belgian Parliament (2008–2009).

[f] Belgian Parliament (2009).

[g] Berghman (2009).

[h] Data from the Banking, Finance and Insurance Commission, analyzed in De Witte, Roels, and Stevens (2009).

Table 7.5 Projected Gross Statutory Pension Spending (% GDP)

Projected expenditures	2000	2007	2020	2030	2040	2050	2060	Peak year
Statutory pension plans								
Total	10.0	10.0	11.8	13.9	14.6	14.7	14.7	2056
Employee plan	5.1	4.9	5.9	7.1	7.6	7.7	7.7	2057
Self-employed plan	0.7	0.7	0.8	0.8	0.8	0.8	0.7	2035
Civil servants' plan	2.9	3.1	4.0	4.8	5.0	5.1	5.2	2060
GIE	0.1	0.1	0.1	0.1	0.1	0.1	0.1	2036
Prepension	0.5	0.4	0.3	0.3	0.3	0.3	0.3	2000
Disability	0.7	0.8	0.8	0.8	0.7	0.7	0.7	2018
Taxes on statutory pension benefits	—	1.3	1.5	1.9	2.0	2.0	2.0	2057

and civil servant plans are jointly responsible for these increases. The other pensions remain stable or decline slightly. Together, the employee and the civil servant plans make up 80 percent of the total public pension expenditure, and this proportion increases to 87 percent in 2060. Because of the rising statutory pensions, tax income on these pension payments will also increase from 1.3 percent of GDP in 2007 to 2 percent of GDP in 2060.

PENSION REFORM PROPOSALS OF THE MAIN SOCIAL AND POLITICAL ACTORS

There is a consensus in Belgium with respect to the necessity of a pension reform. The main social and political actors refer to two problems of the Belgian pension system: budgetary sustainability and social sustainability. However, no consensus exists with respect to concrete pension reform proposals. In fact, very different and opposing ideas exist. This section summarizes the reform proposals of the main social and political actors.

Federation of Enterprises in Belgium

According to the Federation of Enterprises in Belgium (FEB), the insurance character of the statutory pension plan for employees should be enforced (FEB 2010). The FEB wants to change three mechanisms of the employee plan: 1) the early retirement age,[17] 2) the capped benefits,[18] and 3) the so-called free rights.[19] The FEB proposes an increase in the actual and legal retirement age. To increase the actual retirement age, the FEB proposes the valuation of the labor period after the age of 60 at a higher rate (115 percent) and the valuation of periods of inactivity before the age of 60 (unemployment, prepension, etc.) at less than 100 percent. The FEB refers to the Swedish pension system, where individual accounts within the first pillar were introduced, and rising life expectancy has been corrected for by decreasing pension benefits. According to the FEB, the statutory pension plan for civil servants is much too favorable compared to the pension plans of employees (in the public and the private sector) and the self-employed. The calculation of the statutory pension for civil servants should be based on the principles of the statutory pension for employees.

According to the FEB, occupational pension plans are necessary to increase replacement rates. The FEB proposes the facilitation of occupational pension accrual by allowing workers to invest more of their wages directly into their occupational pension plans. In addition, the FEB believes that tax relief for the individual pensions encourages people to save, and it should therefore remain unchanged.

Trade Unions[20]

According to the trade unions, only statutory pension plans guarantee solidarity. Therefore, they should be strengthened. Trade unions claim that statutory pension benefits for employees are too low. Twenty-five percent of the current pensioners in Belgium are poor according to the European poverty standard (i.e., 60 percent or less of the median wage). Increasing the benefits for employees with lower incomes is a priority for the trade unions. They support increasing the GIE to the European poverty standard and the minimum pension to 110 percent of the European poverty standard. In addition, the trade unions also want to increase statutory pensions for employees with higher incomes. The Socialist trade union (FGTB-ABVV) proposes an increase in the statutory employee pension formula, from the current 60 percent of average income to 75 percent of average income. The trade unions do not agree with an increase in the legal retirement age, which will decrease pension benefits. Finally, the trade unions want automatic adjustment of statutory pension benefits to the CPI and real wages (for the moment, adjustment of statutory pension benefits is not automatic and is only related to CPI, not to real wage increases).[21]

To finance the extra expenditures, the trade unions propose three measures: 1) the so-called General Social Contribution, which is an alternative financing mechanism for the social security system (statutory pensions are embedded in this system) that includes social contribution on all types of incomes (instead of only labor income); 2) higher social security contributions for the self-employed; and 3) a phase-out of the tax relief for individual and occupational pension plans.

The trade unions are not opposed to the further development of occupational pensions, as long as those pensions also benefit employees with lower incomes.[22] The Christian trade union (CSC-ACV) proposes a ban on risk-bearing investments in occupational pensions. The Socialist trade union proposes the development of more mandated occupational pensions with solidarity mechanisms (e.g., pension accrual during unemployment and illness). With respect to individual pension plans, the trade unions are unanimous. They believe that tax relief should be abandoned, given the fact that this relief is clearly to the benefit of higher income persons, who do not need these incentives to invest in pensions.

Pensioners

The Advisory Committee for the Pension Sector was created to give recommendations with respect to the organization and reform of the pension system. This Committee covers about 40 pensioner associations in Belgium. The Committee proposes that absolute priority must be given to statutory pension plans. The Committee argues for a minimum pension equal to the minimum salary and an upgrading of the current pension benefits. According to the Committee, current pension benefits have lost their purchasing power as a result of inadequate CPI adjustments. The extension of the occupational pensions is not a solution according to the Committee because these pensions increase inequality and insecurity. Moreover, the Committee says that 1 percent of salary invested in statutory public pensions provides a higher pension benefit than 1 percent of salary invested in occupational pensions.[23]

In order to finance extra expenditures for statutory pensions, the Committee proposes the introduction of a wealth tax. Although the Committee did not make a concrete proposal, it refers to France where such a tax exists. In addition, the Committee proposes a phase-out of tax relief for occupational and individual pension plans.

Government

With an aging population set to put mounting pressure on the budget in the decades ahead, in 2001 the Belgian government created the so-called Silver Fund, which is a budgetary trust fund that was supposed to cover a portion of future pension costs. The idea was to reduce the debt-to-GDP burden in the near term, leaving room for the government to run budget deficits as the population ages and statutory pensions and health care costs rise. The fund was financed by privatization proceeds and budget surpluses. The government's goal was to turn the projected budget deficit of 0.1 percent of GDP in 2001 into a surplus of 0.7 percent of GDP in 2005 and 1.5 percent of GDP in 2010 and thereafter. However, these targets were never met. On the contrary, the recent financial and economic crisis strongly increased the debt-to-GDP burden, and the Silver Fund remains fundamentally empty.

In 2005, the Belgian government tried to increase the actual retirement age. A new early retirement regulation, the "Generation Pact," was enacted. The results thus far have been limited, however. Currently there are no concrete pension reform proposals from the government. Within most political parties, a consensus exists about the guidelines formulated by the EU in Stockholm in 2001, that is, decrease government debt, increase employment and labor productivity, and decrease costs of public pension systems and health care. In the *Green Paper: A Future for our Pensions* (Belgian Secretary of Pensions 2010), the government refers to a series of possible reforms. The following reforms focus on the budgetary sustainability of the system: increased retirement age, decreased pension benefits, decreased tax relief for occupational and individual pensions, and increased taxes. In addition, two reforms that focus on social sustainability were introduced: increased minimum pension benefits and increased participation in occupational and individual pension plans. Some of these proposals are discussed in the next section.

EVALUATION OF THE VARIOUS PENSION REFORM PROPOSALS

Many different reform options are available, and the choice between them is based on ideology and value judgments. To be clear about the evaluation criteria used, I first develop a set of evaluation criteria and then evaluate the various reform proposals discussed above in terms of these criteria.

Evaluation Criteria

In this section, four types of pension accrual are defined: 1) long-term savings, 2) private insurance, 3) social insurance, and 4) social security. These four types are then distinguished on the basis of their intrinsic features, using the following criteria: the degree of redistributive solidarity, the scope of risk sharing, and the degree of protection of pension rights.

Degree of redistributive solidarity

Various forms of pension accrual can be distinguished based on their degree of redistributive solidarity. The four degrees of redistributive solidarity are as follows: 1) no redistribution at all, 2) redistribution based on "probability-solidarity," 3) redistribution based on "risk-solidarity," and 4) redistribution based on "income-solidarity." Redistribution based on probability-solidarity is present when different persons with similar risk profiles are pooled in one group and pay the same pension contributions or insurance premiums. Redistribution in this group is from those who do not actually experience the adverse event (e.g., death in the case of survivor's benefits) to those who do, even though they all share a similar probability of experiencing it. Redistribution based on risk-solidarity is present when different persons with different risk profiles are pooled together and pay the same pension contributions or insurance premiums. In this system, persons with better risk profiles subsidize persons with inferior risk profiles. Redistribution based on income-solidarity involves contribution or premium differentiation based on income, so that persons with higher incomes pay higher premiums for the same benefits. In this system, direct income redistribution takes place, independent of risk profiles. The degree of reciprocity in a system based on income-solidarity can be higher or lower. If there is no link between entitlement to benefits and the payment of contributions in the past, the degree of reciprocity is nil (e.g., the GIE in Belgium). However, in many income redistributive systems, there is some connection between the entitlement to benefits and the payment of contributions in the past (e.g., the statutory pension plans in Belgium). Risk- and income-solidarity are necessarily linked to a certain degree of mandatory membership (Stevens 2002).

Scope of risk sharing

Pension accrual often takes place over a period of decades. Therefore, risk control is a very important issue. As discussed previously, there are five primary risks that threaten pension accrual and four scopes for distinguishing risk sharing (Table 7.3).

Degree of protection of pension rights

The protection of pension rights varies for different types of pension accrual. Protection can be granted on three fields: 1) protection of investment returns, 2) protection against bankruptcy of the pension provider, and 3) protection of the destination as pension (e.g., interdiction of provisions on lump sum payments and early withdrawals). In the protection of the investment returns, three options are available: no guaranteed investment returns, guaranteed investment returns by contract (optional), and guaranteed investment returns by law (mandatory). In the protection against bankruptcy of the pension provider, four degrees of protection are possible: 1) no protection, 2) liability of the sponsor for the payment of the pension benefits, 3) pension protection funds, and 4) state guarantees. In the protection of the destination as pension, three degrees of protection can be distinguished: no prohibition of payout before pensionable age and no prohibition of payout as a lump sum after pensionable age; prohibition of payout before pensionable age, but no prohibition of payout as a lump sum after pensionable age; and prohibition of payout before pensionable age and obligation of payout as an annuity after pensionable age.

Four types of pension accrual

Based on the above-mentioned features, we defined four types of pension accrual. These types are prototypes, which do not necessarily correspond to real forms of pension accrual in Belgium or other countries. We named these types long-term savings, private insurance, social insurance, and social security. Long-term savings is a type of pension accrual without any form of redistributive solidarity, no risk sharing, and no protection of pension rights. Private insurance is a type of pension accrual with redistributive effects based on probability-solidarity, risk sharing at the company level, and limited protection of pension rights. Social insurance is a type of pension accrual with redistributive effects based on risk-solidarity, risk sharing at branch of industry level, and heavy protection of pension rights. Social security, finally, is a type of pension accrual with income-redistributive effects, nationwide risk sharing, and heavy protection of pension rights. A schematic overview of the distinguishing criteria of these four types of pension accrual is shown in Table 7.6.

The various forms of actual pension accrual in Belgium are evaluated in Appendix 7A with respect to their degree of redistributive solidarity, scope of risk sharing, and degree of protection of pension rights. The results of this evaluation are reordered in Table 7.7 to show the various forms of pension accrual in Belgium relative to accrual prototype. The table shows some interesting results. First, it shows that no form of actual pension accrual in Belgium corresponds entirely to one prototype. Each form of pension accrual presents features of different prototypes of pension accrual.

The individual pension plans are entirely based on the long-term savings and private insurance prototypes. Their degree of redistributive solidarity, risk sharing, and protection of pension rights is very low.

The occupational pensions, except for social industry-wide plans, also show many similarities with the long-term savings and private insurance types of pension accrual. This is remarkable, given the fact that occupational pensions are often referred to in Belgium as social insurance systems. The only social insurance features of the occupational pension plans are the risk-solidarity in defined benefit survivor's pensions and social industry-wide pensions, the sharing of bankruptcy and financial risks at the branch of industry level for industry-wide plans (longevity and inflation risk are not shared, see Table 7A.1), and the liability of the sponsor in case of bankruptcy of the pension provider. Moreover, a social security feature is present—the mandatory guaranteed investment return.

As might be expected, the statutory pension plans have the most properties of social security, and the GIE is clearly social security because income redistributive solidarity, without any reciprocity, is present (the entitlement to GIE benefits is not linked to the payment of contributions in the past). For the other statutory pensions, a certain degree of reciprocity is present (benefits are calculated based on earnings in the past). This is a social insurance character of the statutory pension plans for employees, civil servants, and the self-employed. However,

Table 7.6 Four Types of Pension Accrual

Type of pension accrual	Features
Long-term savings	1) No redistributive solidarity 2) No risk sharing 3) No protection of pension rights • No guaranteed investment returns • No protection against bankruptcy of the pension provider • Payment of pension benefits as a lump sum at any moment in time
Private insurance	1) Redistributive effects based on probability-solidarity 2) Risk sharing at company level 3) Small protection of pension rights • Guaranteed investment returns by contract (optional) • No protection against bankruptcy of the pension provider • Payment of pension benefits as a lump sum at the date in the insurance contract
Social insurance	1) Redistributive effects based on risk-solidarity 2) Risk sharing at branch of industry level 3) Medium protection of pension rights • Guaranteed investment returns by contract (optional) • Liability of the sponsor in case of bankruptcy of the pension provider • Payment of pension benefits in the form of an annuity at retirement age

Social security	1) Income-redistributive effects 2) Nationwide risk sharing 3) High protection of pension rights • Guaranteed investment returns by law (mandatory) • Pension protection funds or state guarantee in case of bankruptcy of the pension provider • Payment of pension benefits in the form of an annuity after retirement

Table 7.7 Classification of the Different Forms of Pension Accrual in Belgium

		Individual pension plans		Occupational pension plans				Statutory pension plans	
Types of pension accrual		Pension saving	Individual life insurance	Company plan (DC)	Company plan (DB)	Industry-wide plan (DC)	Social industry-wide plan (DC)	Statutory pensions	GIE
Long term savings	No redistributive solidarity	X		X	X	X			
	No risk sharing	X	X	X	X	X	X		
	No guaranteed investment return	X							
	No protection against bankruptcy	X	X						
	Payment of pension benefits as a lump sum at any moment in time	X							

Private insurance	Redistributive effects based on probability-solidarity		X					
	Risk sharing at company level		X	X	X	X		
	Guaranteed investment return (by contract)	X	X		X			
	Payment of pension benefits as a lump sum at the date in the contract		X	X	X	X	X	
Social insurance	Redistributive effects based on risk-solidarity				X		X	
	Income-redistributive effects (with a certain degree of reciprocity)							X
	Risk sharing at branch of industry level					X	X	
	Liability of the sponsor in case of bankruptcy of the pension provider			X	X	X	X	
	Payment of pension benefits as an annuity at pensionable age							

(continued)

Table 7.7 (continued)

Types of pension accrual		Individual pension plans		Occupational pension plans				Statutory pension plans	
		Pension saving	Individual life insurance	Company plan (DC)	Company plan (DB)	Industry-wide plan (DC)	Social industry-wide plan (DC)	Statutory pensions	GIE
Social security	Income-redistributive effects (without reciprocity)								X
	Nationwide risk sharing							X	X
	Guaranteed investment return (by law)			X		X	X		
	Protection fund or state guarantee in case of bankruptcy of pension provider							X	X
	Payment of pension benefits as an annuity after retirement							X	X

NOTE: DB = defined benefit; DC = defined contribution.

the social insurance character is limited—persons with higher incomes pay higher contributions for, at a certain level, equal benefits. The risk sharing within statutory pensions is nationwide, and the protection of pension benefits is very high.

The classification of the various forms of pension accrual in Belgium, according to their intrinsic characteristics, allows us to evaluate the different reform proposals according to the type of pension accrual they promote.

Evaluation of Reform Proposals

When evaluating each proposal, I also briefly explain the type of reform (parametric or structural),[24] the aim (budgetary or social sustainability), and the cost bearer (government, employers, or employees).

Changing tax relief for occupational and individual pensions

Occupational and individual pensions in Belgium are strongly tax driven. A decrease in the tax relief for occupational and individual pensions is a parametric reform aimed to improve the budgetary sustainability of the Belgian pension system. If implemented, it would probably decrease the proportion of this kind of pension accrual within the Belgium pension system. An increase of the tax relief for occupational and individual pensions is a parametric reform aimed at improving the social sustainability of the pension system. It would probably increase the proportion of this type of pension accrual within the Belgium pension system.

As shown above, individual and occupational pensions are mainly based on the long-term savings and private insurance prototypes (except for the social industry-wide plans). A decrease or increase of individual and occupational pensions will respectively decrease or increase the proportion of long-term savings and private insurance within the Belgian pension system.

Increased retirement age

An increase of the retirement age can take place within statutory pensions, occupational pensions, and individual pensions. However, it will most likely occur primarily within statutory pensions. The increase in the retirement age can be achieved by increasing the legal retirement age or the career length required to obtain full benefits. Increasing the statutory retirement age is a parametric pension reform aimed at improving the budgetary sustainability of the pension system. This reform is at the expense of employees, civil servants, and the self-employed who, in one way or another, will have to work longer for the same statutory pension benefits or receive lower benefits.

Statutory pensions in Belgium are closest to the social security type of pension accrual. An increase in retirement age would mean that the proportion of this type of pension accrual within the Belgium pension system would decrease.

Increased minimum benefits of statutory pensions

An increase of the minimum benefits of statutory pensions (the GIE and minimum pension for employees and the self-employed) is a parametric pension reform aimed at improving the social sustainability of the pension system. Initially, this reform will be at the expense of the government, which will most probably recoup the increased expenditures from taxpayers or decrease other statutory pension benefits.

If the increase in minimum benefits of statutory pensions is compensated for by a decrease in other statutory pension benefits, the proportion of the social insurance type of pension accrual in Belgium would probably decrease in comparison with the social security type. If the increase is financed with increased taxes, the proportion of social insurance and social security types of pension accrual would increase.

Increased statutory pension benefits via a wealth tax

The Advisory Committee for the Pension Sector proposes an increase in statutory pensions by means of a wealth tax. The financing of statutory pensions by means of a wealth tax is a structural pension reform aimed at both the budgetary and social sustainability of the pension system. This reform is at the expense of the wealthiest citizens.

To the extent that the extra tax revenues are used to strengthen the statutory pension plans in Belgium, the proportion of social insurance and social security types of pension accrual would increase within the Belgian pension system.

THE IDEAL PENSION SYSTEM FOR BELGIUM

The Current Main Problem

The benefits of the statutory pension plans are considered too low for employees and the self-employed. Occupational pensions cover only 60 percent of employees, and the benefits are too low, except for higher income persons. Individual pensions cover 37 percent of Belgian residents (15–64 years old), and their total reserves amounted to 45.1 percent of GDP in 2007. This percentage is even higher if tax-driven investments in real estate are taken into account. The main problem of the Belgian pension system at present is not the total amount of investment in pension accrual. The main problem is the large proportion of investment in the long-term savings and private insurance prototypes. The degree of redistributive solidarity, the scope of risk sharing, and the protection of pension rights associated with these types of pension accrual are very low. As a consequence, groups with weak bargaining power (lower income workers, women, and those with atypical careers) are not covered or are inadequately covered. The question we have to ask, then, is which types of pension accrual do we want to promote in the future?

Pensions as Social Goods

In public economics, a distinction is made between three types of goods: public, private, and social. A public good is defined as a good that is non-rivaled and non-excludable. This means that consumption of the good by one individual does not reduce the amount of the good available for consumption by others and that no one can be effectively excluded from it (e.g., clean air, national defense, or public fireworks). A private good is the opposite of a public good. It is excludable, for example, to those who have not paid for it, and consumption by one consumer prevents simultaneous consumption by other consumers. A social good is a private good for which consumption is stimulated by the government for various reasons, including social policy. A government decides that individuals should have a particular social good based on a norm other than responding just to consumer preferences. This norm could be the public interest, common well-being, or general welfare. A social good would be under-consumed in a free market economy. Because of its positive externalities, the government stimulates consumption through social policy measures.[25] Pensions can be considered to be social goods insofar as they meet two conditions: 1) they have to show a certain degree of solidarity, risk sharing, and protection, and 2) they may not exceed a certain percentage of final salary.

The Ideal Pension System for Belgium

I have shown that individual and occupational pension plans in Belgium (except for social industry-wide plans) mainly show characteristics of long-term savings and private insurance. They lack the necessary degree of solidarity, risk sharing, and protection of pension rights to qualify as pensions. If these pension plans are to maintain their tax incentives, they need to integrate more features of social insurance, for example, mandatory payment of annuities instead of lump sums, continued pension accrual during periods of illness or unemployment, risk sharing at the branch of industry level, and protection of pension rights in case of bankruptcy of the pension provider. Moreover, once a certain accumulated sum of total pension provisions is reached,[26] no more tax incentives for individual and occupational pensions should be allowed. In an ideal pension system for Belgium, the statutory pensions would guarantee benefits of 60 percent of final salary. The individual and occupational pensions would cover the difference up to 75 percent of final salary. No tax incentives would be granted for pension provision above 75 percent of final salary. Individual and occupational pensions still would have an important role, but tax incentives would only be granted if minimum degrees of solidarity, risk sharing, and protection of pension rights are met.

Type of Welfare Regime

The underlying ideological matter with respect to the ideal pension system of a country is to what extent the government is responsible for the retirement income of individuals. Three different types of welfare regimes can be distinguished: the liberal, the conservative, and the social democratic (Esping-Andersen 1990). In the liberal welfare regime, the pension system increases inequality. The limits of welfare equal the marginal propensity to opt for welfare instead of work. Entitlement rules are strict and often associated with stigma. Benefits are modest. The government encourages the market, either by guaranteeing only a minimum benefit or by subsidizing private welfare plans. In the conservative welfare regime, the pension system preserves inequality. The redistributive impact of the pension system is negligible. Social insurance typically excludes nonworking wives. The principle of subsidiarity serves to emphasize that the government will only interfere when the family's capacity to service its members is exhausted. In the social democratic welfare regime, finally, the pension system decreases inequality. The government pursues an equality of the highest standards, not an equality of minimal needs. This implies, first, that services and benefits will be upgraded to levels commensurate with benefits of the middle classes. And, second, that equality is furnished by guaranteeing workers full participation in the quality of rights enjoyed by the better-off. The Belgian pension system clearly shows characteristics of the conservative regime. An ideal pension system for Belgium should show more characteristics of a social-democratic welfare regime.

Appendix 7A
Main Features of the Different Forms of Pension Accrual in Belgium

In this Appendix, I briefly evaluate the different forms of pension accrual in Belgium with respect to their degree of redistributive solidarity, risk sharing, and protection of pension rights. The different forms of pension accrual in Belgium are individual pension plans (pension saving and individual life insurance), occupational pension plans (defined benefit or defined contribution plans at the company level, defined contribution plans at the industry level, and social industry-wide defined contribution plans), and statutory pension plans (social security pensions and guaranteed income for the elderly). An overview of the evaluation is presented in Table 7A.1.

Individual Pension Plans

Pension saving in individual pension plans includes no redistributive solidarity, no risk sharing, and little protection of pension rights. In Belgium, the clear distinction between financial institutions and insurance companies or between long-term savings and private insurance has disappeared (specialists often speak of the "bancassurance" as the phenomenon where banks and insurance companies both offer products linked to savings and insurance). Consequently, pension saving in a bank is often linked to insurance products. A guaranteed investment return can be agreed upon. Moreover, the first €100,000 of pension savings in a bank account is covered by a state guarantee. Individual life insurance as a form of individual pension includes no redistributive solidarity with respect to old-age pension accrual. With respect to survivor's pensions, a redistribution based on probability-solidarity is present. Private insurance includes no risk-sharing whatsoever. With respect to the protection of pension rights, a guaranteed investment return is granted by contract (through the insurance mechanism), and pension benefits are paid at the date agreed upon in the insurance contract (early surrender of the policy may be possible).

Occupational Pension Plans

With respect to occupational pensions, defined contribution plans at the company level include no redistributive solidarity and no sharing of risks linked to longevity and inflation. The risks linked to financial markets and bankruptcy are shared at the company level. A medium protection of pension rights is present—there is a guaranteed investment return by law, liability of the sponsor in case of bankruptcy of the pension provider, and no payment of pension benefits before retirement age (early withdrawal of pension benefits is possible for the purchase or renovation of a plan member's own dwelling). Defined benefit plans at the company level include no redistributive solidarity with respect to old-age pensions. With respect to survivor's pensions, a redistribution based on risk solidarity is present (people with different risk profiles are pooled together in one group). The risk of longevity is not shared within defined benefit plans at the company level. The risks linked to inflation, financial markets, and bankruptcy of the pension provider are shared at the company level. As for defined contribution plans, a medium protection of pension rights is present (because the issue is not applicable to defined benefit plans, a guaranteed investment return is provided by law only for defined contribution plans). Industry-wide plans include no redistributive solidarity and no sharing of the risks linked to longevity and inflation. Risks linked to financial markets and bankruptcy are shared at the industry level. The same protection of pension rights applies for both defined benefit and defined contribution plans at the company level. The social industry-wide plans differ from standard industry-wide plans only with respect to their degree of redistributive solidarity. Membership in these plans is mandatory and people with different risk profiles are pooled together. In case of illness, employment, pregnancy, and other circumstances, pension accrual continues, and therefore, redistribution based on risk solidarity is present (for old-age and survivor's pensions).

Statutory Pension Plans

Social security pensions include income-solidarity, nationwide risk sharing, and full protection of pension rights. The difference between social security pensions and the GIE is the degree of reciprocity within the income solidarity. For the GIE there is no link between entitlement to benefits and payment of contributions in the past. For social security pensions, there is some proportional connection between the entitlement to benefits and the payment of contributions in the past.

Table 7A.1 Evaluation of the Different Forms of Pension Accrual in Belgium

			Individual pension plans		Occupational pension plans				Statutory pension plans	
Criteria to evaluate pension accrual			Pension saving	Individual life insurance	Company plan (DC)	Company plan (DB)	Industry-wide plan (DC)	Social industry-wide plan (DC)	Social security pensions	GIE[a]
Degree of redistributive solidarity	Old age pension	No redistributive solidarity	X	X	X	X	X			
		Probability-solidarity								
		Risk-solidarity						X		
		Income-solidarity (R)							X	
		Income-solidarity (NR)								X
	Survivors pension	No redistributive solidarity	X		X		X			
		Probability-solidarity		X						
		Risk-solidarity				X		X		
		Income-solidarity (R)							X	
Scope of risk taking	Longevity	No risk sharing	X	X	X	X	X	X		
		Company								
		Branch of industry								
		Nationwide							X	X

(continued)

Table 7A.1 (continued)

Criteria to evaluate pension accrual			Individual pension plans		Occupational pension plans				Statutory pension plans	
			Pension saving	Individual life insurance	Company plan (DC)	Company plan (DB)	Industry-wide plan (DC)	Social industry-wide plan (DC)	Social security pensions	GIE[a]
	Inflation	No risk sharing	X	X	X		X	X		
		Company				X				
		Branch of industry								
		Nationwide							X	X
	Financial risks	No risk sharing	X	X						
		Company			X	X				
		Branch of industry					X	X		
		Nationwide							X	X
	Bankruptcy of pension provider	No risk sharing	X	X						
		Company			X	X				
		Branch of industry					X	X		
		Nationwide							X	X
Protection of pension rights	Protection of investment returns	No guaranteed investment return	X							
		Guaranteed investment return by contract	X	X		X				
		Guaranteed investment return by law			X		X	X	X	X

Protection against bankruptcy of pension provider	No protection	X	X						
	Liability of the sponsor			X	X	X	X		
	Pension protection funds or state guarantee	X						X	X
Protection of the destination as pension	Payment of pension benefits as a lump sum at any moment in time	X							
	Payment of pension benefits as a lump sum on date in contract		X	X	X	X	X		
	Payment of pension benefits in the form of an annuity at pensionable age								
	Payment of pension benefits in the form of an annuity after retirement							X	X

NOTE: DB: defined benefit; DC: defined contribution; R: with a certain degree of reciprocity; NR: no reciprocity.
[a]There is no survivor's pension linked to the GIE.

Notes

1. For example, a single person who worked 35 years will receive an annuity equal to 35/45 × average (capped) earnings × 60 percent. A married person with a dependent spouse who worked 40 years will receive an annuity equal to 40/45 × average (capped) earnings × 75 percent. In 2008, the wage of 20.1 percent of full-time private sector employees was higher than the wage ceiling (Belgian Secretary of Pension 2010, p. 127).
2. It is possible to retire at the age of 60, provided the person had a minimum career length of 35 years. To stimulate employees to work until the age of 65, a pension bonus has been granted for each working day after the age of 62 or after a career of 44 years. After retirement a person may continue to work, although his or her pension may be adjusted (i.e., reduced) for earnings above certain levels.
3. The calculation of penalties in case of early retirement (before 65) and the absence of a minimum claim per year are examples of the differences. Legal retirement age, the pension bonus, price indexation, and the survivor's pension are similar to the employee plan.
4. Civil servants who have been declared permanently unfit to continue their careers, regardless of their age or seniority, are entitled to a disability pension.
5. New legislation has severely restricted internal funding via book reserves.
6. Belgium has an elaborate network of collective negotiation bodies. In labor matters, employee representatives and employer representative bodies meet at different levels to discuss collective measures. The National Labor Council supervises 200 joint committees, organized by industry type. Therefore, for the companies in a particular industry, there is a body of representatives of both employers and employees that meets to conclude binding collective bargaining agreements or more politically engaging social agreements.
7. According to the OECD, tax incentives for occupational pension plans cannot be preserved because they mainly benefit higher income workers, who have already enough savings for their retirement (OECD 2007, 2009).
8. The maximum statutory pension benefit for a single person who has been an employee during his entire career is €1,800 per month (€2,200 for married persons with a dependent spouse). The maximum is €1,000 per month for a single person who has been self-employed during his entire career (€1,200 for married self-employed persons with a dependent spouse).
9. The replacement rate is the fraction of previous salary that the statutory pension benefits replace. In order to calculate these rates, previous gross salary (or the average of the 5 last years of net income of self-employed) is compared with gross statutory pension benefits, including holiday pay and other supplements.
10. Industry-wide plans in Belgium are always defined contribution plans.
11. Insurance companies can purchase a state guarantee for the first €100,000 of individual pension reserves (Royal Decree of November 14, 2008).
12. Statutory pensions are embedded in the social security system. The social security contributions for the self-employed are capped. The self-employed pay a maxi-

mum of €3,664.49 per quarter (in 2009). This amount corresponds to 22 percent of the income up to €51,059.94 and 14.16 percent of the income above that up to the cap of €75,246.19. This system restricts redistributive solidarity because a self-employed person with a net income of, for example, €80,000 pays the same social security contributions as one with a net income of €300,000. Employees pay social security contributions on their entire salary.

13. About 80 percent of occupational pensions are managed by insurance companies and about 20 percent are managed by pension funds (Hannes 2009; Sommerijns and De Bilderling 2009).
14. These estimates are based on data from the Banking, Finance, and Insurance Commission. The accumulated reserves for voluntary pensions for the self-employed are very limited—they amounted to €28 million in 1996 and €72 million in 2000 (Gieselink et al. 2003).
15. Half of total spending goes to the employee plan (4.9 percent of GDP), and one-third goes to the civil servants plan (3.1 percent of GDP). The rest goes to disability pensions (0.8 percent of GDP), the self-employed plan (0.7 percent of GDP), pre-pensions (0.4 percent of GDP), and the GIE (0.1 percent of GDP).
16. This demographic evolution is mainly present in the Flemish region in Belgium.
17. The average retirement age is 59.5 years for men and 58.2 years for women.
18. Statutory pension contributions are calculated on the entire salary, whereas the benefits of statutory pensions are capped, taking into account a maximum salary of €47,282 (2009). The FEB proposes the introduction of more earnings-related benefits.
19. According to the FEB, one-third of statutory pension benefits are attributed without any social security contribution of the beneficiary.
20. Trade unions play a very important role in Belgium. Seventy-five percent of employees and civil servants are members of a trade union. The two major unions are the Christian trade union (CSC-ACV) and the Socialist trade union (FGTB-ABVV). The third major union is the Liberal trade union (ACLVB-CGSLB), which is much smaller. The pension reform proposal of each union can be found on their websites.
21. According to the trade unions, one reason for low pension benefits in Belgium lies in the indexation rules used to calculate initial benefits. In the Belgian benefit formula, wage histories are brought forward for averaging adjusted for prices rather than wage growth, the latter being the usual practice in most countries. This provision has the effect of gradually reducing per capita benefits relative to per capita wages over time.
22. According to the trade unions, only 2 percent of the employees with the lowest statutory pensions benefit from an occupational pension as compared to 36 percent of the employees with the highest statutory pensions.
23. A study at the University of Leuven, ordered by the Christian trade union, shows that the return or efficiency of statutory public pensions is higher than the return of occupational and individual pensions, as a result of the considerable administration costs of the latter (Pacolet and Strengs 2009).

24. Structural pension reforms are reforms that change essential features of the pension system, for example, the transformation from pay as you go to a funded plan, from defined benefit to defined contribution plans, or from average salary to final salary plans. Parametric pension reforms are reforms that change the value of certain parameters, for example, career length, minimum pension, or the defined benefit percentage. However, some parametric reforms lead to structural changes in the overall pension system. For example, the further development of occupational and individual pensions will also lead to a change in the proportion between funded and pay-as-you-go financing. Obviously, the weight of funded pensions would increase in this situation.
25. Musgrave (1957) introduced the concept of a merit good, but I prefer the notion social good, which is used here. According to Musgrave, different rationales can be found for the existence of merit goods. There may be more acceptance for income redistribution in the form of goods, rather than purchasing power. Consumption of merit goods needs to be stimulated because when consumed, a merit good creates positive externalities (there is a divergence between private benefit and public benefit and most consumers only take into account private benefit) and most individuals are short-term utility maximizers and so do not take into account the long-term benefits of consuming a merit good. Examples of merit goods include education, subsidized housing, and health care.
26. That is, an accumulated sum of statutory pension, occupational pension, and individual pension.

References

AON Consulting. 2007. "2007 European Pensions Barometer. Report: Measuring the pressure on EU pensions systems." London: AON Consulting Ltd.

Assuralia. 2009. "Estimation Market Research Fortis., NPC/GT2." Brussels: Assuralia.

Belgian Parliament. 2009, "Questions and Answers, Chamber of Deputies 2008–2009, QRVA 52 057." Question no. 330, April 14. Brussels: Belgian Parliament.

Belgian Secretary of Pensions. 2010. "A Future for Our Pensions." Green Paper. Brussels: Belgian Secretary of Pensions.

Berghman, Jos. 2009. "Pension Pillars 1-2-3 in Belgium: An Overview." Presentation given to the ACV-CSC (Christian Trade Union) Congress of September 2.

Capretta, James C. 2007. "Global Aging and the Sustainability of Public Pension Systems: An Assessment of Reform Efforts in Twelve Developed Countries." A report of the Aging Vulnerability Index Project. Washington, DC: Center for Strategic and International Studies. http://csis.org/files/media/csis/pubs/pension_profile.pdf (accessed June 23, 2011).

CBFA (Belgian Banking, Finance and Insurance Commission). 2009. *Tweejaarlijks verslag betreffende het vrij aanvullend pensioen voor zelfstandigen* [Bi-Annual Report Regarding the Voluntary Pension for Self-Employed]. Brussels: CBFA. http://www.fsma.be/nl/Supervision/pensions/ap/apzs/Article/reportszs/bisannual.aspx (accessed June 29, 2011).

Dellis, Arnaud, Alain Jousten, and Sergio Perelman. 2001. "Micro-Modeling of Retirement in Belgium." Discussion Paper no. 2795. London: Centre for Economic Policy Research.

de Dessus les Moustier, Colette, and Laurence Masy. 2007. "Pension Survey 2007." London: AON Consulting Ltd.

De Witte, Kim, Paul Roels, and Yves Stevens. 2009. "The Matthew Effect: Why Current Pension Policy Helps the Rich Get Richer." In *Personal Provision of Retirement Income, Meeting the Needs of Older People?* Jim Stewart and Gerard Hughes, eds. Cheltenham, UK: Edward Elgar, pp. 151–175.

Esping-Andersen, Gøsta. 1990. *The Three Worlds of Welfare Capitalism.* Cambridge: Polity Press.

FEB (Federation of Enterprises in Belgium). 2010. "Nationale Pensioenconferentie: de hervorming van de pensioenen is een noodzaak, krachtlijnen VBO-standpunt" [National Pension Conference: Reform of the Pensions Is Necessary. Point of View of the FEB], February 16.

Gieselink, Gerhard, Hans Peeters, Veerle Van Gestel, Jos Berghman, and Bea Van Buggenhout. 2003. *Onzichtbare pensioenen in België* [Invisible Pensions in Belgium]. Gent: Academia Press.

Hannes, Birgit. 2009. "Aanvullende pensioenen: visie van Assuralia" [Occupational Pensions: Vision of Assuralia]. NCP/GT2. Brussells: Assuralia.

Musgrave, R. A. 1957. "A Multiple Theory of Budget Determination." *Finanz-Archiv* 17(3): 333–343.

NIS (National Institute for Statistics in Belgium—Algemene Directie Statistiek en Economische Informatie). 2007. "Statistics Concerning Average Salaries in 2007." Brussells: NIS.

OECD. 2006. *Financial Market Trends* 1(90): 212.

———. 2007. "Pallier l'insuffisance des retraites: le rôle des pensions privées." *L'Observateur Synthèses*. October, p. 6.

———. 2009. "Un plan de relance belge, version OCDE." *L'Echo*, May 13, p. 9.

Pacolet, Jozef, and Tom Strengs. 2009. "Pensioenrendement vergeleken. Vergelijking van de performantie van de eerste versus de tweede en derde pensioenpijler" [Pension Performance Comparison: Comparing the Performance of the First versus the Second and Third Pension Pillar]. Leuven: Katholieke Universiteit Leuven, HIVA.

Pierreux, D. 2009. "Doorlichting sectorale CAO's gesloten in uitvoering van de WAP" [Screening of the Collective Bargaining Agreements Based on the Supplementary Pensions Act). Social Security Administration (FOD Werkgelegenheid], NCP/GT2, April 23.

Sommerijns, Lut, and Fabian de Bilderling. 2009. "Présentation introductive Abip" [Introductive Presentation Abip], NCP/GT2, April 2.

Stevens, Yves. 2002. "Gelijkheid en solidariteit in aanvullende werknemerspensioenen: van loon naar sociale bescherming" [Equality and Solidarity in Occupational Pensions: From Salary to Social Protection]. Doctoral thesis. Leuven: Katholieke Universiteit Leuven.

Wuyts, Gunther, Pierrick Stinglhamber, Christian Valenduc, and Marie-Denise Zachary. 2007. "Saving for retirement in the Third Pillar of the Belgium Pension System." *Forum Financier* 2: 55–62.

8
Toward the Ideal Pension System for France

Lucy apRoberts
Institutions et Dynamiques Historiques de l'Economie, Université de Paris Ouest Nanterre

Pierre Concialdi
Institut de Recherches Economiques et Sociales

The French pension system involves almost no funding. The French savings rate is high and bolstering retirement income is a major motivation for savings, but French people rarely use savings plans that are dedicated to retirement. Public sector employees do not need supplementary pensions since replacement rates provided by the existing pay-as-you-go plans are quite high. In the private sector, the social security retirement plan does not provide an adequate replacement rate. However, all private sector employees are covered by mandatory nationwide supplementary plans that function on a pay-as-you-go basis. Thus, even the main supplementary pension plans do not involve funding. In the private sector, employer-sponsored plans are rare. They exist for employees of a few publicly owned or formerly publicly owned companies, mainly the national railway and gas and electricity companies, but these plans are also run on a pay-as-you-go basis. In addition to mandatory plans, a few large private companies run their own pension plans, but most of these have been closed.

A national pension system can be evaluated in the light of three criteria: 1) the extent of coverage, 2) the degree to which risks are shared, and 3) the adequacy of benefits. The first two criteria, however, do not merit much discussion in the case of France.

Coverage is not an issue—the French pension system provides universal coverage through employment-linked benefits for retired workers plus a means-tested minimum income (*minimum vieillesse*) for people age 65 and over who have worked little or not at all. Whenever workers are employed, they acquire pension rights. However, the unemployment rate is high, and underemployment is common. Therefore, while coverage by pension plans is not a problem, the capacity of workers to find employment at a decent wage is an issue.

Since the French pension system is financed on a pay-as-you-go basis, the question of how financial risks are shared does not arise. Although funded plans have been growing in importance in recent years, their overall contribution to retirement income remains very small. The main form of risk associated with the French pension system—as for most public pension plans in Europe—is "political" risk. Indeed, over the past 20 years, successive governments have implemented a series of reforms that have resulted in a decline in social security pension levels relative to earnings. Moreover, further decreases are currently being recommended by policymakers. Hence, adequacy of benefits has now become the main issue for the French pension system.

The first part of this chapter briefly describes the organization of the French pension system, its main features, and trends in the level of pensions since the 1980s. The second part outlines guiding principles that might be applied to reform the pension system for the better. Possible measures for improving the system are then discussed, including reinstating a target replacement rate, continuing to enable workers to retire at 60, redefining eligibility criteria for retirement that are coherent with the actual functioning of the labor market, and increasing the financial resources of the pension system.

PRESENT SITUATION AND TRENDS

As in many other developed countries, the present pension system started after World War II, with the creation of social security. Pensions for civil servants were established much earlier, in the nineteenth century.[1] Before 1945, there were attempts to set up retirement pension systems for private sector employees, with laws enacted in 1910 and 1930. These arrangements were not successful, largely because the plans were funded and were therefore unable to guarantee benefits in the face of great economic turbulence during the first half of the twentieth century (apRoberts and Concialdi 2009).

Early Development of the Retirement System: 1945 to 1982

In 1945, the government planned to create a universal social security pension plan for all workers, called the *Régime général* or General Plan. However, some categories of workers did not want to join this unified plan. Civil servants and employees of some large public enterprises (the electricity company, EDF; the gas company, GDF; the railroad company, SNCF; etc.) were already covered by occupational plans that were more generous than the new General Plan. They kept their occupational plans and stayed outside the General Plan. These separate occupational plans are called *régimes spéciaux*, or "special plans." The self-employed also did not want to join the General Plan, which they felt would be dominated by trade unions representing employees; they succeeded in establishing their own pension plans, without joining the General Plan.

Higher paid private sector employees were reluctant to join the new General Plan. These employees are referred to as "cadres," a term that encompasses managers and highly skilled technical staff. The new General Plan was to collect contributions and pay out benefits on wages below a ceiling, known as the social security ceiling. Higher paid employees succeeded in keeping this ceiling rather low, well below the wages of most cadres. Therefore, the higher paid employees wanted to establish a supplementary plan, based on their wages above the ceiling. In 1947, when the General Plan began to function, cadres joined it. At the same time, they established a supplementary occupational plan, through a collective agreement, negotiated by employers' associations and trade unions for cadres throughout the private sector.

Supplementary occupational plans came to cover all private sector employees over the following decades.[2] Plans for non-cadres were set up in the late 1950s and early 1960s. A law passed in 1972 made it compulsory for every private sector worker covered by the General Plan to be covered by a supplementary plan. Today, employees contribute to the supplementary plans on total wages, but the contribution rate is higher on wages above the social security ceiling than on wages below it. This partially offsets the fact that the General Plan only takes wages below the ceiling into account. These supplementary plans play an important role in the French pension system: they pay out about one-third of total private sector pension benefits. Unlike supplementary plans in most other countries, French supplementary plans are organized on a pay-as-you-go basis (for a history of their development, see apRoberts and Concialdi [2009] and Lynes [1985]).

The French system also provides a means-tested minimum benefit for the elderly. This minimum was reformed and improved in 1956. Throughout the 1950s and the 1960s, the minimum income for the elderly played an important role. Three-fourths of pensioners were receiving it in the late 1950s, versus fewer than 8 percent today. Its level increased considerably during the 1970s and the early 1980s.

In the 1970s, the rules governing entitlement to and calculation of General Plan pensions were made more generous. Advantages were granted to specific categories of workers (manual laborers) or under specific circumstances (bonuses for women who had reared children). In the mid-1970s, a mechanism of transfers between separate plans was set up to compensate for demographic differences (the ratio of retirees to contributors). This system of transfers was possible because nearly all pension plans are organized on a pay-as-you-go basis.

An important reform took place in 1983. A minimum contributory pension (*minimum contributif*) was created for workers with a full career at low wages. Also the age for retiring with a full rate basic pension was reduced from 65 to 60. Before this reform, workers could retire at age 60, but in that case, they got only half of the full rate. Since 1983, the General Plan has been organized around two key legal ages (for more information about the formula, see Appendix 8A).

Sixty is the age at which workers can start claiming their pension. If they have a full career, they get the full rate of 50 percent of the reference wage. In the 1980s, the reference wage was the average of the highest 10 years of wages below the social security ceiling. If the worker's career is less than full length, the rate of the pension is reduced in proportion to the shortfall in their insurance period.

Sixty-five is the retirement age at which every worker can get the full rate, whether they have had a full career or not. If the worker's career is less than full, the pension is reduced in proportion to the shortfall in the insurance period. However, the pension rate of 50 percent is not reduced.

The improvements described above shaped the French pension system of today. Three main features characterize the current French pension system.

First, pension plans are organized on an occupational basis. As a consequence, the system is fragmented by socio-professional status (making it a "Bismarckian" system in international comparisons). There has been a trend toward less fragmentation. In 1945, there were more than 200 different basic pension plans whereas there are only about 20 today.

Second, all mandatory plans, including the main supplementary plans, are organized on a pay-as-you-go basis. Funded plans—employer-provided or individual—play a very marginal role, providing less than 3 percent of total pension benefits in 2008. Workers do not bear any financial risk.

Finally, the system of compulsory pay-as-you-go plans provides a replacement rate that is among the highest in Europe. For retirees with a full career, average replacement rates (first pension benefit received divided by end-of-career wage level) were 76 percent for civil servants and 83 percent for private sector employees in the second half of the 1990s (Direction de la recherche, des études, de l'évaluation et des statistiques [DREES] 2004).[3] The difference between civil servants and private sector employees is mainly due to the fact that, on average, civil servants are more highly qualified and have higher wages than private sector employees.

These replacement rates reflect the level of pensions achieved by the French pension system by the 1990s. Many changes have been enacted in the pension system, including major legislation passed in 1993, but their impact is not reflected in these replacement rates since the reforms have been implemented gradually.

Reforms since the Late 1980s

For decades, contribution rates rose as the level of pensions and the coverage of workers improved. Beginning in the 1980s, concerns were expressed that further rises in contribution rates would place an unbearable burden on French companies and handicap them in international competition. Received wisdom on the part of both right- and left-wing governments currently holds that contribution rates should not rise.

Occasionally, recourse to other sources of financing is proposed, for example, taxes on property or profits and eco taxes.[4] Up until now, however, practically all pensions are financed by contributions levied on earnings, and it seems unlikely that there will be massive recourse to other sources of financing.

The refusal to increase contribution rates, coupled with the stagnation of real wages over recent decades, has led to the only alternative, namely, reduced benefits. This has been done through a series of changes in the rules governing the distribution and the level of pension benefits. Over the past two decades, four major changes can be identified:

1) the introduction of social contributions levied on pensions,
2) the 1993 reform of the General Plan for private sector employees,
3) the 2003 retirement system reform, which concerned most mandatory plans, and
4) agreements between social partners concerning supplementary pensions for private sector employees.

In addition to these changes, the minimum income for people aged 65 and over has dropped in relation to other sources of income since the mid-1980s. As a percentage of median income, the minimum income for retirees fell from 50.7 percent in 1984 to 40.2 percent in 2008. The 2008 level is well below the European poverty threshold of 60 percent of median income.

Furthermore, in 1980, General Plan pensions became subject to a social security health insurance contribution of 1 percent (the contribution rate was 2 percent for supplementary pensions and 2.25 percent for civil service pensions). The contribution rate was increased in 1987, 1991, and 1997. Today, total social contributions levied on pensions amount to 7.1 percent of the gross pension. For retirees with low incomes, this rate is reduced to 3.8 percent. Those who are not subject to income tax are completely exempt from making these contributions. The increase in social contributions for retirees is tantamount to reducing net pensions.

The 1993 reform of the General Plan

The 1993 reform changed the rules governing the calculation of benefits for the General Plan, which mainly concerns private sector employees. It was a so-called parametric reform. We do not go into all the details of this reform here, but the major changes are summarized below.

The main mechanism by which pensions have been reduced was to slow down increases by changing the method of indexation. This mechanism was actually introduced in 1987 but it did not become law until 1993. Pensions in payment are now indexed to prices, whereas they used to be indexed to wages. In addition, past wages used to calculate the pension level at the time of retirement under the General Plan are now indexed to prices instead of wages. Furthermore, the reference wage was changed from the average of the highest 10 years of wages to the average of the highest 25 years of wages.

The other main mechanism by which pension levels have been reduced was to increase the number of years of contributions required for a full pension, without changing the age at which workers can start claiming their pension (60 years of age since the 1980s). This change is equivalent to an across-the-board decrease in pensions at all retirement ages, similar to the consequences of the rise in the full retirement age in the U.S. Social Security retirement system.

The 1993 reform also created a public fund[5] that is separate from all other pension plans and funded through various earmarked taxes. This fund pays for pension benefits that are considered "noncontributory." Such benefits include means-tested minimum income for the elderly, bonuses for pensioners that have had at least three children, and pension credits for periods without contributions (unemployment, sickness, disability, military service, or child rearing).

The 2003 retirement system reform: A further reduction in pensions

After several months of protest demonstrations, a retirement reform law was passed on August 21, 2003. It is not possible to summarize the long and complex legal text in a few sentences. Instead, we focus here only on the rationale behind the reform, whose main goal was to increase work life and delay the effective retirement age.

The insurance period needed to qualify for a full rate pension had already been increased from 37.5 to 40 years in the private sector between 1994 and 2003. The 2003 reform increased the number of years of employment required for a full pension for civil servants from 37.5 in 2003 to 40 years by 2008. This insurance period will continue to increase in both sectors and reach 41 years in 2012. After that date it should increase in line with increases in life expectancy. It is consequently expected that the insurance period required for a full rate pension should be around 42 years by 2020 and approximately 44 years by 2040.

The changes enacted in the pension system will reduce future pensions. For this reason, the 2003 law encouraged the development of voluntary retirement savings through new exemptions on taxes and contributions.

The 2003 reform applied to all pension plans, with the exception of the "special" plans of some large public enterprises, which were reformed in the second half of the 2000s. The main measures of these reforms were to increase the contribution period required for a full pension, to index pensions to prices, and to introduce penalties for workers retiring without a full career before a certain age.

Changes in supplementary pension plans for private sector workers

On average, supplementary pension plans for private sector workers provide around one-third of total pensions. Changes in these supplementary plans have a strong impact on the level of pensions.

In the supplementary pension plans, an employee is awarded a number of points each year, which depends on the contributions paid. (The employee "earns" pension points at a certain "price" equal to the amount of contributions required to acquire one point.) When the employee retires, the plan adds up all the points acquired over the career and multiplies them by the value of the point at the time of retirement. The result is the amount of the pension benefit. In such a system, the key parameters are the price of the point while working and the value of the point during retirement. The value of a point and hence the pension can change during retirement. Agreements negotiated by employers' organizations and labor unions in the 1990s have increased the price of the point and simultaneously decreased the value of the point. Hence, supplementary pension plans for private sector workers have become less generous. This change will hit high wage workers the hardest, since supplementary pensions can amount to more than 60 percent of their total pension. If the current indexing arrangement were to be renewed, supplementary plan replacement rates would be halved over the next 40 years.

Trends and Current Proposals

The main consequence of all the pension system "reforms" implemented over the past 20 years in France is that the pension system has become less generous. As a result, more and more new retirees are getting only the minimum contributory pension: 57 percent of women and 26 percent of men retiring in 2005 were in this situation, whereas the proportions were 50 percent for women and 20 percent for men in the mid-1990s (Figure 8.1). The proportion of all General Plan retirees getting the minimum contributory pension rose from 8 percent in 1985 to 36 percent in 2005. It is expected that 40 percent of General Plan pensioners will be receiving the minimum contributory pension in 2010. In 2004, 75 percent of pensioners receiving the minimum contributory pension had a total pension (including supplementary pensions) that was well below the minimum wage (DREES 2008).

The growing incidence of low pensions will affect the youngest generations the most. The generosity of the pension system will decrease over time, but we do not have data on changes in replacement rates over time. In order to evaluate the generosity of the pension system as a whole, we compare average pension expenditure per older person to per capita GDP, that is, to the average income of the whole population (Figure 8.2). This indicator measures the proportion of total income spent on public pensions in relation to the proportion of older people in the population.

Over the next 40 years, the generosity of the pension system will decline in proportion to per capita GDP. In 2050, the ratio of average pension expenditure per older person to per capita GDP is projected to be about 45 percent, that is, the same level as in the mid-1970s. At that time, 35 percent of retirees were poor in France, versus less than 10 percent today. If current legislation is left unchanged, the result will be future impoverishment of retirees. Nonetheless, the new reform pro-

Figure 8.1 Proportion of New Retirees Receiving the Minimum Contributory Pension

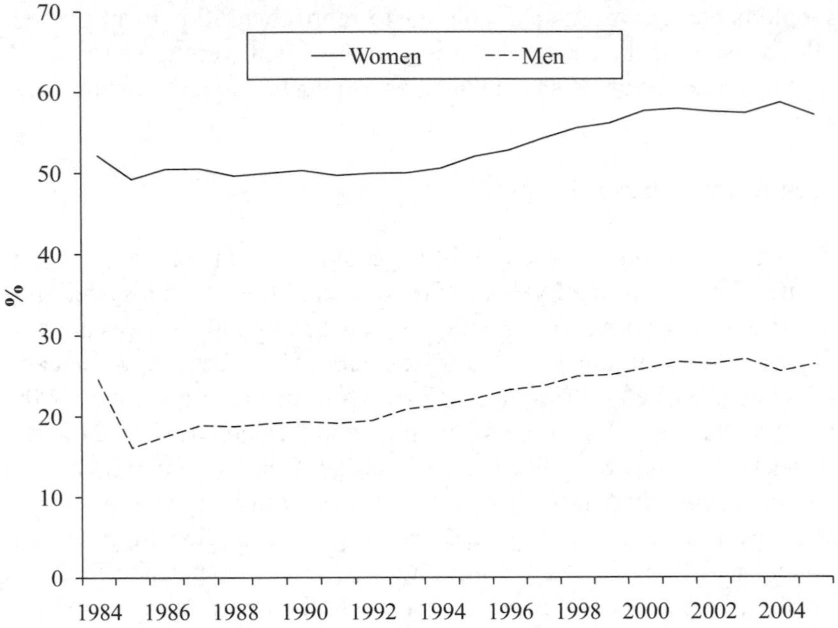

SOURCE: Caisse nationale d'assurance vieillesse (CNAV) (data cover Metropolitan France and exclude early retirement).

posal of the current government would worsen further the situation of future retirees.

At the end of 2009, the government announced that a law on pensions would be passed in 2010. The main objective of the new law, which was passed by Parliament in the autumn of 2010, is to further slow down pension expenditure through new cuts in benefits. The main measure is to raise the legal retirement age by 2 years, increasing the minimum age from 60 to 62 and the age at which people may retire without a penalty from 65 to 67. The increase is supposed to take place very quickly—the minimum age is to increase over the next 6 years so that people born in 1956 will have to wait until age 62 to retire in 2018.[6] Although the government is planning for a slight increase in the financial resources of pension plans, this will not be sufficient to cover future

Figure 8.2 Generosity of the Pension System (Average Pension Expenditure per Older Person/per capita GDP)

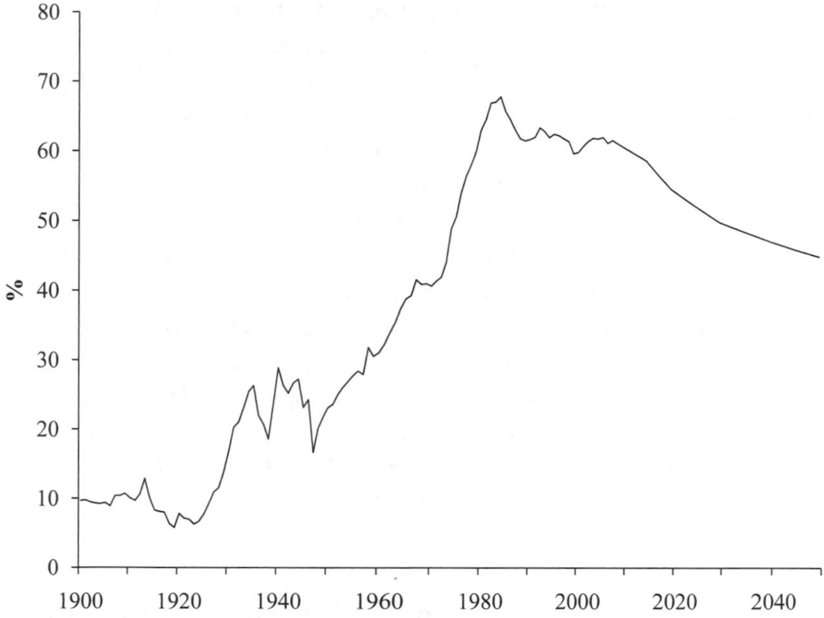

NOTE: An older person is defined as age 60 or over.
SOURCES: Reimat (2001), for the period 1900–1995; COR (2010) for the period 1996–2050; Institut national de la statistique et des études économiques (INSEE) for demographic projections.

pension expenditure. The new law is not designed to finance future pensions, but to reduce pension expenditure. As a result of the new law and previous reforms, by 2050, the ratio of average pension expenditure per older person to per capita GDP will fall to the same level as in the late 1960s.

There is no economic constraint that justifies such a dramatic decline in the standard of living of retirees. According to official long-term projections, the total population should increase by 12 percent over the next 40 years. Over the same period, real GDP is expected to roughly double (projected growth ranges from 95 percent to 115 percent depending on macroeconomic assumptions). There is thus ample leeway to increase the standard of living of the entire population, in all age groups. The crucial issue behind the debate on pensions deals with how current output is shared between retirees and the rest of the population.

Over the past 60 years, gains in labor productivity have been used to increase real wages, to finance social protection via increases in social contributions and to reduce the duration of work time (Table 8.1). However, we may distinguish two different periods, 1950–1979 and 1980–2008. Productivity gains were much higher during the first period than the second one. During the first period, 75 percent of productivity gains were used to increase real wages, 15 percent to reduce work time, and a little more than 10 percent to finance social protection. The profit share, the share of factor income going to capital, remained fairly stable. Over the second period, productivity gains were used in about equal proportions to increase real wages (31 percent) and to reduce work time (29 percent). About 15 percent was used to finance social protection. Since the late 1970s, productivity gains have also fueled a rise in the profit share, as is also true in many other countries around the world (Ellis and Smith 2007).

Table 8.1 Past and Projected Distribution of Productivity Gains (Annual Increase, %)

	1950–1979	1980–2008	Official retirement system projections 2009–2050
Real net wage per worker	3.97	0.64	1.6 –1.8
Reduction in average annual work time	0.80	0.61	0
Increase in social contributions	0.55	0.31	0
Change in profit share	−0.08	0.48	0
Hourly labor productivity	5.24	2.04	1.6 –1.8

NOTE: Figures show average annual increase. For example, from 1950 to 1979, the real net wage per worker increased by 3.97 percent per year on average.
SOURCE: INSEE, national accounts (authors' calculations).

The French government's scenario for the future in retirement projections is quite different from patterns of the past. The government claims that there will be no increase in social contributions and no reductions in work time, despite the persistence of massive unemployment. Since the profit share is at a historically high level, no one is suggesting future increases. The implicit assumption behind official retirement system projections is therefore that all productivity gains should translate into an increase in real wages. In the short run, it might be desirable to increase wages faster than other sources of income. However, such a policy is not sustainable, either politically or socially, over the medium or long run. Other approaches to distribution of productivity gains might help in thinking about how to reform the French pension system for the better.

REFORMING THE FRENCH PENSION SYSTEM FOR THE BETTER

Changes made to the French pension system over the past 20 years have gradually altered the way workers acquire pension rights. Researchers often classify France as a country that has carried out parametric pension reforms, a term which gives the impression that the fundamental principles that govern the distribution of pensions have not changed. However, if they stay in place, these reforms will result in drastic reductions in pensions, similar in scope to those that will result from the Swedish systemic reform. Therefore, we argue that the French pension system is in the midst of a fundamental change. We also argue that a reform of the French pension system is needed, not only to restore an adequate level of pensions, but also to modernize the French pension system in line with changes that have taken place in the labor market. Such a reform would provide an opportunity to strengthen the principles that have guided the construction of the French pension system up to now.

Guiding Principles for the Pension System

One of the principles underlying the French pension system up until the late 1980s is that pensions are equivalent to continued payment of wages. Retirees received a periodic payment throughout their remaining lives, a payment that represented a proportion of their highest wages. This pension allowed retirees to maintain the position they held in the hierarchy of earnings before reaching retirement, not only upon retirement but also beyond, since the pension kept pace with current wages. In keeping with this principle, the pension was calculated on the basis of wages, not on the basis of savings or contributions, hence the importance of the replacement rate.

A second principle is that pensions are financed through socialization of wages, which is the underlying rationale of a pay-as-you-go retirement system. The concept of socialization of wages refers to social protection systems in which contributions are paid to a common fund, so they are not the property of individual workers but rather belong collectively to contributing workers and beneficiaries. In the case of pensions, such a system does not involve a buildup of savings. Instead, it is based on the acquisition of pension rights by workers over the course of their careers. The financing of the pension system is geared to "paying for pensions," the title Tony Lynes gave to his study of the French retirement system (1985), rather than saving for retirement.

A pension system based on socialization of wages can attribute pension rights in many ways, as shown by the large variety of rules used under such systems in different countries. Pensions may be calculated on the basis of wages over the whole duration of working life, a portion of working life, or career end wages. The French system traditionally based pensions either on career end wages (as in the public sector) or the highest wages of the career (as in the private sector General Plan). The age at which the pension is first drawn may affect its amount, as does the number of years of contributions. Workers with high earnings may get a lower replacement rate than those with low earnings. Under a system based on socialization of wages, pension rights can be attributed not only on the basis of earnings but also for periods spent outside employment, for example, during unemployment, child rearing, and schooling. Such a system may even attribute extra pension rights to workers who have been engaged in physically taxing occupations.

With the correct rules, a system based on socialization of wages can guarantee a high replacement rate for retirees. It can also ensure that retirees share in the gains in productivity achieved by active workers, as was the case for many years in France, before the reforms enacted since the 1980s. As national output increases, both retirees and active workers can share in the increase, both seeing the purchasing power of their remuneration—their wage or their pension—rise. The French system could be reformed in such a way as to guarantee a high level of pensions throughout retirement, with a high replacement rate and pensions in payment indexed to current wages.

Another way of sharing the results of gains in productivity is to cut back on the time devoted to employment over a lifetime. This can be done through a decrease in work time during the career (shorter work weeks, more vacation days, and increased use of sabbaticals or other forms of leave) and through a cutback in the number of years spent in employment, by increasing the age at which young people begin to work and/or decreasing the retirement age. Such a reform is economically feasible if labor productivity is increasing because fewer hours of work can produce the same or more output.

Ways to Reform the Pension System for the Better

We now turn to measures that could improve the French pension system. The first is to reinstate the replacement rate as the system's main objective. The second is to ensure that the system continues to reduce work time over the life cycle. Finally, we examine ways to augment system finances.

Reinstate the replacement rate as the main objective of the retirement system

The retirement system should guarantee a clearly defined replacement rate for people who have worked over a full career, along with a definition of a full career that is attainable for the majority of workers. Successive reforms have obscured changes in the effective replacement rate by changing the parameters used in the formula for calculating pensions. This is especially true for the General Plan. It is also the case to some extent in the plan for public sector workers. The supplementary plans do not use a replacement rate to calculate pensions; however, until the 1990s, their pensions more than kept pace with wages, resulting in a rise in replacement rates over time.

In the General Plan, several key parameters—indexation of past wages, the number of years used to calculate the reference wage, the number of years of work required for a full pension, and indexation of pensions payments—have been changed in such a way as to lower replacement rates. However, the drop in replacement rates has been obscured by the fact that the rate of 50 percent of wages under the social security ceiling has been maintained in the formula for calculating pensions.

The plan for public sector employees has maintained the same full replacement rate, namely 75 percent for a full career. The reference wage in the public sector has remained the wage of the last six months of the career. However, as in the General Plan, the number of years of work considered to constitute a full career has increased. Furthermore, indexation of pensions in payment has switched from indexation on current public sector wages to indexation on prices.

The outlook for replacement rates guaranteed by supplementary plans is particularly bleak. If current trends continue, the replacement rate of supplementary plans will drop even further than that of the General Plan or the plan for public sector employees (Conseil d'orientation des retraites [COR] 2007, p. 64). If labor unions are unable to negotiate increases in contribution rates, supplementary pensions will decrease more quickly and more drastically than General Plan pensions. This implies a particularly large drop in overall replacement rates for private sector workers whose wages are above the social security ceiling, which is equal to about 1.3 times the average wage. The only way to maintain overall replacement rates for private sector workers would be for the General Plan to compensate by raising its replacement rates.

Labor unions sometimes call for a target replacement rate. In the case of private sector plans, the target includes both General Plan pensions and supplementary pensions. In the early 1980s, when the Socialist Party came to power, the labor union objective was 70 percent for workers with wages below the social security ceiling—50 percent from the General Plan plus 20 percent from the supplementary plans (Lynes 1985, p. 37), with more for low-wage workers. At the end of the 1980s, the target replacement rate cited by one major labor union, the Confédération générale du travail (CGT), was 75 percent for a career of

37.5 years (Castel 2009, p. 88). In 1992, another major union, the Confédération française démocratique du travail (CFDT), claimed that the replacement rate should be 75 percent of the wage over the 10 highest years for a full career for most workers, with a slightly higher rate for those with low wages (Castel 2009, p. 179). In recent years, there have been fewer calls for a target replacement rate, in part because successive reforms have obscured real replacement rates. Nonetheless, unions continue to demand a replacement rate of at least 75 percent for a full career.

As the unions demand, the replacement rate is somewhat higher for those with wages close to the minimum. In 1984, just after the minimum contributory pension was introduced, the replacement rate for workers who had always earned the minimum wage came to about 87 percent—67 percent from the General Plan (the minimum contributory pension) plus 20 percent from the supplementary plan ARRCO. Subsequently, the minimum contributory pension declined in relation to wages. The 2003 retirement system reform law promised a replacement rate (the minimum contributory pension plus a supplementary pension) of 85 percent for workers with a full career at the minimum wage.

In recent statements on retirement policy, the administration has focused on the purchasing power of retirees, rather than on the relationship between pensions and wages. A discussion document released in the spring of 2010 in preparation for the 2010 reform law states that pension levels will improve, since the average pension of all retirees is projected to outpace inflation. Indeed, official projections foresee a rise in pensions, net of social contributions, of about 20 percent above inflation between 2008 and 2030 (COR 2010, p. 30). The government discussion document states: "This improvement in pension levels results from the guarantee of purchasing power for retirees granted by law and from improvements in pension levels of future retirees due to increases in wage levels" (Government of France 2010, p. 5). The document does not mention that the same projections foresee a rise over the same period of between 30 and 40 percent in real wages net of social contributions, depending on the assumptions used. This implies that the ratio of the average net pension to the average net wage will decline by between 7 and 14 percent. Far from enabling retirees to share in productivity gains, pensions are projected to drop steadily in relation to wages.

In keeping with the idea that a pension is a continued wage, we include in the notion of the replacement rate not only the initial pension paid out upon retirement but also pensions paid throughout the period of retirement. In the past, pensions in payment were indexed to current wages, but they are now indexed to prices. This policy will result in a lowering of pensions in relation to current wages for all categories of retirees. If continued, this policy will deprive retirees of a fair share of gains in labor productivity and increases in national output.

The 2010 government discussion document states that the purchasing power of retirees will be guaranteed, meaning that pensions in payment will keep pace with inflation: "pensions will not decrease in euros . . . their purchasing power will continue to be guaranteed, as is the case today, thanks to yearly indexing of retirement pensions to inflation. This guarantee of purchasing power despite price increases is . . . essential to maintaining confidence in our retirement system" (Government of France 2010, p. 5). The government thus explicitly puts forward constant purchasing power, rather than a constant replacement rate, as the norm for the retirement system.

The quest for a new norm other than the replacement rate has motivated an interest among some members of Parliament in a radical transformation of the whole retirement system into one based either on accumulation of points, such as is done in the French mandatory supplementary plans, or on notional accounts, such as those used in the new social security pension system of Sweden. One attraction of such systems is that they entail no explicit reference to replacement rates.

Gearing the pension system to wages implies that the means-tested minimum old-age income for people age 65 and over (as well as to those who have attained the age of 60 and are considered unable to work) should be indexed to wages. However, at present it is set to rise in line with prices, a policy that will leave more retirees in poverty (COR 2007, p. 98). Governments may enact exceptional increases to raise it more quickly, as the Sarkozy government has done. By 2012, after the exceptional increase, the minimum old-age income will be equal to only about 48 percent of median income, well below the poverty threshold of 60 percent of median income (Concialdi 2010, p. 163). It is essential that the minimum income for the elderly, like pensions, be indexed to wages to prevent poverty and enable older people to enjoy the same general rise in the standard of living as the rest of the population.

As labor unions have demanded, the replacement rate should be about the same for the public sector and the private sector. Currently, debates on retirement policy for the two sectors tend to center on decreasing pensions for the public sector rather than improving pensions in both sectors.

The 2003 reform launched an experiment in funded pensions for the public sector, a change that can hardly be considered to further convergence with private sector plans. In the public sector, bonuses, which represent 20 percent of pay on average, are not included in pensionable salary. The 2003 reform did not integrate bonuses into pensionable salary. Instead, the 2003 law created a mandatory funded defined contribution money purchase pension plan financed by employer and employee contributions levied on bonuses.[7] The level of pensions under this plan will vary with returns on pension fund investments. Since the plan is funded and defined contribution, public sector employees now close to retirement will receive very little from this arrangement. It will take many years for the new plan to pay out a full benefit. Rather than experiment with a mandatory funded plan, it would be preferable that bonuses be integrated into pensionable salary. If bonuses were recognized as part of wages in the context of the pay-as-you-go system, public sector workers would quickly see their pensions rise.

Reduce work time over the life cycle

In France, as in other wealthy industrialized countries, the duration of the average work week has been dropping ever since the industrial revolution. This trend affects the legal length of the work week, now 35 hours for most French employees, the number of days in a year that employees work, and the number of years they work over a lifetime. Some of the reductions in work time take the form of unemployment or underemployment, which strikes individuals unequally. In an economy with productivity gains, a collective reduction in work time is one way to share the gains equally. Collective forms of work time reduction—reductions in the work week, increases in the number of days of leave, and increases in the duration of retirement—can further social justice and help to prevent unemployment (Concialdi 2010, pp. 155–158).

Since 1993, the number of years of contributions required to receive a full pension has risen. The 2003 retirement reform law formulated a rule by which the requirement for the years of contributions is henceforth to be adjusted. The rule is ostensibly designed to maintain a constant ratio between work time and retirement time. The number of years of contributions required for a full pension is to increase in line with increases in life expectancy: for every three additional months of life expectancy at 60, the insurance period required for a full pension is to be extended by about two months (COR 2007, fiche 11). This rule for splitting gains in life expectancy between work and retirement is not the only possible norm. Gains in life expectancy could be entirely allocated to retirement.

In any case, the length of a "full" career as defined by the retirement system does not necessarily correspond to actual work lives. Many people retire with less than a full career and some retire after working longer. As the requirement for a full career lengthens, people will not necessarily work longer or retire at a later age. Many may retire as early as possible, at 60, with less than a full career. The requirement for a full career does not determine how long employees will actually work and contribute to the retirement system.

Why not lengthen the period of retirement still more, as has been the case historically? This is a question of social choice. Do people prefer to devote more time to employment, which might contribute to an increase in total output and hence an increase in consumption of goods and services? Or do people prefer to spend more time in retirement, that is, free of the bonds of employment but receiving a continued wage?

Up until now, most people retiring at 60 have reached a "full" career for retirement purposes. However, the average age at which people begin to contribute is rising. A Ministry of Labor study examines the employment record of different birth cohorts at age 30. For the cohort born in 1942, more than 40 percent of men and more than 60 percent of women had not reached a full career of 40 years by age 60 (in 2002). For the cohort born in 1974, 75 percent of men and 80 percent of women will not have reached a full career by age 60 (in 2034) (Concialdi 2010, p. 117). As the number of years of contributions required for a full pension increases, retirement with a full pension at 60 will become impossible for many people, mostly due to the fact that younger people devote more years to studies. As the requirement for a "full" career lengthens, many employees may find it difficult or impossible to meet.

The current administration has sponsored a legal increase in the age at which workers may begin to draw a pension, from 60 to 62. The same law will increase by the same increment of two years the age at which a full rate pension is awarded to people with short careers. That age is now 65 and it is scheduled to increase to 67.

Currently, the vast majority of employees (about 80 percent) begin to draw a pension either at 60 or at 65. Those who begin to draw a pension at 60 have generally contributed over enough years to qualify for a full pension as of that age. Those who begin to draw a pension at 65 have generally not contributed long enough to qualify for a full pension; therefore, they wait to get their pension until age 65, since an incomplete career is less heavily penalized after that age. Most of the people in the first group are men, and most of those in the second group are women (Concialdi 2010, p. 111). An increase in the retirement age would probably have a strong impact on retirement behavior: those with a sufficient insurance period would tend to retire at the new higher minimum age, and those with an insufficient insurance period would tend to wait until age 67.

Pushing back the age at which an employee may begin to draw a pension from 60 to 62 would be particularly hard on those who began to work young enough to reach a full career by 60. It would also be hard on those whose life expectancy is low, since their "retirement expectancy" (the length of time they can expect to spend in retirement) would be reduced. Retirement expectancy is correlated to gender, since women live longer than men on average, and to income level. An increase in the earliest retirement age would have a great impact on employees with relatively low incomes, whose life expectancy is generally low.

What is the rationale behind increasing the retirement age? On the face of it, the objective is to increase the number of workers contributing to the retirement system and reduce the number of pensioners. Yet it could be argued that maintaining the age of 60 would enable older workers to profit from gains in productivity in the form of time free from employment. It could also help to contribute to full employment.

Another issue at stake is simply the well-being of retirees. Retirement should be a time when individuals are in sufficiently good health to take advantage of freedom from employment. In other words, it should be a period of true *jubilación*, as the Spanish say, rather than a period of retreat (*retraite* in French) from life.

One aspect of retirement that has given rise to ongoing controversy in France is the treatment of workers who have been subjected to physically demanding work conditions. Such conditions include carrying heavy loads, working at night, and exposure to excessive noise, extreme temperatures, and toxic materials. All of these conditions can lead to health problems, decrease life expectancy, and increase the incidence of physical handicaps. The 2003 reform law stated that physically harmful work conditions should be taken into account upon retirement, but the questions of the definition of such conditions and how they would be taken into account were left up to negotiations between national employers' organizations and labor unions. Discussions broke off in 2008 and no agreement was reached.

The employers' position is that, in order to qualify for retirement advantages, an employee must obtain a medical certificate attesting that past working conditions have caused the employee to suffer from health problems, a point of view the government currently supports. Labor unions demand a collective definition of physically harmful work conditions and compensation in the form of early retirement for workers who have been exposed to such conditions. The unions focus on work conditions rather than on individual employees' health status. According to the unions, if a worker has been exposed over a certain length of time to physically harmful conditions, he or she should be entitled to retire early, whether or not the conditions have caused health problems prior to retirement. This is in keeping with the idea that retirement should be a period of freedom from the constraints of employment rather than a period of inactivity for people who are no longer capable of working.

The French retirement system accords pension rights on the basis of periods devoted to certain activities other than employment, notably for mothers who have raised children. Pension rights are also awarded for periods of unemployment, which count as periods of insurance for the calculation of career length. However, a recent revaluation of the minimum contributory pension, enacted by the 2003 retirement reform law, excludes insurance periods that do not give rise to payment of contributions, such as child care or unemployment. In other words, pension rights awarded for such activities are considered noncontributory. It can be argued that such periods are contributory in that they contribute to the economy and to the retirement system. The tradition of attributing pension rights for activities other than employment could be maintained and even expanded. For example, pension rights could be attributed for periods devoted to studies.

Increase pension system revenues

A reform of the retirement system for the better is financially feasible. Increases in national output due to gains in labor productivity could be used in part to finance higher pensions over a longer lapse of time. It would still be possible to increase consumption for the population below retirement age.

A number of specific measures could increase the revenues of the retirement system. Certain forms of remuneration for private sector workers are partially or totally exempt from contributions to the retirement system. This is the case for profit sharing (*intéressement, participation*), employer payments to employee savings accounts, including employee retirement savings accounts (PERCO), stock options and company stock distributed to employees, employee retirement plans, and other employee benefit plans (e.g., supplementary health and disability insurance). If exemptions on all of these forms of remuneration were abolished, the revenues of the General Plan would increase considerably.[8]

Furthermore, the purpose of some of these exemptions is to encourage company retirement benefit plans, namely employee retirement savings plans and company pension plans. When such plans give rise to exemptions from contributions to mandatory plans, they undermine mandatory plans by depriving them of revenues. Abolition of such exemptions would help to protect the finances of mandatory pension plans.

Contribution rates could rise over time without causing hardship for current workers. The government's 2010 discussion document on pension reform excludes the possibility of increasing workers' contributions. It states that an increase in contribution rates would be detrimental to the economy. It would reduce workers' net income, and "such a reduction in households' standard of living would affect growth and employment, through its impact on consumption" (Government of France 2010, p. 7). The document neglects to mention that pensioners also live in households whose consumption contributes to growth and employment.

CONCLUSION

In France, employer-provided and individual pension accounts play a marginal role in the distribution of pension benefits, which are organized on a pay-as-you-go basis. However, income from property accounts for a large share of retirees' incomes, around 30 percent. With such a system, the standard of living of French retirees is roughly the same today as that of other households, a result that can be considered fair.

As in other countries, however, this picture will change over time. The reforms implemented over the past 20 years are due to dramatically reduce the generosity of pension benefits. One of the main consequences of the downsizing of social security pensions is that market forces will become more powerful, subjecting workers to more market risk. Insofar as the main goal of social protection systems is to protect workers from these risks, an ideal pension system should counterbalance this trend. The French experience shows that pension systems can protect workers without prefunding, so that workers do not have to bear financial risks. Reinforcement of public pay-as-you-go plans should be one of the main goals of an "ideal" pension system.

Employment is another key issue. Workers can acquire social security pension rights mainly by participating fully in the labor market. Whatever conception of social security we may have, full employment is a condition for providing economic security to workers. As stated by William H. Beveridge in 1944 in his book *Full Employment in a Free Society*, full employment is one "of the assumptions of Social Security: the assumption that employment is maintained and mass unemployment prevented." Hence, when thinking about the ideal pension system, we also have to consider the functioning of the labor market as a whole. Pension systems can be seen as powerful tools for reducing work time. As such, they can promote full employment.

The organization of pension systems raises crucial issues concerning distribution of both incomes and paid work. Since the industrial revolution, productivity gains have allowed workers to achieve better living standards while working less over their lifetimes. It is impossible to predict how large these productivity gains will be in the future. However, we can reasonably assume that trends observed over the past

20 or 30 years will not suddenly come to a stop. Hence, the question of how to share these gains will remain on the political agenda. In fact, it is possible to continue to improve standards of living, both for retirees and for the population as a whole.

Appendix 8A
General Plan

Length of Insurance Period and Calculation of the Pension

In calculating the pension, the French General Plan for private sector employees takes into account both the age at which the pension is awarded and the number of years of contributions. This appendix describes the rules before application of the reform enacted in the autumn of 2010, which will gradually increase the age at which workers may begin to draw a pension and the number of years of contributions required for a full pension. Before this reform goes into effect, workers may begin to draw a pension as of age 60. If a retiree has contributed over the insurance period required for a full pension, the pension is equal to 50 percent of the reference wage.

The formula for calculating the pension is $T \times W^* \times D/D^*$, where T is the pension rate, equal to 50 percent for retirement at age 60 with a full insurance period. W^* is the reference wage, currently the average of the highest 25 years of wages under the social security ceiling, with past wages revalued in line with prices. D^* is the insurance period required for a full pension at age 60, currently 40 years for private sector workers turning 60 between 2003 and 2008 (born between 1943 and 1948). D is the worker's actual length of insurance, limited to D^* for the calculation. People who work more than the full insurance period get a separate pension bonus. The pension is reduced if the person has worked less than the duration required for a full pension. Whatever the age at which the person begins to draw a pension, the pension is reduced by a fraction equal to the number of quarters of contributions divided by the number of quarters required for a full pension (D/D^*).

If a person has worked less than the duration required for a full pension and begins to draw a pension before age 65, the pension is further reduced by reducing the pension rate. The reduction of the rate is equal to 1.25 percent multiplied by one of the following, whichever is smaller: the number of quarters of contributions missing in relation to the full insurance requirement or the number of quarters by which the individual's age is short of age 65.

For example, the pension for a person born in 1944 and retiring in 2008 at age 64 with 152 quarters of insurance would be calculated as follows: $D^* = 160$ quarters and therefore $D/D^* = 152/160 = 0.95$. $T = 0.50$, but it must be adjusted, in this case, by the number of quarters the individual is short of 65 years of age: 0.50 – (0.0125 × 4 quarters) = 0.45. The pension therefore is 0.45 × W^* × 0.95 = W^* × 0.4275.

Notes

1. The main law establishing pension plans for civil servants dates back to 1853.
2. The plan for cadres is AGIRC. Today, a second plan, ARRCO, covers all private sector employees.
3. For private sector employees, on average, the General Plan provided a replacement rate of 49 percent and the supplementary schemes provided an additional 34 percent.
4. Since the early 1990s, income from property has been taxed to some extent to finance health insurance.
5. Called the Fonds de solidarité vieillesse or FSV.
6. The age at which people may retire without a penalty is set to begin increasing in 2016. People retiring in 2023 and after will have to wait until the age of 67.
7. This plan is called the RAFP (Régime additionnel de la fonction publique). Contributions are equal to 10 percent of bonuses, limited to amounts below 20 percent of salary. The employer and the employee each pay 5 percent.
8. According to an official report published in 2007 (Cour des Comptes 2007), in 2005, exemptions from contributions granted to various forms of employee remuneration (for low wages, profit sharing plans, employee savings plans, stock options and distribution to employees of shares, and company benefit plans for employees) resulted in a net loss for the social security system (retirement, family allowances, health insurance, etc.) of €13.5 billion. The same year, social contributions paid to social security came to €152.2 billion; total revenues of social security amounted to about €244 billion (Commission des comptes de la sécurité sociale 2006).

References

apRoberts, Lucy, and Pierre Concialdi. 2009. "Pension Reform and Personal Provision of Retirement Income in France." In *Personal Provision of Retirement Income: Meeting the Needs of Older People?* Jim Stewart and Gerard Hughes, eds. Cheltenham, UK: Edward Elgar, pp. 15–37.

Beveridge, William H. 1944. *Full Employment in a Free Society*. London: George Allen and Unwin.

Castel, Nicolas. 2009. *La retraite des syndicats: Revenu différé contre salaire continué*. Paris: La Dispute.

Commission des Comptes de la Sécurité Sociale (CCSS). 2006. "Les comptes de la sécurité sociale: Résultats 2005, Prévisions 2006–2007." Rapport Tome 1. Paris: CCSS.

Concialdi, Pierre. 2010. *Retraites, en finir avec le catastrophisme. Idées neuves contre un déclin programmé.* Paris: Editions Lignes de repères.

COR. 2007. "Retraites: 20 fiches d'actualisation pour les rendez-vous de 2008." Fifth report of the Conseil d'Orientation des Retraites. Paris: Conseil d'Orientation des Retraites.

———. 2010. "Retraites: Perspectives actualisées à moyen et long terme en vue du rendez-vous de 2010." Eighth report of the Conseil d'orientation des retraites. Paris: Conseil d'Orientation des Retraites.

Cour des Comptes. 2007. "Rapport sur l'application des lois de financement de la sécurité sociale." Paris: Cour des Comptes.

DREES. 2004. "Le taux de remplacement du salaire par la retraite pour les salariés de la génération 1934 ayant effectué une carrière complète." Etudes et résultats no. 312. Paris: Direction de la Recherche, des Études, de l'Évaluation et des Statistiques.

———. 2008. "4,4 millions de pensionnés au minimum contributif en 2004." Études et résultats no. 639. Paris: Direction de la Recherche, des Études, de l'Évaluation et des Statistiques.

Ellis, Lucy, and Kathryn Smith. 2007. "The Global Upward Trend in the Profit Share." BIS Working Paper no. 231. Basel: Bank for International Settlements. http://www.bis.org/pub/work231.pdf (accessed June 24, 2011).

Government of France. 2010. "Document d'orientation sur la réforme des retraites." Paris: Government of France. http://www.travail-emploi-sante.gouv.fr/IMG/pdf/Document_d_orientation_sur_la_reforme_des_retraites.pdf (accessed June 24, 2011).

Lynes, Tony. 1985. "Paying for Pensions: The French Experience." STICERD Occasional Paper no. 9. London: Suntory and Toyota International Centers for Economics and Related Disciplines.

Reimat, Anne. 2001. "Histoire quantitative de la prise en charge de la vieillesse en France, XIXe et XXe siècles: Les régimes de retraites." *Economies et sociétés* 28(July–August): 1097–1193.

9
Aging in the Shadow of the Three Pillars

A Generation of Pension Debates in Switzerland (1972–2010)

Matthieu Leimgruber
Paul Bairoch Institute of Economic History, University of Geneva

THE BEST PENSION SYSTEM IN THE WORLD?

Since its consecration by the World Bank in its well-known report, *Averting the Old Age Crisis* (1994), as well as its adoption a decade later in an EU directive on pension funds, the three-pillar doctrine has been one of the potent metaphors of contemporary pension reform (Coron 2007; Tausch 2002). The principles underlying this model are well known: state pay-as-you-go pensions (first pillar) should remain a basic component, to which occupational (second pillar) and individual (third pillar) prefunded pensions should be added. This structure may seem at first a neutral and factual depiction of the inherent nature of modern pension systems. Yet, the pillar doctrine has a strong normative dimension: it aims both to contain the scope of pay-as-you-go state (social security) pensions and to favor funded solutions whose management is devolved to private financial institutions.

Switzerland occupies a special position in this reform discourse. Indeed, the country is a pioneer of the three-pillar doctrine, whose principles have been anchored in the Federal Constitution since 1972. In early 2010, a leading pension consultancy firm even awarded Switzerland, and in particular its mandatory second occupational pillar, a gold medal, designating it as the "best pension system in the world" (Mercer 2010).[1] This ranking underscored the enthusiasm for the Swiss pension system among the financial actors who are involved in its management. Consider this somewhat arrogant statement from a Swiss Re economist: “The Swiss pension system comes off rather well in comparison to the rotten social insurance systems of its European neighbors [and] rightly deserves the high esteem it receives from abroad: its foundations are properly laid” (Trauth 2000). More could be said of the international diffusion of the multi-pillar doctrine, notably on the role played by Swiss insurers in this process before the 1994 adoption of the doctrine by the World Bank (Leimgruber 2009). Moreover, as is often the case when foreign national examples are summoned and designated as models, accolades and rankings often remain silent on the controversies and struggles that structure these national systems.

On March 7, 2010, a large majority (72.7 percent) of Swiss voters turned down a proposed reduction in the conversion rate that determines the calculation of second pillar benefits, which would have effectively reduced those benefits.[2] This reduction, which had been presented as a necessity to ensure the long-term financing of occupational pensions facing demographic aging and uncertain financial returns, was supported by the Federal Council (the executive branch), right-wing parties—who enjoyed a comfortable majority in the Federal Parliament at that time—as well as business associations, the pension lobby, and the insurance industry. The main Swiss trade union (UNIA), the Socialist Party, and consumers’ associations strongly opposed the proposed cut in pension benefits. As soon as the conversion rate had been accepted by Parliament in late 2008, these forces launched a popular referendum that gathered 125,000 signatures in 30 days, whereas only 50,000 in 90 days were necessary.[3] A stormy political debate preceded the March 2010 vote. The main Swiss business association, Economiesuisse, allegedly spent 10 million Swiss francs (CHF) in favor of a “yes” vote (Wuthrich 2010).[4] However, the well-oiled campaign of political power, mainstream media, and business associations floundered: the denunciation of “pension theft” and of the meddling of financial interests into pensions carried the day.

The long-term impact of the referendum vote is still uncertain, but its importance cannot be underestimated. First, the referendum underscores the increasing polarization of occupational pension debates, after decades during which these had remained confined to experts. The March vote also has a historic dimension. It is the first time since

1972, when the three-pillar doctrine was added to the Constitution, that Swiss voters have expressed their views on the second pillar. After a generation of maturation, occupational pensions now occupy a central position in Swiss old age provision. This chapter analyzes these three aspects so as to place the March 2010 vote in a larger historical context and to highlight the antagonisms that currently agitate the discussions of the Swiss second pillar.

THE TRAJECTORY OF THE THREE-PILLAR DOCTRINE IN SWITZERLAND

This chapter cannot retrace the century-long trajectory of Swiss occupational pensions (see Box 9.1 for a short summary). I will instead underline five key features that have shaped the pension system (see Table 9.1 for more information on the different pillars).

First, the histories of the different pillars of the Swiss pension system have always been deeply interconnected. The existence of a strong private pension lobby has contributed both to the belated introduction of the Old-Age and Survivors' Insurance (AHV, the first pillar, introduced in 1947) and to the moderate expansion of this pay-as-you-go basic social security pension during the postwar growth decades. This moderation favored the gradual and selective development of pension plans and enabled them to remain largely autonomous vis-à-vis the federal state. The 1972 vote on the three-pillar doctrine not only aimed to improve pensioners' incomes by granting a supplementary benefit to almost all wage earners. It first and foremost aimed to contain (in the anticommunist meaning of the period) the development of the pay-as-you-go AHV and to preserve funded pensions from being marginalized by the "people's pensions" project. The three-pillar doctrine succeeded in blocking this alternative path and steered the pension system in another direction. From 1972 onward, all future improvements of pensions have been dependent on the expansion of funded occupational pensions (the second pillar). I will return below to the long-term consequences of this crucial crossroads, but we can immediately grasp its importance by examining Figure 9.1. Since the 1970s, old-age pensions have represented about half of overall social expenditures. However,

Box 9.1 Origins of the Three-Pillar Doctrine in Switzerland[5]

1918–1948: A divided pension system

With the exception of a handful of pioneering firms and public administrations, the "big bang" of occupational provision can be dated from 1916. A federal tax on war profits enacted that year introduced special deductions for firms that created a pension or welfare fund for their workers. By the end of World War I, life insurance companies sold their first group pension contracts and participated in the development of the pension market. By 1930, 18 percent of the nonfarm workforce was covered by funded plans with reserves that represented 26 percent of GDP in 1937. The development of occupational pensions was facilitated by the failure to enact state pensions at the federal level (old-age and survivors' benefits, or AHV) in 1931. After slowing down during the economic depression of the 1930s, the expansion of pension plans accelerated during World War II. The federal government also launched a new AHV project during the war, which was finally overwhelmingly accepted by the voters in 1947. The first AHV pension checks were modest (amounting to 10–15 percent of wages), so as neither to compete with existing pension plans nor hinder the creation of new ones.

1948–1972: The three-pillar doctrine versus the people's pensions

During the postwar growth decades, an informal division of tasks was established between the AHV (the future first pillar) and occupational plans (the future second pillar). While the AHV provided a basic pay-as-you-go benefit, occupational plans increased their coverage from 20 percent (1955) to 30 percent (1970) of all wage earners, offered very differentiated benefits, and played a key role in personnel management. The financial reserves of the occupational plans were already considerable and reached 40 percent of Swiss GDP by 1970. The three-pillar doctrine was elaborated during the 1960s. This concept was favored by the political right, business, and insurers and aimed to anchor occupational plans in the old-age retirement system and thus contain the expansion of the pay-as-you-go AHV. It was also supported by trade unions seduced by the idea that they might obtain a larger say in firm management through the boards of pension plans. The "people's pensions" was an alternative proposal favored by the left wing of the Socialist Party and other far-left groups. Its aim was to expand the pay-as-you-go component (AHV) of the pension system to the detriment of its funded plans. The three-pillar doctrine, at the core of which is the idea of mandatory second pillar occupational pensions, was finally accepted by a large majority of voters in 1972. The leadership of the Socialist Party, as well as trade union secretaries, contributed to this victory by convincing their rank and file of the necessity to implement a state mandate so as to guarantee pensions that would be both generous and partly co-managed by workers' representatives.

Unresolved issues on the scope and content of occupational plans were later addressed in the Federal Law on Occupational Pensions (BVG, 1982–1985), but this law did not address the demands made a decade earlier by the left and largely preserved the autonomy of occupational pension plans.

the relative importance of each pillar has changed. While AHV expenditure (as a percentage of GDP) has remained stable since 1980, second pillar expenditures have more than doubled during the same period, and prefunded pension expenditures now exceed those of the AHV. These numbers do not tell us anything about the respective importance of each pillar in pensioners' income, but they clearly illustrate the maturation of occupational provision. Today, as during the twentieth century, the pension pillars do not evolve in isolation. Unfortunately, the policy cycles followed by the AHV and the second pillar are seldom synchronized, which may blur a proper understanding of their enduring interconnections.

Second, despite state regulations, occupational provision remains a domain in which private interests retain a great deal of influence. Despite its institutional fragmentation (over 2,000 pension plans were in operation in 2010) and the existence of large pension plans in the public sector, occupational provision is dominated by a powerful lobby, composed of large autonomous corporate plans, a handful of life insurance companies, and various pension experts and consultancies. Insurers in particular have nurtured an important pensions market since the 1920s and have played a key role in shaping business perspectives on old-age provision.[6] By 2010, group insurance pension contracts covered about 40 percent of wage earners affiliated with mandatory second pillar pensions (BVG). Insurance companies also managed one-fifth of second

Table 9.1 The Swiss Three-Pillar Pension System (2010)

	Old-age and survivors' insurance (AHV, 1st pillar)	Occupational pensions (BVG, 2nd pillar)	Individual savings (3rd pillar)
Key institutions and actors	Confederation	2,430 pension plans: autonomous corporate plans, group contracts, and "collective foundations" (multi-employer plans)	Life insurance companies and banks
Coverage	Universal coverage	About 90 percent of the workforce Wage entry floor = CHF19,890 of annual income or 75% of a maximum AHV pension	Voluntary affiliation: approximately half of the working population subscribes to a "linked" 3rd pillar account ("3a account," see below)
Financing mode	Pay as you go: payroll tax (8.4% levied on all wages without ceiling, provides 75% of financing needs), state subsidies (20%), and AHV reserve fund (5%)	Funded: payroll tax (8–10% of wages); the wage ceiling above which the BVG payroll tax is not levied is equal to three times the maximum AHV pension.	Funded individual savings: voluntary contributions are capped. Wage earners with BVG coverage may contribute CHF6,566 per year, while self-employed without BVG coverage may contribute CHF32,832 per year.

Benefits	Ranging between CHF1,140–2,280 per month, mixed indexation (wages and prices) State authorities provide supplementary means-tested old-age assistance (AHV Ergänzungsleistungen; AVS)	Benefits and indexation procedures vary among pension plans. Benefits can also take the form of lump sums.	Annuities or lump sums
Reserves and assets	Approximately one year of expenditure (about CHF3 billion)	About CHF600 billion	About CHF60 billion
Replacement income	Combined AHV and BVG benefits should offer replacement rates of at least 60 percent of wages.		Negligible role in old-age provision, but key tax deduction for higher income population. Tax expenditure for 3rd pillar accounts cost CHF450 million to the Confederation each year.

Figure 9.1 Social Expenditure and Pension Expenditure (% of GDP, 1970–2007)

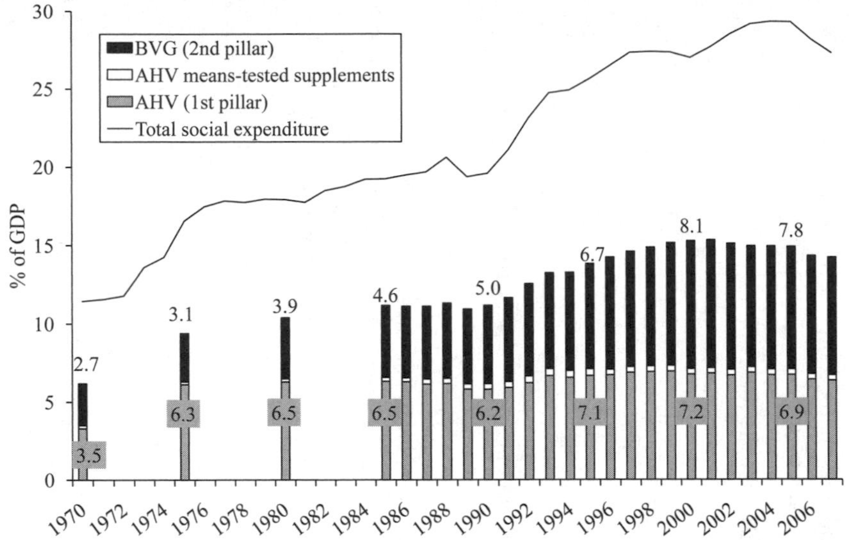

pillar pension reserves (about CHF125 billion). Occupational provision is the source for half of life insurance premiums levied in Switzerland.[7] Life insurers' prominence has been, and is still, a source of tension among business interests. Small- and medium-size entrepreneurs often resent the conditions imposed on them by insurance actuaries. However, the main business associations and actors of the pension industry agree on defending the basic principles of the three-pillar doctrine.

Third, the integration of trade unions into management of occupational pensions has led to ambivalent outcomes. Pension comanagement and workers' participation on pension boards was a longstanding union demand and has constituted a major activity for union representatives. These boards have increased trade union acquiescence toward business personnel management goals while making impossible any genuine "workers' control" of pension funds. Union participation in the three-pillar doctrine has thus reinforced funded old-age provision to the detriment of more redistributive pay-as-you-go provision.

Fourth, old-age benefits are only one facet of the second pillar. Since their inception, occupational plans have been used by employers to favor "labor peace" and facilitate personnel management. Tax deductions for pension plans have always been an important incentive for business. Fifth, the funded reserves of the second and third pillar are considerable. The pillar structure thus offers a profitable business activity for the insurance companies and banks that participate in the management and investment of pension reserves. For the reasons mentioned above, life insurers are particularly well entrenched at the core of occupational pension provision. Unsurprisingly, this situation has been criticized by the left and trade unions, which underscores the contradictions between the growing role of occupational provision in retirees' incomes and insurers' profit goals.

Finally, it is important to consider the Swiss pension system in an international comparison. Switzerland belongs to the leading OECD countries in terms of private social expenditure for health and pensions (Table 9.2). The Swiss pension system bears little resemblance to its French and German neighbors, but is much more similar to those in the Netherlands as well as the United Kingdom and the United States. The decentralization of Swiss occupational provision and insurers' involvement in pensions is similar to the systems in the United Kingdom and the United States, but the post-1972 expansion of the mandatory second pillar has brought Switzerland closer to the Dutch system, with one important difference. Large multi-employer plans linked to collective bargaining are central to Dutch occupational provision, while such institutions play a marginal role in Switzerland.

The elements enumerated above underscore the critical role of the mandatory second pillar in the Swiss pension system. After the 1972 vote, the history of occupational provision can be divided into three periods. From 1972 to 1982, the outcomes of the political negotiations on BVG legislation favored the expansion of pension plans while maintaining a mild regulatory framework. In a second phase, from 1982 to 2000, occupational pension provision continued to expand among the workforce while the issue of its regulation remained off the political agenda. These first two periods are briefly analyzed in the next section, and as we will see in the fourth section of this chapter, the current radicalization of second pillar controversies from 2000 onward is a direct consequence of this long-term maturation process.

Two opposing dynamics structure the post-1972 period. The first dynamic, fueled by demands from the political left and trade unions, has aimed to reinforce the collective and redistributive elements of the

Table 9.2 Private Social Expenditure: An International Comparison

	Mandatory and voluntary private social expenditure (% GDP, 2005)		Private social expenditure as a share of total social expenditure (%, 2005)	Pension funds assets (% GDP, 2007)
	Old age, health and disability	Only old age		
United States	10.1	3.8	38.9	140.6
Switzerland	8.4	5.3	29.3	151.9
Netherlands	8.3	4.1	28.5	149.1
United Kingdom	7.1	4.7	25.1	96.4
OECD average (30 countries)	2.9	1.5	11.8	111.0[a]
France	3.0	0.2	9.3	17.9
Germany	3.0	0.8	10.1	6.9

SOURCE: Federal Office of Statistics (OFS), Federal Social Insurance Administration (OFAS), and Financial Market Authority (FINMA).

[a] Pension fund assets as a percentage of overall OECD GDP.

second pillar, to bolster solidarity between their members, and to submit pension plans to stricter state regulation. Contrary to these aims, business forces and the pension lobby have fought to safeguard the autonomy of pension plans, develop the pension market, and limit the solidaristic dimensions of the second pillar. These two antagonistic dynamics are riddled with internal contradictions. How indeed is it possible to increase "social solidarity" in a second pillar whose original aim was to limit solidarity and redistribution? At the same time, recent pension controversies underscore how it is difficult for proponents of pension funding to disentangle themselves from the growing social obligations linked to the maturation of the second pillar.

THE THREE-PILLAR DOCTRINE IN PRACTICE (1972–2000)

The decade that followed the 1972 vote witnessed the abandonment of the pursuit of a second pillar system that had universal coverage, offered benefits modeled on the best pension plans of the time (mostly public service defined benefits plans), and had extensive co-management procedures and robust state regulation. These objectives, all of which had figured among the arguments presented in 1972 by the Socialist Party leadership as a substitute for the people's pensions, faced considerable obstacles. Indeed, the political right, businesses, and the pension industry worked to safeguard the autonomy of existing plans and to allow plans to choose freely between defined benefit or defined contribution structures (which were then in the majority among private sector plans). These groups also downplayed the constraints of the state mandate by introducing into the Federal BVG law a wage floor under which low-wage workers would not be covered by the second pillar as well as a wage ceiling above which firms could freely organize supplemental benefits for handpicked categories of employees.

The turn toward austerity that followed the economic crisis of the 1970s, continued business determination to limit the scope of the state mandate, and the abandonment of the people's pensions alternative all were factors in the legislative debate that led to the adoption of the 1982 BVG law on the mandatory second pillar. The complexity of occupational provision also contributed to keeping these debates buried in experts' commissions and away from public scrutiny (Hafner 2004; Lusenti 1989; Rechsteiner 1984). In 1978, a first BVG draft failed to obtain a parliamentary majority. Even if they had pushed for the BVG, insurers were not dissatisfied by this outcome, which was the result of increased business resistance toward too much state regulation of pension plans. Considering this failure as "non-tragic," the directors' board of Winterthur Life, a leading group pension provider, underscored in December of that year that "efforts to simplify the law [were] in the interest of [our] company."[8]

The outcomes of the state mandate implemented in 1982 have remained ambiguous. The immense majority of wage earners were now covered by pension plans, but lower wage workers and temporary workers, primarily women, struggled to overcome the wage floor limiting participation in the mandatory pensions system. The constitutional aim stating that AHV (social security) and BVG occupational pension benefits should reach a combined replacement rate of 60 percent of former wages remained insufficient for those with low incomes. The level of BVG benefits, as well as their indexation, continued to vary considerably. Finally, the institutional decentralization of occupational provision, its opacity, the gradual phasing in of portability rights, and the absence of labor-management boards among the myriad of group pension contracts covering small- and medium-sized firms only reinforced the complexity of the pension system. In parallel to the implementation of the BVG pension law, AHV social security benefits were de facto frozen. Their replacement rate (about one-third of wages) has not improved since the eighth AHV revision enacted in 1973–1975. The introduction of benefits indexation in 1978 has only maintained this level. The mandatory second pillar has acted as a Trojan horse by anchoring in the middle of the pension system institutional and funding mechanisms that counteract the redistributive and solidaristic dimensions of social insurance.

While the BVG pension law has had an ambivalent impact on the quality and level of benefits, notably for low-wage workers and women, it has spurred the pension market and notably life insurers' activities. Between 1983 and 1985, or the time that elapsed between the final parliamentary vote on the BVG and its implementation, the annual profits of Rentenanstalt/Swiss Life tripled (Hafner 2004; Hepp 1993). The expansion of the second pillar mostly concerned small- and medium-sized firms that instituted group pension contracts to comply with the mandatory requirement. Banks and insurance companies also benefited from the financial flows generated by the opening of individual third pillar savings accounts. The third pillar today plays an important, though mostly symbolic, role. The concept of personal responsibility and individual savings is included in the pension system, which offers tax deductions to people with higher incomes, while playing a negligible role in most pensioners' overall incomes.

In the end, the "constraints of obligation" introduced by the BVG pension law have remained mild and the law, according to economist Graziano Lusenti (1989), respected the "traditional framework" of occupational provision and limited itself to "minimal dispositions" and "half measures." The number of persons receiving BVG mandatory pension benefits to supplement their AHV social security pension remained rather low until the 1990s. At the same time, the buoyant financial markets of the 1980s and 1990s offered a favorable context for the maturation of the second pillar. Pension plans could easily comply with one of the framework regulations introduced in 1985, namely the obligation to guarantee a minimum 4 percent rate of return on invested BVG pension assets. During this period, pension funds consolidated their positions as key institutional investors (Theurillat, Crevoisier, and Corpataux 2006). The experience gathered by Swiss insurance companies in the domain of occupational provision also enabled them to participate in foreign markets (e.g., in Eastern Europe and Latin America), where a transnational social security reform campaign orchestrated by financial international organizations was taking place (Lordon 2000; Orenstein 2008). Renewed demands from the parliamentary left for an amelioration of the BVG pension law long remained without concrete impact, and until the late 1990s, the second pillar continued its development without enduring much political scrutiny. This below-the-radar evolution highlights the asynchronous nature of pension debates, which mainly focused on the AHV pension during the 1990s. A brief overview of these controversies is useful as it reveals dynamics that are currently at play in the second pillar.

Even though AHV pension benefits were frozen, attempts to improve them continued and focused in particular on pension inequalities between men and women. In a context characterized by recurrent economic crises and continuing austerity pressures, these efforts culminated in a tenth revision of the AHV, implemented in 1995. This revision introduced several improvements for women, including replacing "couple benefits" with individual ones and introducing pension bonuses that accounted for years spent raising children. It also inaugurated the first increase in the retirement age for women (from 62 to 64 years) as well as cuts in widowers' benefits. A proposed eleventh AHV revision envisioned annual cuts in benefits amounting to about CHF1 billion. The revision was condemned by the left and trade unions as antisocial and challenged through a strong referendum campaign, and floundered in early 2004. A new draft of the revision faced much controversy before being buried again in autumn 2010. This transition from compromise to clear-cut conflict underscores the hardening of pension debates in Switzerland and notably the resistance to austerity cuts presented as necessary consolidation measures.

AHV social security benefit reform packages combining improvements and cuts have attracted the attention of political scientists (Bertozzi, Bonoli, and Gay-des-Combes 2005; Bertozzi and Gilardi 2008; Bonoli 2004). Yet they have only recently integrated the second pillar in their analyses. This renewed interest is linked to the current maturation of occupational provision and attempts to reform the system in a period of demographic and financial uncertainty.

While the number of pension plans has fallen steeply since the late 1970s as a result of consolidation, the basic institutional structures of the second pillar have not fundamentally changed (Table 9.3). Despite the losses incurred during the dot com crash and the financial crisis that started in 2008, second pillar pension assets still exceed Swiss GDP. Occupational provision is still dominated by a few dozen large pension plans managed by leading firms and public administrations, as well as a few insurance companies. Leading pension providers, such as Swiss Life or AXA-Winterthur, cover about half of the 1.6 million persons covered by group contracts (FINMA 2009). By contrast, mandatory participation in the second pillar has led to a threefold increase in the number of pension beneficiaries and a resulting increase in benefit payments. This maturation constitutes an obvious source for the growing controversies that have characterized occupational pension provision in the recent period. Second pillar pension institutions have not been spared the challenges of rising life expectancy, especially in a period riddled with recurring financial crises and sluggish economic growth.

Table 9.3 The Maturation of the Second Pillar (1978–2008)

	1978	2008
BVG pension plans	>10,000	around 2,400
Insured persons—millions (as a % of the workforce)	1.3 (50%)	3.6 (>85%)
Of which: coverage by group pensions	40%	40%
BVG pensioners—millions	0.3	0.9
As a comparison: AHV pensioners—millions	1.0	2.0
BVG benefits—CHF billions	4.0	28.4
As a comparison: AHV benefits—CHF billions	9.8	33.5
BVG assets—CHF billions (as a % of GDP)	82 (54%)	660 (123%)
As a comparison; AHV reserve fund—CHF billions	9.7	38.3

SOURCE : *La prévoyance professionnelle en Suisse. Statistique des caisses de pension*, various years, Swiss Federal Statistical Office.

Moreover, popular expectations of second pillar pensions have remained high. This is the case not only because mandatory BVG pensions play a growing role in pensioners' benefits, but it is also the result of two decades of alarmism about the sustainability of AHV pensions, which has shifted popular views of the alleged safe haven of occupational benefits. The hopes that people have in terms of pension provision from the second pillar may well contradict the priorities of the pension providers. This evolution sets business and life insurers in a tricky situation. They have successfully contained the AHV social security program and redirected pension development toward funded solutions, but after having cashed in on the expansion of occupational provision caused by the BVG pension law, the pension plans now have to face increasing obligations.

Finally, the political left and trade unions have pursued their efforts to improve BVG pension benefits, which they consider as insufficient for many low-wage workers. These forces disapprove of financial consolidation measures to reduce pensioners' incomes, underscore the hefty management costs of pension plans, and disapprove of their lack of transparency. The long-term maturation of the second pillar as well as the contradictory demands faced by the system have spurred a shift from a fragile political quid pro quo to open confrontation. The recent controversy on the BVG benefits conversion rate thus constitutes the second act of an ongoing controversy that began a decade ago during the first BVG revision.

FROM COMPROMISE TO DIRECT CONFRONTATION (2000–2010)

Although the political rhythms of the first two pension pillars remain disjointed, debates focused on one of them have often, even if belatedly, been echoed in the other. Thus, in the wake of the tenth AHV revision, proposals to improve the second pillar have also focused on the situation of women. From the end of the 1990s onward, the left has repeatedly demanded a better integration of low-wage earners in the BVG pension system through lowering the minimum wage requirement for pension coverage as well as an extension of joint management procedures to group pension contracts. The Federal Parliament finally acceded to these demands in 2003 but not without adding a reduction of the BVG conversion rate (from 7.2 percent to 6.8 percent by 2014, resulting in reduced pension benefits) to ensure long-term financing. This compromise enabled the passage of the first BVG revision and insulated it from a potential referendum campaign. During the same period, the eleventh AHV revision faced heated controversies and failed to pass the referendum hurdle.

The BVG pension law compromise reached in 2003 combined contradictory evolutions. On one hand, the lowering of the BVG wage floor (from 100 percent to 75 percent of a maximum AHV pension) partially took into account atypical work situations (primarily temporary and part-time work) as well as women's structural under-participation in pension plans (Leimgruber 2010). On the other hand, the reduction of the conversion rate constituted a first attack against a key feature determining the level of BVG benefits. Moreover, while the argument of financial consolidation has been systematically used to frame pension debates for the last 20 years, the financial crises of the early twenty-first century have also weighed on reforms implemented outside the scope of the BVG.

The dot com stock market crash of 2000–2001 caused the first losses in overall BVG assets since 1985. This financial crisis also served as the background for an intense campaign by insurers eager to disentangle their companies from BVG constraints. In other words, the debate about the consolidation of the second pillar is also a battle led by private interests to preserve their influence and autonomy in this domain. The 2003 compromise was thus accompanied by important measures that escaped the referendum mechanism. After sustained lobbying from insurers, the Federal Council lowered the guaranteed minimum BVG pension rate of return on investment from 4 percent (the level fixed in 1985) to 3.25 percent in 2003; then it was allowed to fluctuate (reaching 2.25 percent in 2004 and then 2.75 percent in 2008, before falling to 2 percent in early 2010). Insurance companies also unilaterally lowered the conversion rate used for benefits above the BVG ceiling. Because of the complexity and institutional decentralization of the second pillar, resistance against these two measures has been largely ineffectual. In 2004, the Federal Council granted insurance companies the controversial right to keep 10 percent of the investment returns of BVG assets. This decision, which generates about CHF500 million annually in revenues to insurers, has been denounced by pension experts who consider it to be contrary to the nonprofit goal of the BVG (Killer 2009; Molo 2009).

All of these measures enacted in parallel with the first BVG revision underscore the permeability of the second pillar to private interests that have extensive means to shape the pension system. By contrast, these measures also underscore the fragile position of trade unions. Forced to accept "realist" compromises that end up having a negative impact on pensioners, trade unions have less leverage to counteract such dynamics.

Since 2000, public sector pension plans have faced increasing consolidation pressures as well. These pressures are part of the offensive against the few progressive dimensions of the second pillar. Because public sector plans tend to offer more generous benefits than those in the private sector, submitting them to financial consolidation requirements is a powerful weapon linked to fiscally conservative campaigns waged against public budgets. Derided as onerous privileges, public sector pension plans face recurrent attacks and relentless austerity drives (Guex 1998).

Finally, the resurgence of radical reform proposals signals the hardening of debates about pensions and their future. Left-wing critics of the three-pillar doctrine have continued to argue in favor of an exit strategy from costly pension funding and a reinforcement of the pay-as-you-go AHV social security system. However, such positions remain minority opinions confined primarily to the left wing of trade unions (Swiss Trade Union Federation 2006). On the other side of the political divide, several free-market economists have repeatedly criticized the collectivist dimension of the second pillar and advocated the introduction of free choice in occupational pension provision. This option would lead to an individualization of the second pillar by severing the link between job contracts and pension plan affiliation (Gerber 2004). For the moment, this proposal has attracted only limited support among employers' associations. Fearing that free choice might reopen the Pandora's Box of alternative pension proposals and lead to endless conflicts with trade unions, employers' associations recognize the pertinence of the idea but are loath to follow this path (Hasler 2003). Experts have also lambasted the option as inappropriate because it would disorganize and imbalance the present system (Pittet, Pittet, and Schneider 2005). In the meantime, individual retirement accounts have continued to expand—no less than 2.7 million persons (out of a population of 8 million) have a third pillar individual account. However, contributions to these accounts (whose reserves are estimated at CHF60 billion) are very unequal. The first serious study on the subject done by the Federal Tax Administration in late 2009 confirmed that the main beneficiaries of the system are the banks, which offer low rates of return while having access to a steady flow of contributions, and the upper middle class, who benefit the most from the tax deduction granted to individual retirement accounts. These tax subsidies represent annual losses of CHF450 million for the Confederation, while these individual third pillar accounts play only a minor role in pension provision, even among higher income retirees (Peters 2009; see also NZZ 2009).

CONCLUDING COMMENTS

In retrospect, the March 2010 vote should not be viewed as an isolated event, but rather an important moment in a particularly turbulent phase of social policy development. As early as 2002, insurance companies had already argued in favor of a benefit conversion rate of 6.4 percent. The fact that the first BVG revision settled at 6.8 percent was not considered sufficient, and pressures to further reduce the rate continued. The controversial decision to lower the rate in late 2009 had little to do with the financial crisis that began in 2008 even if proponents of the decrease used the crisis to stress the urgency and necessity of lowering the conversion rate. In a context that witnessed costly state intervention in favor of Swiss banks such as UBS, business appeals to implement financial consolidation impacting pension benefits have caused resentment among the general public, even among the traditional electorate of right-wing parties.

While the unequivocal result of the March 7 vote represents a clear disavowal of the reform favored by the political right and business, its medium-term impact remains to be seen. Immediately after the vote, the political left and trade unions tried to capitalize on the referendum success to present a series of demands aiming both to improve pension benefits for low-wage earners (e.g., an increase in the combined replacement rate of the first and second pillar to 80 percent of past wages, compared to 60 percent today) and to more closely regulate life insurance companies offering group contracts. Pressure remains high on insurers, as illustrated by a recent parliamentary motion that demands their eviction from the BVG pension system and their confinement to supplemental benefits of higher paid employees. However, such proposals will have much difficulty to get beyond the point of political gesturing. Less than two weeks after the March 7 vote, the left already had to focus its forces on a new referendum—this time to oppose cuts in unemployment insurance. While commentators briefly feared a repeat of the March vote, the unemployment insurance reform cleared the referendum hurdle in September. A few weeks after, the new version of the eleventh AHV revision floundered in the Federal Assembly, after failing to clear a final vote. The left had already announced its intention to oppose the revision, and its minority position was bolstered at the last minute by votes from the Swiss People's Party. This important right-wing populist group was in favor of cuts in AHV pensions but preferred to vote down the revision rather than allow the left to launch a referendum campaign that might have been a distraction to the political right during the run-up to the federal elections of Autumn 2011 (NZZ 2010c,d).

These contradictory outcomes show that the March referendum victory was not sufficient to block the long-term offensive against the level of pension benefits. As is often the case in Switzerland, the multiplication of referendum campaigns might drain and splinter left-wing forces in struggles against an agenda set by the political right and business interests. Indeed, these forces have not abandoned the objective of the financial consolidation of the second pillar. They still dictate the agenda and rhythm of reforms, not only in old-age provision, but also in the other domains of social protection. Several elements hint that business forces and the right are not ready to disarm. Before prudently backtracking a few weeks before the March 7 vote, the Liberal-Radical party (the main center-right party) discussed the possibility of launching a popular initiative to demand automatic cuts in social insurance programs in case of budget deficits. The idea of a "deficit brake," which might help disarm referendum campaigns and "depoliticize" social debates, has also been taken up by the main business associations. In a similar vein, the Federal Council has spoken in favor of linking the evolution of the BVG benefit conversion rate to economic and demographic variables, which will also exert automatic downward pressure on the rate (NZZ 2010d).

Whatever issues these ongoing debates might have, they confirm the increasing centrality of the second pillar provision in present and future pension debates. Despite the controversies that may surround it, the three-pillar doctrine still remains the foundation of the Swiss pension system. In this context, submitting the core principles of the doctrine to a thorough critical analysis and untangling what is at stake in supposedly technical reforms is absolutely necessary.

Notes

1. The 13 countries considered were all important pension markets. Switzerland topped the ranking, followed by the Netherlands, Australia, Sweden, and Canada. Other countries mentioned were the United Kingdom, the United States, Chile, Singapore, Germany, China, and Japan. See http://www.mercer.com/globalpensionindex and *Neue Zürcher Zeitung* (NZZ 2010a). This preranking seems to have been leaked to the main Swiss financial newspaper to serve as an argument in the referendum campaign analyzed in this paper. In the final index, published on October 20, 2010, Mercer split the highest award between Switzerland and the Netherlands (see NZZ 2010b; Mercer, 2010).

2. The BVG conversion rate is used to calculate the annual BVG pension from the overall BVG assets accumulated during a work life. Let us consider an employee whose BVG assets amount to CHF600,000 at the age of 65. With a 7.2 percent conversion rate (the rate between 1985 and 2004), her annual pensions would have amounted to CHF43,200. With a 6.8 percent rate (the rate enacted in 2004 and to be implemented in 2014), her pension would be lowered to CHF40,800. The proposed new law would have further reduced the conversion rate to 6.4 percent.
3. Feuille Fédérale (2009, p. 2937); see also http://www.swissvotes.ch.
4. As of August 2010, CHF1 = \$0.96 = €0.72.
5. See Leimgruber (2008).
6. The Swiss Pension Funds Association (Association suisse des institutions de prévoyance, ASIP) is the direct heir of the first pension funds association founded in 1922. See also Leimgruber (2006).
7. See Swiss Financial Market Supervisory Authority (FINMA) at http://www.finma.ch.
8. Winterthur Directors' Board, December 5, 1978, quoted in Jung (2000).

References

Adema, William, and Maxine Ladaique. 2009. "How Expensive Is the Welfare State? Gross and Net Indicators in the OECD Social Expenditure Database (SOCX)." OECD Social, Employment, and Migration Working Paper no. 92. Paris: OECD.

Bertozzi, Fabio, Giuliano Bonoli, and Benoît Gay-des-Combes. 2005. *La réforme de l'Etat social en Suisse. Vieillissement, emploi, conflit travail-famille*. Lausanne: Presses Polytechniques et Universitaires Romandes.

Bertozzi, Fabio, and Fabrizio Gilardi. 2008. "The Swiss Welfare State: A Changing Public-Private Mix?" In *Public and Private Social Policy: Health and Pension Policies in a New Era*, Daniel Béland and Brian Gran, eds. Basingstoke, UK: Palgrave, pp. 207–227.

Bonoli, Giuliano. 2004. "The Institutionalization of the Swiss Multi-Pillar Pension System." In *Rethinking the Welfare State: The Political Economy of Pension Reform*, Martin Rein and Winfried Schmähl, eds. Cheltenham: Edward Elgar, pp. 102–121.

Coron, Gaël. 2007."Le prisme communautaire en matière de retraites: La diffusion à travers le droit européen de la théorie des piliers." *Retraite et Société* 50(1): 250–277.

Feuille Fédérale. 2009. "Reférendum contre la modification du 19 décembre 2008 de la loi fédérale sur la prévoyance professionelle vieillesse, survivants en invalidité." Bern: Swiss Federal Chancellery. http://www.admin.ch/ch/f/ff/2009/2937.pdf (accessed June 24, 2011).

FINMA. 2009. "Comptabilité de la prévoyance professionnelle en 2008." Berne: Swiss Financial Market Supervisory Authority.

Gerber, Daniel S. 2004. "Freie Pensionskassenwahl mit Grossem Nutzen. Von den Grenzen Betrieblicher Sozialromantik." *Neue Zürcher Zeitung*, March 9.

Guex, Sébastien. 1998. *L'argent de l'Etat. Parcours des finances publiques au 20ème siècle*. Lausanne: Editions d'En bas.

Hafner, Wolfgang. 2004. *Im Strudel der Finanzmärkte: Pensionskassen in der Schweiz*. Zurich: Rotpunktverlag.

Hasler, Peter. 2003 "Keine freie Wahl der Pensionskasse. Überforderte Aufsicht und ratlose Arbeitnehmer." *Neue Zürcher Zeitung*, September 2.

Hepp, Stefan. 1993. *The Swiss Life Insurance Industry: The Main Beneficiary of the Trend towards Collective Savings*. London: Morgan Stanley.

Jung, Joseph. 2000. *Die Winterthur: Eine Versicherungsgeschichte*. Zurich: NZZ Verlag.

Killer, Martin Kuert. 2009. "Le rôle douteux des compagnies d'assurance vie dans le deuxième pilier." *Travail Suisse* 4(March). http://www.travailsuisse.ch/fr/node/1927 (accessed June 24, 2011).

Leimgruber, Matthieu. 2006. "La politique sociale comme marché. Les assureurs vie et la structuration de la prévoyance vieillesse en Suisse (1890–1972)." In *Geschichte der Sozialversicherungen: L'histoire des assurances sociales*. Schweizerisches Bundesarchiv. Zürich: Chronos, pp. 109–139.

———. 2008. *Solidarity without the State? Business and the Shaping of the Swiss Welfare State, 1890–2000*. Cambridge: Cambridge University Press.

———. 2009. "Bringing Private Insurance Back In: A Transnational Insurance Think Tank for the Post-Keynesian Decades." In *European Economic Elites between a New Spirit of Capitalism and the Erosion of State Socialism*, Friedrike Sattler and Christoph Boyer, eds. Berlin: Duncker & Humblot, pp. 473–495.

———. 2010. "Caisses de pension et rapports sociaux de sexe en Suisse au XXe siècle." In *Die Produktion von Ungleichheiten: La Production des Inégalités*, Thomas David, Valentin Groebner, Janick-Marina Schaufelbühl, and Brigitte Studer, eds. Zürich: Chronos, pp. 49–64.

Lordon, Frédéric. 2000. *Fonds de pension, piège à cons? Mirage de la démocratie actionnariale*. Paris: Raisons d'agir.

Lusenti, Graziano. 1989. *Les institutions de prévoyance en Suisse, au Royaume-Uni et en Allemagne fédérale. Placements financiers et politique sociale*. Genève: Georg.

Mercer. 2010. *Melbourne Mercer Global Pension Index 2010*. Melbourne: Mercer.

Molo, Romolo. 2009. "La grande duperie du legal quote." *Le Temps*, February 4.

NZZ (*Neue Zürcher Zeitung*). 2009. "Die Profiteure der Säule 3a. Der Steuerabzug subventioniert vor allem obere Einkommensklassen und Banken." November 20.

———. 2010a. "Goldmedaille für das Dreisäulensystem." February 24.

———. 2010b. "Das Schweizer Dreisäulenmodell ist wetterfest." October 21.

———. 2010c. "Die Linke ergreift das Referendum. Nationalrat stimmt Sanierung der Arbeitslosenversicherung zu." March 19.

———. 2010d. "Gegen subventionierte Fühpensionierungen. Der Nationalrat lehnt neue Ausgaben bei der 11. AHV Revision ab." March 3.

———. 2010e. "Burkhalter tritt nicht auf die Reform-Bremse." March 8.

Orenstein, Mitchell. 2008. *Privatizing Pensions: The Transnational Campaign for Social Security Reform*. Princeton, NJ: Princeton University Press.

Peters, Rudi. 2009. "Les cotisations au pilier 3a Une étude descriptive des données de l'imposition 2005." Berne: Administration fédérale des contributions.

Pittet, Meinrad, David Pittet, and Jacques-André Schneider. 2005. "Faisabilité du libre choix de la caisse de pensions. Étude comparative sur l'individualisation et le transfert du risque à l'assuré." OFAS Research Report no. 10/05. Berne: Office Fédéral des Assurances Sociales.

Rechsteiner, Rudolf. 1984. *Das 200-Milliarden-Geschäft: Pensionskassen in der Schweiz*. Zürich: Unionsverlag.

Swiss Trade Union Federation. 2006. "Endlich existenzsichernde Renten: Erste Säule stärken—3000 Franken Rente für alle." Dossier 34. Bern: Schweizerische Gewerkschaftsbund. http://www.zora.uzh.ch/3979/ (accessed June 24, 2011).

Tausch, Arno. 2002. *The Three Pillars of Wisdom? A Reader on Globalization, World Bank Pensions Models, and Welfare Society*. Huntington, NY: Nova Publishers.

Theurillat, Thierry, Olivier Crevoisier, and José Corpataux. 2006. *L'impact des caisses de pension sur les circuits de financement et de contrôle de l'économie suisse (1985–2003)*. Neuchâtel: Institut de Sociologie, Groupe de Recherche en Économie Territoriale.

Trauth, Thomas. 2000. "Schweizer Sozialsystem als Vorzeigemodell? Notwendigkeit der Fokussierung auf die Kernaufgaben." *Neue Zürcher Zeitung*, October 13.

World Bank. 1994. *Averting the Old Age Crisis: Policies to Protect the Old and Promote Growth*. New York: Oxford University Press.

Wuthrich, Bernard. 2010. "Deuxième pilier: Les assureurs montent au front." *Le Temps*, January 8.

10
The Role of Occupational Pension Plans in an Optimal Polish Pension System

Marek Szczepański
Poznań University of Technology

In spite of a radical and comprehensive reform of the public pension system in Poland that took place in 1999,[1] an adequate and sustainable retirement income for Polish citizens remains a major challenge.

This chapter focuses on occupational pension plans and their role in the current and in an optimal pension system in Poland. The current, relatively new pension system is analyzed and evaluated in terms of its three main goals: 1) improving coverage, 2) sharing risks, and 3) providing adequate benefits. The analysis of the current system then leads to conclusions about the role of employer-sponsored pension plans in an ideal Polish pension system.

INSTITUTIONAL ARCHITECTURE OF THE NEW PENSION SYSTEM

The institutional architecture of the Polish pension system is complicated. Since the implementation of pension reform in 1999, two statutory employee pension systems have been operating in Poland: the old one, which is organized on a pay-as-you-go defined benefit basis, and a new, multi-pillar pension system, organized on a defined contribution basis (Figure 10.1). The new multi-pillar pension system consists of 1) a state-run pay-as-you-go Notional Defined Contribution (NDC) first pillar, 2) a fully funded second pillar (so-called open-ended pension funds, or OFEs, managed by private, commercial institutions) with a financial defined contribution formula,[2] and 3) a voluntary third pillar (employee pension plans, PPEs, and personal pension accounts, IKEs). The old system will cease to operate in 2034.

The new pension system is based entirely on individual accounts, with annuitization of account values at retirement. It is financially neutral and actuarially balanced and should be, according to the reform leaders, much more effective and fair than the old system. The new pension system is not redistributive across generations and will not result in hidden public debt. The reform package has been described as achieving "security through diversity."

In theory, the new statutory pension system in Poland looks very good. Twelve years after the implementation of this reform, some advantages are obvious, but there are also many shortcomings and risks connected with the new system.

Barr and Diamond (2010, p. 26) stated that a pension system should accomplish two core purposes: 1) "offer a mechanism for consumption smoothing . . . and provide insurance against low income and wealth in old age" and 2) "relieve poverty and redistribute income and wealth." A well-designed pension system should therefore not only guarantee protection from poverty, but also income maintenance. With an expected gross replacement rate of about 60 percent for men and 40 percent for women in Poland, only relief from poverty can be achieved under the current system (Szumlicz 2005, p. 266; OECD 2011). The average earnings in Poland are only about 1/3 of the average earnings for EU-27,[3] and the gross replacement rate of 40–60 percent does not guarantee a decent level of retirement income.

According to the analysis prepared for the European Commission (2010), Poland belongs to the group of EU-27 members with the largest expected decline in net replacement rates from the public pension social security system. Also the benefit ratio (the average benefit from public and private pensions as a share of the economy-wide average wage) will fall from 56 percent in 2007 to 31 percent in 2060 (European Commission and Economic Policy Committee 2009).

The design of the new statutory pension system is favorable for people with long uninterrupted careers, but it is particularly poorly designed for atypical workers and generally poor for women. The new statutory pension system increases the risk of social exclusion for many groups, including people who experience unemployment (the current

Figure 10.1 Design of the Old-Age Pension System in Poland since 1999

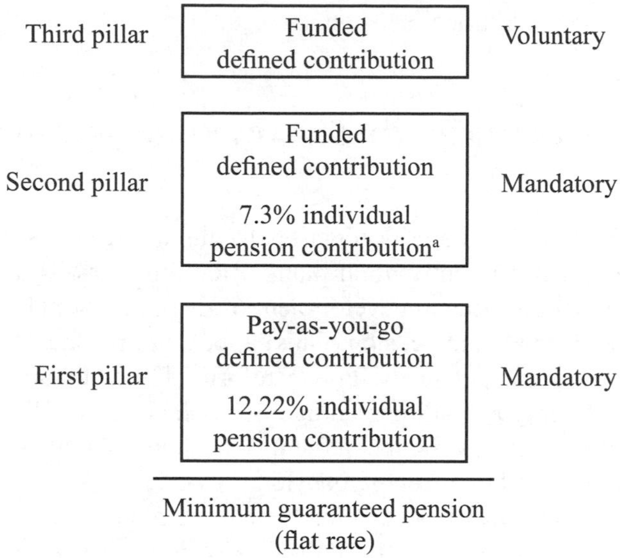

[a] On March 25, 2011, the Polish Parliament (Sejm) decided to reduce contributions to the funded part of the public pension system from 7.3 percent to 2.3 percent and increase pension contributions to the pay-as-you-go part of the system to 17.22 percent, starting May 1, 2011. The defined contribution pension formula remains unchanged for both parts of the system.

unemployment rate in 2011 is 13 percent), part-time workers, freelance workers, and temporary workers. The system also increases the risk of inadequate pensions for a considerable number of workers with stable, long-term employment but with below average incomes. There is no intragenerational redistribution or solidarity between high-wage and low-wage workers (as used to exist in the old pay-as-you-go pension system through the defined benefit formula). Low levels of actuarially strict mandatory defined contribution benefits inevitably will lead to low-wage workers receiving low or very low pensions, quite often the minimum guaranteed pension. Even entrepreneurs and the self-employed can expect limited benefits from the new statutory pension system because most of them declare only the lowest level of pension contributions calculated for minimum wages. As a result, they also will receive very low retirement benefits. But even average- or high-wage workers will not achieve acceptable income maintenance levels in retirement without additional pension savings.

PROBLEMS WITH THE VOLUNTARY THIRD PILLAR

Both the individual and occupational voluntary pension plans are fully funded, defined contribution plans offered in various forms (see Table 10.1), but insufficient development of these additional plans (especially the occupational pension plans) appears to be one of the most important disadvantages of the Polish reform. The voluntary pension systems cover only a small percentage of the labor force: PPEs cover only 2 percent and IKEs about 6 percent. Thus, these voluntary pension options play only a minor role in pension provision.

The development of occupational pension plans has been rather slow since 1999 (Figure 10.2). The only exception occurred in 2004, when many group life insurance programs were transformed into pension plans when the new Law on Occupational Pensions came into effect. But, even in 2004 and afterwards, the development of employer-sponsored pension plans was not sufficient to improve coverage.

In addition, participants in existing occupational pension plans organized on a Financial Defined Contribution (FDC) basis bear numerous types of financial market risks, and there is no minimum guaranteed

Table 10.1 Number of Occupational Pension Plans in Poland by Plan Type, 2010

Life insurance	795
Investment fund	285
Company pension fund	33
Foreign management companies	0
Total	1,113

SOURCE: Pracownicze programy emerytalne w 2010 roku [Occupational pension plans in 2010], Polish Financial Supervision Authority (KNF), available at http://www.knf.gov.pl.

Figure 10.2 Development of Occupational Pension Plans in Poland, 1999–2009

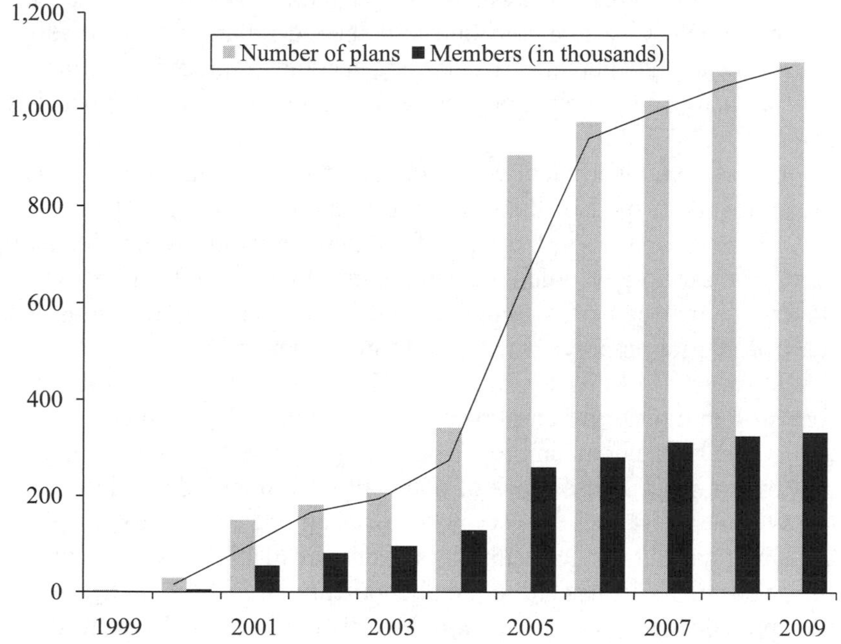

SOURCE: Author's calculations based on data from the Polish Financial Supervision Authority (http://www.knf.gov.pl, accessed June 15, 2010).

rate of return for the savers. There is also no mutual insurance fund in case of the bankruptcy of the plan sponsor.

Barriers to the Development of Employee Pension Plans

Key barriers to the development of employee pension plans in Poland can be divided into exogenous factors of an institutional nature, exogenous factors of a noninstitutional nature (primarily macroeconomic determinants), and endogenous factors attributable to the employer (Szczepański 2010, p. 179). Because employees generally show little interest in employee pension plans, the endogenous factors connected with employees play a lesser role in practice and can be regarded as secondary factors influencing the development of employee pension plans.

Exogenous institutional factors

The reformed pension system retained a high level of contributions to the obligatory system (the first and second pillars, which together receive nearly 20 percent of salaries), leaving limited space for the development of supplementary systems, including employee pension plans.

In addition, insufficient economic and fiscal incentives are offered to employers to sponsor the plans and to employees to join them. Especially problematic are the lack of an income tax allowance for plan participants who pay voluntary supplemental premiums and an unattractive capital gains tax allowance whose threshold is too high and inaccessible for employees with medium and lower incomes.

There is also little flexibility and limited selection of institutional forms of administering employee pension plans. This includes the inability to administer an employee pension plan as a defined benefit plan or a hybrid plan. Those types of plans allow a more balanced division of investment risk and other types of risks among employers, employees, and financial services suppliers than is available under the current Polish system. This has led to the phenomenon of institutionally driven nonoptimal risk allocation. A more flexible market-based system theoretically would reduce transaction costs.

Plan participants are given insufficient legal and institutional disclosures about currently executed strategies in asset management and the levels of risks related to these strategies. This has led to information asymmetry, as described in agency theory, between plan participants and the financial institutions hired to manage employee pension plans. In addition, there is little institutional support for helping current and potential employee pension plan participants and employers to compare offers from financial services providers in terms of costs and investment results.

There are no institutional solutions protecting the interests of participants in different age groups. Older and younger age groups (demographic cohorts) have different needs in employee pension plans. One institutional solution could take the form of subfunds that invest in safe assets to which pension savings would be transferred in a specified time period, such as 5 years before the employee is 60 years old or is eligible to receive benefits. Another solution is the use of packages of properly selected pension funds within employee pension plans, ensuring an optimal allocation of premiums for participants in different life-cycle phases, taking into account individual needs and approaches to risk. Such a role could be played by aggressive funds, aimed at younger people, that have a higher proportion of more risky but potentially more profitable assets, balanced funds, and more conservative but potentially less profitable funds. Multi-fund solutions could play the role of automatic stabilizers, reducing the risk of erroneous selection of a fund by plan participants who generally have to select one of several investment funds available in employee pension plans or unit-linked insurance plans. This would be particularly helpful to people who do not want to choose a fund on their own.

Other barriers to the development of employee pensions include:

- An inability to differentiate the amount of the basic premium paid to employee pension plans by the employer for employees. This makes it difficult to use qualified pension plans as an efficient salary policy instrument or incentive factor.
- Unresolved legal and institutional issues connected with the creation of employee pension plans in institutions belonging to public finance.
- The lack of regular and wide-scale educational activities about employee pension plans managed by state institutions.
- A lack of requirements for financial results of institutions servicing employee pension plans. Such requirements could be modeled after solutions used in other countries, where a minimum return rate is specified (e.g., with reference to the inflation rate or other external macroeconomic parameters).
- An insufficient level of coordination of transferability of benefits or pension entitlements between employee pension plans existing in different countries, at least within the EU.
- An insufficient level of coordination related to the security of employee pension plan participants in the EU. For example, there are no unified requirements of financial service providers for such plans and the requirements specified in EU directives are too general and interpreted in different ways in different countries.

Exogenous noninstitutional factors

Poland has a high unemployment rate, and most employers are not interested in taking on additional financial obligations aimed at retaining employees. One such obligation would be creation of an employee pension plan.

In general high costs have been associated with the adaptation activities connected with the transformation of Poland's economic system. Entrepreneurs have been focused on gaining and maintaining market share and face ever-increasing competition connected with Poland's entry into the EU. Other issues, including supplementary employee benefits such as an employee pension plan, have presumably been of secondary importance. Workers in Poland already have a significantly lower average salary as compared to the EU average, which has resulted in relatively low levels of average disposable income and average household savings.

Finally, the global financial crisis negatively influenced the investment results of financial institutions that service employee pension plans as well as the value of assets accumulated in the plans.

Endogenous employer-related factors

In general there is little competitive pressure for employers to provide pensions because most businesses do not offer these types of nonwage benefits to their employees. Therefore, employers do not feel obliged to bear the additional costs of creating employee pension plans. There is also insufficient pressure from employees and their organizations to force employers to create pension plans.

Employee pension plans are nonwage long-term incentives that do not directly influence labor productivity growth. Instead, they improve the working environment and relations between employers and employees, help build loyalty and employee attachment to the company, but they do not, at least in the short and medium term, increase financial benefits (e.g., profits or growth in company market value) for the employer.

The employee pension plans are also inflexible in terms of employee compensation and administration. As stated previously, employers do not have the flexibility to shape the amount of the employer's contribution so that premiums can be individualized, depending on the appraisal of a given employee. In addition, the employer is obligated to register plans with a national supervisory body, which especially discourages small- and medium-sized companies with a small staff base. Plan administration also poses additional accounting, financial, and human resource obligations.

There is an agency problem in the relationship between employers financing a plan and the financial institutions managing it, including information asymmetry and transaction costs connected with sometimes suboptimal choices in the plan and the provider.

Endogenous employee-related factors

The level of pension awareness is generally low, although recent research has shown it to be slowly increasing. In general, people still prefer current consumption over savings, particularly people with lower incomes. Most employees perceive existing incentives to participate in employee pension plans (highlighted above in the discussion of institutional barriers) as too weak, and for many individuals, participation is simply unaffordable.[4]

The awareness of the risk connected with investing in financial markets has grown as has awareness of the differences in interests between plan participants and the financial institutions managing the plans. To date, these factors have not had a significant influence on the development of employee pension plans, but they may become a barrier in the development of employee pension plans in Poland unless new solutions to limit risk to employees are introduced to the plan structure.

Variables Stimulating the Development of Employee Pension Plans

Exogenous institutional factors

Legal, institutional, and administrative factors related to employee pension plans have evolved in the past decade and helped with plan formation. Employers were allowed limited engagement in plans and to exit them in the case of deterioration of a company's financial standing. Restrictive penalties were lifted for failing to observe formalities connected with the registration and administration of a plan. The legal changes made in 2004 were particularly profound and stimulated employee pension plan development. One factor, the expansion of available institutional forms of running employee pension plans to permit their management from abroad, has not yet helped develop employee pension plans because no such program has yet been registered. During the same period, regulations were adopted governing the operations of financial institutions providing employee pension plan services to meet EU legal requirements, which increased the security of the financial operations and asset management.

Tax relief was withdrawn for unqualified pension plans, which had been run in the form of group life insurance programs or payments into investment funds. This was an incentive for some companies to convert them into qualified employee pension plans.

At the same time, the base portion of the reformed pension system was defined. The new system uses different methods of financing and pension capital accumulation in the base portion (both the pay-as-you-go and the funded systems). The system assumes that future benefits should come from at least two obligatory segments and that benefits should be supplemented by additional savings accumulated in the third pillar (i.e., in employee pension plans and in individual retirement accounts). Understood narrowly, the third pillar is limited to systems of supplementary pension savings covered by systemic fiscal and social incentives offered by the state, but the third pillar is an integral part of the new system.

Exogenous noninstitutional factors

A factor that might have contributed to the creation of employee pension plans at least in some sectors of the economy (e.g., in construction and transportation) was the increased possibility of economic migration to other EU states (particularly after Poland's entry into the EU in 2004) and the desire to keep employees in Poland by offering them additional benefits. However, analyses show that there is no clear positive correlation between periodic economic migration and an increase of employee pension plan participants (Szczepański 2010, p. 377). Entrepreneurs that wanted to retain current or recruit new employees to replace the ones who went abroad seemed to use other methods, particularly salary increases.

European integration, which included the creation of jobs in Poland in companies with foreign capital or in international corporations, contributed slightly to the creation of company pension plans (both qualified and nonqualified plans). Foreign employers running employee pension plans were mainly driven by non-economic motivations (e.g., organizational culture, corporate social responsibility, and image) rather than by fiscal or cost incentives because the latter in Poland are very modest as compared to other countries. Because of the low level of flexibility and an inability to individualize base premiums paid by the employer, many domestic and foreign employers preferred to start nonqualified plans,[5] which gave them more freedom in shaping this form of nonwage employee benefits.

Finally, competition among financial institutions providing financial services for employee pension plans was stronger than in the capital segment of the public pension system. There was a much higher number of competing entities, leading to more differentiation of premiums and investment results.

Endogenous employer-related factors

Employers generally had an overall positive assessment of many aspects of employee pension plans, including their structure, legal limitations, and relaxed administrative oversight. The general structure of employee pension plans as defined by statute was viewed positively, as was the quality of service provided by financial institutions servicing employee pension plans. Also viewed positively were legal and institutional changes that allow premium limits, temporary suspension of the payment of premiums, and the possibility of plan liquidation if the company's financial standing deteriorates. Employers also supported the reduced supervision by state institutions.

The awareness of nonwage remuneration elements has gradually grown, as have the opportunities to use them as an instrument in human resource management policy. The concept of corporate social responsibility in company management has also become stronger. Many employers stated that their desire to ensure supplementary pension security for employees as an element of this social responsibility was a decisive factor when starting a plan.

Endogenous employee-related factors

The fact that the base premium in the plan is paid by the employer is viewed positively by employees. There has been a high participation rate (70–80 percent) in employee pension plans in the few companies that have plans. Awareness of the need for pensions and of the need to accumulate supplementary savings for old age has grown, especially among younger and better educated people. Although it generally occurs too late for individuals to accumulate sufficient supplementary savings, the fear of a decline in one's financial standing after retirement can contribute to an employee's desire to be part of a pension plan.

Since the implementation of pension reform in Poland in 1999, there generally have been more barriers than stimulants to the development of employee pension plans. It is therefore not surprising that development has been slow and limited and that such a small share of employees is covered.

THE IDEAL PENSION SYSTEM IN POLAND

The ideal, or at least the optimal, Polish pension system should guarantee more secure and adequate income for future retirees. But an adequate income should also be combined with the long-term sustainability of the system and better protection of pension rights, especially for women and people with atypical work careers.

The general idea of the 1999 pension reform, risk diversification between the labor and the financial markets (Security Through Diversity), should be retained. The institutional architecture of the new statutory pension system, consisting of two separate, individual pension accounts with defined contribution formulas (in the pay-as-you-go first pillar and the fully funded second pillar) also should be retained. This multi-pillar approach should ensure long-term sustainability, and the defined contribution formula should guarantee actuarial adjustment of the pension system. A separate issue is the insufficient development of the voluntary pension plans in the third pillar.

The new statutory pension system in Poland is actuarially balanced, and this is an important achievement that should neither be disregarded nor discarded. Nevertheless, many changes should to be introduced to improve adequacy and risk sharing in that system. The following changes should enable the Polish pension system to achieve the following goals: improved coverage, improved adequacy, and greater mitigation of financial market and cohort risks.

Improved Coverage

The ideal Polish pension system should be based not only on a compulsory (statutory) pension system (divided into two pillars), but also on occupational pension plans for the majority of workers, especially low-wage workers. The extremely low coverage rates for voluntary occupational and individual pension plans in Poland (the third pillar) illustrate the need for a new approach to the design of old-age pension plans. Attractive tax incentives, especially personal income tax exemptions, could be too expensive and create negative microeconomic side effects. Therefore, automatic enrollment of workers into occupational pension plans with an opt-out option seems to be a more promising solution. High-wage workers should have more opportunities to engage in individual pension savings. The existing individual savings accounts, which typically are in the form of separate bank accounts, investment funds, life insurance, or brokerage accounts should be supplemented with new financial products dedicated to long-term savings for older persons. For lower income individuals and those with atypical working careers, a zero pillar should be created that is tax financed, with benefits at a higher level than the current minimum guaranteed pensions.

Improved Adequacy

To improve the adequacy of future pensions without increasing pension benefits, the statutory retirement age of women (currently 60) should be equalized with that of men (currently 65). To stimulate competition and better performance in the funded second pillar of the statutory pension system, fees and charges should be capped and the use of internal benchmarks should be eliminated. Fees and charges should be connected to investment results. The best-performing pension funds should be rewarded with a "success" fee. In addition, OFEs should not have the right to aggressively advertise for participants.

Mitigation of Financial Market and Cohort Risks

The risks connected with the investments of pension plans should be mitigated, especially in the statutory pension system. The oldest cohorts of participants in the OFEs should be enrolled into sub-funds that invest in less risky financial assets (e.g., participants within 5 to 10 years of retirement age). Young participants in OFEs should be offered more investment options, with more or less aggressive and potentially profitable financial asset portfolios. Participants who do not want to make their own investment choices should be enrolled into low-risk, age-appropriate funds. All participants should be provided with more information than is currently available regarding investment strategies, risks, and potential profits and losses connected with particular funds.

Participants in occupational pension plans should also have more influence on investment choices and strategies of the financial institutions that provide the services for workplace pensions. The participants should receive comprehensive, up-to-date information about risks and potential profits and losses connected with different kinds of investments. A special guarantee fund should be created in case of the bankruptcy of the employer sponsoring the plan. Because of the proposed quasi-obligatory status of the occupational pension plans, the cost of insurance against employer bankruptcy would be limited.

An Alternative Approach

An alternative and more drastic approach would involve the liquidation of the compulsory fully funded second pillar and a return to a one-pillar statutory pay-as-you-go pension system with more incentives for additional pension plans (occupational and individual savings for retirement). Such a modified statutory pension system, with pay-as-you-go financing of a notional defined contribution benefit as the first pillar, fully funded defined contribution occupational pension plans as the second pillar, and voluntary fully funded defined contribution personal pension plans as the third pillar, would be safer for participants because such a system would reduce the financial market risks in the statutory pension system. Such a solution would be difficult to implement, however, and very expensive. The institutions that currently manage OFEs would most likely sue the Polish government and demand compensation for the lost profits that would result from implementation of this scheme. In addition, opinion polls show that most Polish citizens prefer a multi-pillar pension system with a fully funded component over a one-pillar statutory pension system with voluntary additional plans. Bad experiences with unfavorable changes in pension rights and entitlements in the old pension system and different indexation rates of individual accounts in the state-managed first pillar of the new system have provoked this lack of confidence. A multi-pillar system with a funded component and a mechanism to reduce financial market risks would generally be much better perceived and accepted in Poland than a one-pillar system with a high degree of political risk. From the Polish perspective, it seems to be more aligned with the Polish mentality and experiences, and closer to the ideal system design.

Generally, Poles do not trust policymakers, prefer to accept financial market risks rather than political risk in the pension system, and do not want to be entirely dependent on state institutions for their retirement income. When imaging the ideal Polish pension system, one should take these preferences into consideration.

Notes

1. In March 2011, 12 years after the implementation of pension reform, some important elements of pension design have been changed. The amount of pension contributions to the funded part of the new system has been reduced from 7.3 percent to 2.3 percent, and the amount of pension contributions paid to the pay-as-you-go part of the system has been increased (see note to Fig. 10.1). New incentives for additional, voluntary pension savings will be offered beginning January 1, 2012.
2. The old pay-as-you-go pension plan applies to people older than 50 on the first day of the enforcement of the reform (January 1, 1999), and the new one applies to those who were 50 or younger as of that date. Participants in the new pension system are subdivided into two groups: 1) people below the age of 30, who have compulsory coverage in both public and private plans, and 2) people aged 30–50, who can choose whether to remain in the NDC plan only or to take part in both tiers.
3. According to Eurostat, the average monthly full-time equivalent gross earnings in EU Member States in 2006 was €1,695, whereas it was €573 in Poland. Annual income data presented in OECD (2011) confirm this relation.
4. There was an exemption from capital gains tax of supplementary premiums paid into employee pension plans up to PLN12,000 in 2008. The average disposable

income per person in a household was about PLN1,000 (monthly) during the same period, and average spending was PLN900 (monthly). So an average earner clearly gains little benefit from the capital gains tax exemption. That tax incentive is much more favorable for high-income workers who are much more likely to save more and make full use of this tax incentive.

5. It is difficult to give the exact number of nonqualified employee pension plans because there is no nationwide register of such plans. Qualified plans are listed in a register maintained by a central state administration body.

References

Barr, Nicholas, and Peter Diamond. 2010. *Pension Reform. A Short Guide.* New York: Oxford University Press.

European Commission. 2010. "Towards adequate, sustainable and safe European pension systems." Green Paper. Brussels: European Commission. http://ec.europa.eu/social/BlobServlet?docId=5551&langId=en (accessed June 27, 2011).

European Commission and Economic Policy Committee. 2009. *2009 Ageing Report. Economic and Budgetary Projections for the EU-27 Member States (2008–2060).* European Economy, No 2. Luxembourg: European Commission. http://ec.europa.eu/economy_finance/publications/publication13782_en.pdf (accessed June 16, 2010).

OECD. 2011. "Pensions at a Glance 2011: Retirement-Income Systems in OECD Countries, Online Country Profiles, including Personal Income Tax and Social Security Contributions." Paris: Organisation for Economic Co-operation and Development. http://www.oecd.org/dataoecd/33/53/47273023.pdf.

Szczepański, Marek. 2010. *Development of Occupational Pension Schemes in Poland. Barriers and Drivers*. Poznan, Poland: Wydawnictwo Politechniki Poznańskiej.

Szumlicz, Tadeusz. 2005. *Ubezpieczenia społeczne: Teoria dla praktyki* [Social Insurance: Theory for Praxis]. Bydgoszcz-Warszawa: Oficyna Wydawnicza Branta.

11
How to Establish a Better Corporate Pension System in Japan

Noriyasu Watanabe
Rissho University and
International Pension Research Institute

BACKGROUND

In 2010, Japan had 22,219 private sector companies that had been in operation for more than 100 years, the largest number of any country. Of these, 39 companies had been in operation for at least 500 years, 435 companies for at least 300 years, and 1,191 companies for at least 200 years. The Kongou-Gumi Company, the oldest continuously operating company in Japan, was established in the year 578 as a construction company of temples and shrines.

There are two primary reasons that so many companies have been able to remain in operation for so long in Japan: 1) Japanese companies have traditionally respected *Wa* (harmony) more than profits not only with their customers, but also with society and their employees, and 2) according to historical documents, they established severance lump-sum payment systems for the highly paid staff beginning in the seventeenth century. Because of these two features, they have been able to overcome many economic, social, and technological changes and have enjoyed long prosperity.

Following the Meiji Revolution in 1868, the Japanese government opened Japan to the western world. Along with many other concepts, ideas about western corporate systems and corporate pension systems were introduced. The Kanebou Cotton Spinning Company voluntarily established the first western-style occupational pension plan in Japan in 1905. Soon after, the Mitsui Company, a trading company, and many other companies established pension plans for highly paid and middle-income employees.

Development of Defined Benefit and Defined Contribution Plans

In 1962, the corporate tax law and income tax law were amended, and the Tax-Qualified Pension (TQP) Plan was introduced to provide defined benefit plans to employees. Many large- and mid-sized employers changed all or some of their pension contributions from the severance lump-sum payment system to a TQP plan, which is a corporate pension contract between employers and financial companies. To receive favorable tax treatment, the content of the TQP contract must be approved by the Commissioner of the National Tax Agency.

The postwar period of high inflation decreased the real value of pension benefits of the Employees' Pension Insurance (EPI), which is Japan's social security plan. Therefore, in 1965, the Employees' Pension Fund (EPF) plan was established by amendment of the EPI law to allow employers to increase pension benefits. In 1967, the Employees' Pension Fund Association (EPFA) was also established.

Because the increase in EPF plan benefits increased costs for employers, sponsoring employers and their employees are exempted from paying a portion of EPI plan contributions to the government, and instead pay them to their EPF plan. The EPF plans also provide additional benefits on top of the portion that replaces EPI (social security) benefits.

Compared with the TQP, EPF plans have received more favorable tax treatment because EPF plans act as a substitute for part of the EPI. EPF plans were mainly established by large employers (1,000 or more employees) to provide lifetime benefits. TQP plans were mainly established by medium and small employers, typically paying benefits for a limited number of years. Many employers that hoped to establish higher quality employee benefit systems established both plans, each of which is a defined benefit plan that played a major role in providing retirement income for private sector employees until 2001.

As of April 2011, Japan had not enacted a basic corporate pension law establishing fiduciary responsibility, such as ERISA in the United States and *Die Alter Renten Gesetz* in Germany. Because of the collapse of Japan's "bubble" economy in the 1990s and changes in the Japanese economy resulting from changing world economic conditions, however, the New Corporate Pension Amendment was established in 2001, which amended the EPF and TQP systems, which had huge deficits (20 trillion Japanese yen [¥]). In addition, the Defined Benefit Corporate Pension Law and the Defined Contribution Pension Law, the first law governing defined contributions in Japan, were enacted. Before the 2001 laws, many pension scholars had recommended the development of defined contribution plans, using terms such as "self responsibility," but the recommendations did not include full disclosure of the financial risks associated with these types of plans. The Employers' Association and the Conservative government at the time accepted this idea, and the Confederation of Labor did not oppose it, so the new laws were enacted.

Although the defined contribution plans were necessary, the laws regulating them suffered from several weaknesses because they were enacted too early with too few protections. The weaknesses included the following:

- Defined contribution plans should be marketed and managed under strict fiduciary responsibility, but there were no such regulations in the basic corporate pension act.
- Defined contribution plans require fair and transparent financial markets—the financial markets in Japan are neither fair nor transparent, and many financial organizations have sustained large losses or declared bankruptcy.
- Defined contribution plans require enhanced tax regulations and accounting rules, but these were not established.
- Participants of defined contribution plans need to receive financial information and education, but these types of information and education were never provided.
- The act does not contribute to retirement income security for participants—it only helps employers decrease costs and financial corporations increase gains.

In this reform, EPF plans were allowed to stop acting as a substitute or replacement for the EPI plan by returning the corresponding EPF money that would have been paid into the EPI plan to the government. No new TQP contracts were allowed after April 2002. Existing TQPs had to be converted to another form of occupational pension by the end of March 2012 because they would no longer receive favorable tax treatment starting in April 2012. In March 2001, TQPs had 9.9 million members and assets of ¥22.3 trillion. The government intended to change TQPs to another type of corporate pension because of the huge deficits and weaker economy. Because there are no pension benefit guarantees for TQPs, it is not clear whether these participants will receive another corporate pension in the current weaker economy.

With these reforms, corporate and personal defined contribution plans were first introduced in Japan. Employees who have no occupational pension plan from their employer can establish a personal defined contribution plan using their own contributions.

CURRENT SOCIAL SECURITY AND CORPORATE PENSION SYSTEMS

Social Security

The National Pension Insurance (NPI) is a flat-rate pension that is part of the Japanese social security system. Self-employed, "non-regular" employees (e.g., part-time or temporary workers), unemployed, and nonworking spouses of insured workers in the earnings-related public pensions (the EPI in the private sector and the Mutual Aid Associations' Pension Insurance [MAAPI] in the public sector) pay a fixed monthly contribution (¥15,020 in 2011, increasing to ¥16,900 in 2017) to the NPI and receive a fixed monthly pension benefit (¥65,741 with 40 years of contributions as of 2017) starting at 65 years of age. In addition to the NPI, employees in the private and public sectors participate in the earnings-related EPI and MAAPI, respectively.

Corporate Pension System

In the private sector, the Japanese pension system is composed of defined benefit and defined contribution pensions. The defined benefit corporate pensions are the EPF plans, the defined benefit corporate pension plans (established by the 2001 law), and the soon-to-be-discontinued TQP plans. As discussed previously, the 2001 reform also introduced corporate and personal defined contribution pension plans.

The composition of pension plans has shifted tremendously in the past decade. The occupational pension system had its largest amount of assets, ¥63.3 trillion (present value), at the end of March 1998. The EPF system had 1,884 plans, 12.2 million participants, and pension fund assets of ¥44.9 trillion. The TQP system had 90,243 plans, 10.6 million participants, and pension fund assets of ¥18.4 trillion. By the end of March 2010, however, the EPF system only had 608 plans (a 67.7 percent decline), 4.6 million participants (a 62.3 percent decline), and pension fund assets of ¥29.0 trillion (a 35.4 percent decline). The TQP system had 17,184 plans (an 81.0 percent decline), 2.5 million participants (a 76.4 percent decline), and pension fund assets of ¥6.4 trillion (a 65.2 percent decline).

The corporate defined benefit system, which did not even exist in the late 1990s, had 7,405 plans, 6.5 million participants, and pension fund assets of ¥39.0 trillion at the end of March 2010. At the same time, corporate defined contribution plans had 13,222 plans, 3.6 million participants, but incomplete pension fund asset information was available. Personal defined contribution plans had only 0.1 million participants, and pension fund information was also not available. At the end of March 2008, however, the total fund amount for corporate and personal defined contribution plans was only ¥3.7 trillion.

According to official statistics as of the end of March 2010, the number of participants in all defined benefit plans (EPF, TQP, and corporate defined benefit) decreased from 22.8 million at the end of March 1998 to 13.6 million (40.4 percent decline). Pension fund assets increased slowly from ¥63.3 trillion at the end of March 1998 to ¥74.4 trillion (17.5 percent increase), and per participant pension fund assets increased from ¥2.8 million to ¥5.5 million. The total number of participants of corporate and personal defined contribution plans was 3.5 million, fund assets totaled ¥3.9 trillion, and the per participant fund amount was ¥1.1 million. At the end of March 2007, the average monthly contribution was ¥11,400.

This means that small- and mid-sized employers have quit offering defined benefit plans and that almost all employees working for these companies are not covered by any type of pension, whether defined benefit or defined contribution.

Only employees of large companies and good mid-sized companies have sustainable pensions with good benefits. Many employees in large companies have not only a variety of defined benefit plans but also corporate defined contribution plans.

Because of the recent unstable financial markets and weak earning power of financial institutions, corporate pension funds suffered average investment losses of 9.8 percent in FY2007 and 17.2 percent in FY2008. They gained 13.8 percent in FY2009, but lost 6.2 percent in April–August FY2010.

Because of the weak economy, underfunding of corporate pensions increased to ¥13 trillion as of March 2009, and it was no doubt even higher in March 2010. A government accounting committee has discussed strengthening regulations for reporting unfunded liabilities on the balance sheet of employers beginning in 2012.

Many employers with underfunded pension plans have gone bankrupt. In September 2010, Japan Air Line Co. Ltd (JAL) reorganized under the Corporate Reorganization Act with the infusion of ¥350 billion of public money, a debt waiver of ¥522 billion (87.5 percent) by financial corporations, and personnel reductions of 16,000 employees (19.3 percent). Prior to the reorganization, former employees had been receiving EPF, TQP, corporate defined benefit, and corporate defined contribution plans with total pension benefits of more than ¥200,000 per month after retirement.

But JAL had a huge underfunded liability of ¥331.4 billion for its corporate pension plans as of March 2010. Unlike the EPF pension plans, the TQP and corporate defined benefit plans have no pension benefit guarantee system. After difficult negotiations, the decision was made to cut future benefits of active employees by 53 percent with the required consent of at least two-thirds of employees and to cut benefits to current beneficiaries by 30 percent with the required consent of at least two-thirds of beneficiaries.

The Board of Directors of JAL's pension funds has an equal number of members representing the employer, active employees, and beneficiaries. The board maintained a projected investment return rate of 4.5 percent even in the recent period when a more reasonable long-term rate would have been 1.0 percent. They did not adequately perform their fiduciary duties, but no pension law clearly establishes strict pension fiduciary responsibility in Japan.

CURRENT PENSION CONDITIONS

Establishing a better, sustainable retirement income security system is one of the biggest political and social problems in Japan. This better and sustainable system should be established harmoniously as a three-pillar retirement income system: a public pension system (first pillar), corporate pension systems (second pillar), and individual financial products (third pillar). The focus here is primarily on the structure and poor governance of the second pillar.

The OECD (2009) reported that "private pensions are an important part of retirement-income provision in Japan, covering 45 percent of the workforce." According to the official employment report, the number of active workers in Japan was 62.7 million in July 2010, and the unemployment rate was 5.2 percent. In 2009, the number of active nonfarm workers totaled 49.1 million, excluding 5.0 million public sector employees. Participants of all corporate pension plans numbered 17.2 million at the end of March 2009, or 35.0 percent of active nonfarm workers. The coverage rate of 45 percent in the OECD report may have been correct in 1998, but it certainly is incorrect in 2009 and later.

Because of the weaker economy and the cost-oriented employment policy in Japan, the use of non-regular employees (i.e., part-time or temporary workers) has been increasing. The number of non-regular workers increased from 8.7 million in 1990 to 16.9 million in 2010. Over one-third of the workforce is now considered to be non-regular. At the same time, the number of regular workers decreased from 34.7 million to 33.3 million, mainly because of the weaker economy.

According to Ministry of Health, Labor, and Welfare statistics, the average monthly earnings of regular male employees in 2008 was ¥345,300 compared with ¥224,000 for non-regular employees. The average for women was ¥243,900 for regular workers and ¥170,500 for non-regular workers. Contrary to the basic principles of equal opportunity and treatment, part-time employees cannot participate in earnings-related EPI plans or other corporate pension plans, only in the flat-rate NPI plan. As a result of an amendment of the labor law in 2006, companies can employ non-regular employees for up to three years.

According to a survey on people's knowledge of financial matters conducted by the Bank of Japan in 2008, 71.8 percent of people said that they have little knowledge about stocks and bonds; only 4.9 percent answered that they have sufficient knowledge about stocks and bonds. Approximately 83.6 percent of those surveyed answered that they have not heard about defined contribution plans (50.8 percent) or have heard about them but do not know what they are (32.8 percent). It is clear that seven years after the Corporate Pension Reform in 2001, the government, financial organizations, and employers had not done a good job informing people about defined contribution plans.

In September 2010, the government and the Japan Pension Service revealed that the Japan Pension Service had mismanaged basic data, including the name, date of birth, basic salary, and years of membership, to the extent that about 2.6 million EPF members are at risk of losing at least part of their EPF benefits.

NECESSARY POLICY CHANGES

The Japanese corporate pension system has many fundamental problems. The following sections examine policies that should be established to address these problems.

General Reforms

In general, employers and employees need to understand that the harmonization of corporate profits and the employee welfare system is necessary. Employers, in particular, need to exercise corporate responsibility and develop a better employee welfare system, particularly with respect to their corporate pension plans in Japan's current aging society.

In political terms, pension regulations are quite complicated and cause management inefficiencies in the huge social security and corporate pension funds in Japan. Many high-ranking pension-related governmental staff members take high-ranking positions with financial institutions or financial-related corporations after their retirement, which increases the political risks for the retirement income system in Japan. It is a main reason why pension policies are not fair, transparent, or efficient as compared with western countries. New laws should be enacted to regulate the movement of former high-ranking pension bureaucrats into high-paying jobs in related financial fields.

The government in Japan has established many committees, particularly in the pension field. Pension scholars are generally eager to be members of the committees because they can gain access to detailed government information and are well paid. Newspapers have reported that members of these committees are paid from ¥4 to 17 million to attend 5 to 10 meetings a year. The Salary Act enacted in 1949 regulates the salaries of some members of government committees, and the limit in 2011 was ¥936,000. Some scholars are members of several committees, so the work is very lucrative. Members of these committees generally accept policy proposals from bureaucrats with little opposition—they are really nothing more than well-paid "shadow bureaucrats" and are not independent from the government. Pension policymaking in general could be strengthened by strictly and reasonably regulating the pay structure of government committees.

In the labor field, we should observe the basic principles of the International Labour Organization (ILO 1951) concerning equal opportunity and treatment and amend related laws to strictly regulate salaries for similar types of labor.

Reforms in the Corporate Pension System

Several reforms need to be made in the corporate pension system.

- A minimum mandatory corporate pension system should be established to supplement the earning-related social security pension system and establish a better and more stable retirement income security system.
- A Basic Corporate Pension Act should be enacted to include enhanced fiduciary responsibilities and a pension benefits guarantee system.
- Taxation of pension investment income should be abolished.
- To improve accounting regulations, rules from the International Financial Reporting Standards and the Financial Accounting Standards Board should be introduced in Japan, particularly present value accounting.

- To improve financial gains, the financial markets should be reformed to become more transparent and more efficient. Financial corporations should establish higher profit-gaining powers and lower fee structures.
- The government, financial corporations, and employers should provide more and better financial information and education to employees and the general public.

CONCLUSION

Japanese corporate pension policy has not been successful in terms of coverage or creating a sustainable pension system. There has been a focus on small technical subjects and a general neglect of basic problems in Japan's aging society in the twenty-first century.

Employers and employees need to understand the importance of better and more stable employee welfare systems, particularly regarding corporate pension plans, as a way of increasing corporate profits and supporting the social security pension system. The social security and other pension systems need to be reviewed and restructured with a mutual understanding of the importance of public and corporate pension governance and to establish fair, transparent, and efficient markets and regulations in pension-related fields. An ongoing evaluation of policies, government agencies, pension funds, and financial corporations should be conducted to ensure excellent performance.

Japan should return to a basic guiding principle—there should be no long-term development of a company without a stable employee welfare system, particularly in terms of corporate pension plans in the twenty-first century.

References

International Labour Organization. 1951. "C100 Equal Remuneration Convention, 1951." Geneva: ILO. http://www.ilo.org/ilolex/cgi-lex/convde.pl?C100 (accessed May 24, 2011).

OECD. 2009. *OECD Pensions at a Glance 2009: Retirement-Income Systems in OECD Countries*. Paris: Organisation for Economic Co-operation and Development.

Authors

Lucy apRoberts is an associate researcher at the University of Paris Ouest Nanterre, at the IDHE, a social science laboratory. She previously worked for the French national advisory council on retirement, the Conseil d'orientation des retraites, the International Social Security Association, and the IRES, a social science institute that serves French labor unions. Her research focuses on the interplay between government-run social protection and occupational benefit plans.

Pierre Concialdi is working as an economist at the IRES, a social science institute that serves French labor unions. He previously worked as a deputy director at CERC, a French official body analyzing trends in income distribution. He is also a member of the executive committee of the ENRSP (European Network for Research on Supplementary Pensions). His studies have focused on income distribution, social protection and pensions, the financing of social security, tax progressivity, and low-wage employment.

Bryn Davies is a director and actuary in the U.K. at Union Pension Services Limited, a consultancy on occupational pensions specializing in those for trade unions. He was previously pensions officer at the Trades Union Congress and a partner in a leading firm of consulting actuaries. He has published many articles on pension issues.

Kim De Witte is a researcher and associate lecturer in the law faculty of the Katholieke Universiteit Leuven. His research and teaching focus on pension law and policy.

Gerard Hughes is an economist and a visiting professor at Trinity College Dublin. His current research interests include pension reform, autoenrollment private pension schemes, the cost and distribution of tax expenditures on private pensions, and the effectiveness of public and private pension systems in delivering pensions.

Matthieu Leimgruber is a research fellow with the Swiss National Science Foundation and a lecturer at the University of Geneva's Paul Bairoch Institute of Economic History. He has published several books and articles on the history of social policy in Switzerland and on the comparative development of private and social insurance in Western Europe and the United States.

Dana Muir is Arthur F. Thurnau Professor of Business Law at the Ross School of Business at the University of Michigan. Her research on policy matters related to pensions and investments has been cited by the U.S. Supreme Court and other federal courts. She has been appointed by two U.S. presidents to serve in positions to provide advice to policymakers regarding investment and benefits issues. She also has studied the Australian superannuation system.

Finn Østrup is a professor at the Center for Financial Law, Copenhagen Business School. He has previously worked at the Danish Ministry of Economic Affairs and as a financial attache as part of the Permanent Representation of Denmark to the European Union.

Markus Roth is a professor of law at Philipps University Marburg, fellow of MaxNetAging, and a member of ENSRP. Previously, he was senior researcher at the Max Planck Institute for Comparative and Foreign Private Law. His main areas of research and writing are corporate governance, private pensions (occupational pensions, individual pensions: insurance law, and investment law), labor law, banking and capital markets law, private law, and comparative law.

Jim Stewart is a senior lecturer in finance at the School of Business, Trinity College Dublin. He has published a number of peer-reviewed articles. His research interests include corporate finance and taxation, pension funds and financial products, financial systems, and economic development.

Marek Szczepański is an assistant professor at the Department of Economic Science at Poznań University of Technology. His research focuses on old-age pension systems in postsocialist countries, especially on occupational pension schemes. He also has 11 years of work experience in financial institutions in Poland (mainly in the banking sector, as a bank spokesman and bank manager) and is the author of more than 50 articles, chapters, and books on the Polish pension system.

John A. Turner is director of the Pension Policy Center, which provides research and consulting on social security and pension policy. He has also worked in research offices at the U.S. Social Security Administration and the U.S. Department of Labor, where he was deputy director of the pension research office for nine years. He taught as an adjunct lecturer in economics at George Washington University and at Georgetown University in the Public Policy Institute. Turner, who has published 12 books and more than 100 articles, has a PhD in economics from the University of Chicago.

Noriyasu Watanabe is a professor at the Graduate School for Social Welfare, Rissho University and president of the International Pension Research Institute, which is an associate member of the International Social Security Association in Geneva. He specializes in the comparative study of public and private pension systems.

Index

The italic letters *b, f, n,* and *t* following a page number indicate that the subject information of the heading is within a box, figure, note or table, respectively, on that page. Double italics indicate multiple but consecutive elements.

About the Institute

The W.E. Upjohn Institute for Employment Research is a nonprofit research organization devoted to finding and promoting solutions to employment-related problems at the national, state, and local levels. It is an activity of the W.E. Upjohn Unemployment Trustee Corporation, which was established in 1932 to administer a fund set aside by Dr. W.E. Upjohn, founder of The Upjohn Company, to seek ways to counteract the loss of employment income during economic downturns.

The Institute is funded largely by income from the W.E. Upjohn Unemployment Trust, supplemented by outside grants, contracts, and sales of publications. Activities of the Institute comprise the following elements: 1) a research program conducted by a resident staff of professional social scientists; 2) a competitive grant program, which expands and complements the internal research program by providing financial support to researchers outside the Institute; 3) a publications program, which provides the major vehicle for disseminating the research of staff and grantees, as well as other selected works in the field; and 4) an Employment Management Services division, which manages most of the publicly funded employment and training programs in the local area.

The broad objectives of the Institute's research, grant, and publication programs are to 1) promote scholarship and experimentation on issues of public and private employment and unemployment policy, and 2) make knowledge and scholarship relevant and useful to policymakers in their pursuit of solutions to employment and unemployment problems.

Current areas of concentration for these programs include causes, consequences, and measures to alleviate unemployment; social insurance and income maintenance programs; compensation; workforce quality; work arrangements; family labor issues; labor-management relations; and regional economic development and local labor markets.